Shakespeare's Storyt

By the same author

The Novels of George Eliot: A Study in Form
The Appropriate Form: An Essay on the Novel
The Moral Art of Dickens
The Exposure of Luxury: Radical Themes in Thackeray
(*Peter Owen*)
A Reading of Jane Austen (*Peter Owen*)
Tellers and Listeners: The Narrative Imagination
The Advantage of Lyric
Particularities: Readings in George Eliot (*Peter Owen*)
Forms of Feeling in Victorian Fiction (*Peter Owen*)
Narrators and Novelists: Collected Essays
Swansea Girl: A Memoir (*Peter Owen*)
London Lovers (*Peter Owen*)
Henry James: The Later Writing

Shakespeare's Storytellers

Dramatic Narration

BARBARA HARDY

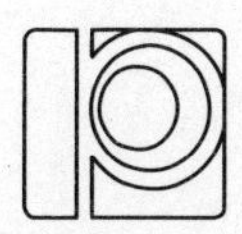

PETER OWEN
London & Chester Springs

PETER OWEN PUBLISHERS
73 Kenway Road London SW5 0RE
Peter Owen books are distributed in the USA by
Dufour Editions Inc Chester Springs PA 19425–0007

First published in Great Britain in 1997

A catalogue record for this book is
available from the British Library

ISBN 0–7206–0963–1
0–7206–1053–2 (pbk)
Printed in Great Britain by Biddles of Guildford and King's Lynn

This book is dedicated to my grandchildren
Rhiannon, Simon and Nathan
with my love

Contents

Preface

'Nature, not art, makes us all story-tellers,' I wrote in 'The Nature of Narrative' (*Novel*, 1968, vol. 2, no. 1), an essay drawing on a lecture given in May 1959 to the London Association for the Teaching of English, at the invitation of colleagues in the University of London Institute of Education, James Britton and Nancy Martin, who, with John and Mollie Dixon and other colleagues in teaching, continued to encourage and publicize my thinking about narrative and imagination. In 1974, after giving the Ewing Lectures at UCLA, on narrative imagination and on narration in James Joyce, I visited Brown University, where the novelist John Hawkes drew my attention to Michel Butor's *Essais sur le roman* (Paris, 1969, p. 7), which makes the same emphasis:

> Le roman est une forme particulière du récit. Celui-ci est un phénomène qui dépasse considérablement le domaine de la littérature; il est un des constituents essentiels de notre apprehension de la réalité.

I began with the narrative display and implicit analysis of narrative modes in prose fiction, but my inquiry expanded to take in drama, particularly Shakespeare, on whose narration I touched briefly in *Tellers and Listeners* (London, Athlone, 1975). I first discussed Shakespeare's construction and analysis of narrative in a paper published in *Papers from the First Nordic Conference for English Studies*, Oslo, 1980, and subsequently in lectures given in the universities of Birmingham, Bochum, Bonn, Dundee, Emory, Furman, Lethbridge, London, Loughborough, North Missouri State at Kirksville, Münster and Oxford, Christ Church College, Canterbury, and the Shakespeare Institute, Stratford-upon-Avon, the Open University, the European Council of International Schools, the

Institute of Education in the University of London, Elizabeth Harwood's course, 'Literature in Context', the Shakespeare Society in Stratford-upon-Avon, the Shakespeare Society of Japan and graduate and undergraduate classes in Birkbeck. I am grateful to colleagues and students in these institutions for hospitality, questions and suggestions. As always, I am grateful to the staff of the British Library and Birkbeck College Library and have particular reasons to thank the staff of the University of London Library and the Hornton Street branch of Chelsea and Kensington Public Libraries.

I was taught Shakespeare by three English teachers at Swansea High School for Girls, Myfanwy Jones, Nansi Evans and Dr Winifred Mountford, who never revealed that she had done a doctoral thesis on Elizabethan drama but who drew on her scholarship in all her teaching, and later by Charles Jasper Sisson, whose knowledge of the Elizabethan stage, printing-house, law and social history seemed at the time less relevant to texts and performances than it subsequently proved, and by Winifred Nowottny, whose classes on textual scholarship and bibliography were daunting but invaluable and with whom I had many conversations about Shakespeare. I was appointed to my first academic post by Geoffrey Tillotson, who believed that all his post-medievalist colleagues should teach Shakespeare's texts.

I am indebted to the British Academy for the assistance of a research grant (1987). I am extremely grateful to several Shakespearean colleagues, Stanley Wells, Barbara Everett and Emrys Jones, who carefully read the book and offered the advantage of their scholarship and critical judgement, and to Lois Potter, for letting me see her essay 'Nobody's Perfect: Actors' Memories and Shakespeare's Plays of the 1590s' before it was published in *Shakespeare Survey* (42, 1990). Richard Ellmann discussed the subject and the plays with me at various stages of reading, planning and writing. Toru Sasaki made valuable suggestions about gender-impersonation in drama. With Murray Cox and Alice Theilgaard, remarkably Shakespearian psychologists, I have talked about narrative, Shakespeare, memory and phenomenology with pleasure and profit. Over many years Kurt Tetzeli von Rosador provided ideas, examples, encouragement, doubts and practical help of many kinds. I am also most grateful to two of his graduate students in the University of Münster (Gabriele Bloom and Elke Lehmann) for providing a translation of the two German books on the subject, Kurt Schluter's *Shakespeares dramatische Erzahlkunst* (Schriftenreihe der deutschen Shakespeare-Gesellschaft, N.F. 7 [Heidelberg, 1958]) and the pioneer work, Karl Obmann's *Der Bericht im deutschen Drama* (Giessener Beitrage zur deutschen Philologie, 12 [Giessen, 1925], s. 43–75). Graham Handley, Janet El-Rayess and Amanda Auckland gave valuable help with references and checking. I must also thank the following friends and colleagues for brilliant help of many kinds – talk, response, suggestions, criticism, encouragement and invitations: Martin Dodsworth, Jerome Beaty, Muriel Bradbrook, Philip Brookbank, Jean Brooks, Tom Healy, Samuel Hynes, Gus Martin, Sally Minogue, Peter Mudford, Richard Proudfoot, Fleur Rothschild, Kristian Schmidt, Michael Slater and Katharine Worth. Mary McGowan and Willard Pate have been encouraging and provokingly doubtful about aspects of the subject.

Chapter 1 draws in part on *Shakespeare's Self-conscious Art*, the F.E.L. Priestley Lecture, 1989, University of Lethbridge; Chapter 3 on the Kathleen Banks Memorial Lecture, University of Loughborough, 1984, (unpublished); Chapter 5 is a revised version of 'Arts and Acts of Memory', the F.W. Bateson Lecture, *Essays in Criticism*, vol. XXXIX, no. 2, April 1989; Chapter 6 a revised version of 'Telling the Future: Forecasts and Fantasies in Shakespeare's Narrative' published in *Chaucer to Shakespeare: Essays in Honour of Shinsuke Ando* (Woodbridge, Boydell and Brewer, 1992); a few pages of Chapter 7 draw on 'The Talkative Woman in Shakespeare, Dickens, and George Eliot', *Problems for Feminist Criticism*, ed. Sally Minogue (London, Routledge); Chapter 8 is a revised version of 'Narration in *King Lear*' (*Deutsche Shakespeare-Gesellschaft West, Jahrbuch*, 1987); Chapter 9 a revised version of 'The Figure of Narration in *Hamlet*, *A Centre of Excellence: Essays Presented to Seymour Betsky*, ed. R. Druce (Amsterdam, Costerus, Rodopi, 1987); and Chapter 10 a revised version of *The Narrators in Macbeth*, the Hilda Hulme Lecture, 1988, University of London.

I have approached the subject of Shakespeare's use of narration through art, theme and three individual plays, but my analysis does not try to be exhaustive, and the list of narrative topics, techniques and – particularly – plays is highly selective. I have discussed narrative themes – memory, fantasy and gender – which occur in all the plays and discussed *Hamlet*, *King Lear* and *Macbeth* in detail, and there is a little – I hope not too much – overlap and repetition. The many plays I have not considered in detail I have discussed, at length or briefly, in the analysis of craft and theme. Narrative structures and topics I have not isolated as distinct categories – for instance, news, gossip, boast, encomium, lies and slander – I have mentioned when looking at individual plays and at stagecraft. My occasional references to performances, on stage and screen, in no way pretend to inclusiveness or stage history but are mere personal asides about examples that have struck me over the years in which I have been thinking about the subject.

Unless otherwise indicated, quotations from Shakespeare's plays are taken from the Arden Shakespeare (London, Methuen), and quotations from Shakespeare's sources are from Edward Bullough, *Narrative and Dramatic Sources of Shakespeare*, 8 volumes (London, Routledge and Kegan Paul, 1957–75).

Introduction

Narrative in Life and Art
'You have often
Begun to tell me . . .'

Nature, not art, makes us all storytellers, but narrative art reflects and explores the nature of storytelling, in art and in life outside art. Narrative art takes many different forms: drama is one of those forms.

Drama is a narrative as well as a dramatic genre. In Shakespeare there is the story, or stories, narrated by the play as a whole, like the story of Lear and his daughters, Hamlet and his revenge, and Macbeth and his murders, and there are stories and fragments of story within these over-arching narratives, narrated by Shakespeare's gifted storytellers, like Edmund, Edgar, Hamlet, the Ghost, Gertrude, Ophelia, Macbeth, Malcolm and the witches. The internal narratives are designed to be performed, on the stage, by actors constructed to speak eloquently and plausibly, for the most part in the voices of individual characters.

Plays, like novels, inspect the nature of narrative, as they construct languages and patterns for private and public acts and arts. Narrative goes beyond art, as a major constituent of human consciousness, relationship and inquiry, but we may go to narrative artists to find out about narrative, and Shakespeare is one of the great narrative artists. We may also go to his plays to find out about the dramatic modes and languages of life outside the theatre and to his lyrical poetry to learn about emotional expression and form, but my present concern is narrative, the telling of a sequence of events.

Shakespeare's subtle and sustained inquiry into human behaviour covers the psychological and sociological life-forms of narrative:

memory, fantasy, report, dream, daydream, truth-telling, lying, slander, boast, confession, confidence, gossip, rumour, news and messages. It inquires, often self-consciously and conspicuously, into the narrative forms of theatre too: exposition, summary, retrospect, anticipation, fantasy, message, joke, short tale, long story. I do not suggest that Shakespeare sets out with such inquiry in mind. Like the novelist, he scrutinizes narration because he is an artist using narrative to write a drama of character in society. You cannot render either character or society without presenting the intimate and public forms of telling in which we conduct and construct private and social lives. Human beings are storytelling creatures, gossiping, lying, trying to tell the truth, dreaming, daydreaming, remembering, planning, historicizing, testifying, telling and reading true and wild stories to our children, reporting good and bad news, influenced and manipulated by society's narrative, creating and responding to the stories of art, mixing the modes, serializing, correcting and reinventing our life-story as long as we live. In reciprocity, we are listening creatures too. Art's telling and listening are part of this wider psychological and political activity, reflecting it and reflecting on it.

Days begin with snatches of the night-narratives. Waking, we recall dreams to ourselves or others. In Act 1, scene 4 of *Richard III*, Clarence wakes up showing signs of 'dismal terror' which provoke the Keeper's questions and his own story of a dream. His terror is the effect of the dream, and perhaps also its cause, as Coleridge insisted dream was. He saw dream as the irrational creation of stories and images for feeling and passion, hit-and-miss objective correlatives supplied by the sleeping mind. In a Coleridgean way, Shakespeare does not always show a rational causality for his dreams but stresses the dream's mood and emotion. The exiled Romeo's sleeping mind finds a story for a mood of happiness, in a joyful dream of being woken up from death by Juliet's kiss. The dream is misleading – she kisses him after death, but not to wake him – partly prophetic in ways which we can see but which he never fully knows, and Shakespeare makes an interesting separation between the personal cause-and-content and the thematic cause-and-content.

But in *Richard III* the dream is purposively rational. Moral cause-and-content and dramatic cause-and-content go hand in hand. Theatre is more important here than dream psychology, and Clarence's nightmare anticipates what lies ahead, but makes some concession to the nature of dream-narrative. It is a medley, whose sequence and vividness are dreamlike. Gloucester pulls Clarence overboard to drown, with surreal and symbolic imagery representing dream's truth and drama's theme:

> Methoughts I saw a thousand fearful wrecks;
> Ten thousand men that fishes gnaw'd upon;
> Wedges of gold, great anchors, heaps of pearl,
> Inestimable stones, unvalu'd jewels,
> All scatter'd in the bottom of the sea.
> Some lay in dead men's skulls, and in the holes
> Where eyes did once inhabit, there were crept –
> As 'twere in scorn of eyes – reflecting gems,
> That woo'd the slimy bottom of the deep,
> And mock'd the dead bones that lay scatter'd by.
> (I.4)

As usual, Shakespeare makes narration into dialogue, and the Keeper's surprise that the dreamer could find time for leisurely observation, in a dream of death, brings out both the improbability and the oddity of dream-time – or time in dream-memory. The action is thematic and didactic but surreal in sequence and movement – for instance, the time-jump from drowning into the afterlife, and the abrupt cut from the appearance of Warwick, Clarence's father-in-law, to the ghost of Prince Edward, Clarence's victim at Tewkesbury. Its vivid and phantasmagoric imagery, like Edward's ghost's 'shadow like an angel, with bright hair/Dabbled in blood', is dreamlike too. The emotional aftermath of dreaming is emphasized, though perhaps obscured – like the threat from Richard – by Clarence's awakened conscience. But as narrative it is much more coherent than real dream-memories, being ordered, like all dreams in art, by artistic purpose, while glimpsing something of the structural, visual and emotional strangeness of dream-story. Harold F. Brooks, in his fascinating source-study '*Richard III*:

Antecedents of Clarence's Dream' (*Shakespeare Survey*, 32, 1979), collected images and motifs of literary dreaming which may have given Shakespeare materials, but none of them seem comparably interesting as an attempt to relate a dream, impressive in its brilliant individual images, but above all in the way it places and displaces them, in emotional unity and narrative discontinuity.

We construct dream-narrative in waking memory, and the nature of memory fascinated Shakespeare, who instructed and inspired Freud. Shakespeare dramatizes many kinds of memory, from Prospero's precise bitter recall of betrayal and exile to Hotspur's hot-headed, patchy reminiscences of war. What is true of Clarence's dream is true of all his author's acts of telling: packed and implicit in the particular act of narration is a scrutiny of the social and psychic genre of narration and of the theatrical medium.

The narrative form may be a dream, dreamt about the future, and recalled as the past, like Clarence's phantasmagoric story. To construct it characters may piece together dream images, as Clarence does. The narrative may be a memory, and to construct it the characters may organize remembered episodes into a continuity of beginning, middle and end, like the controlled Othello and Prospero or, in a more fragmentary form, like mad Ophelia and Mistress Quickly rambling away inconsequentially – as it may seem – in *Henry IV, Pt 2*, *Henry V* and *The Merry Wives of Windsor*. The narrative may be a fantasy in which characters look ahead to the future, like the terrified Juliet taking the Friar's drug and cool greedy machiavellian Richard of Gloucester eyeing the crown, appropriating it in imagination. The narrative may be a lie, persuasively particularized, like Iago's erotic tale of dreaming Cassio and treacherous Edmund's pretence of loyalty to his brother. It may be good news, self-deprecatingly summed up by the three fascinated gentleman who see the meeting of Leontes and Perdita, or bad news, reluctantly revealed by the hapless messenger Cleopatra hales furiously up and down. It may set – or try to set – the record straight, like self-judging suicidal Othello summing up his life and Kate the reformed and politic shrew telling the 'correct' story about dutiful women and ideal husbands. It may be a public oration, encomium or testimonial, like the specious praise of triumphant Octavius Caesar at the end of *Antony and Cleopatra* and the skilful but sincere speech of loyal Cominius as he backs Coriolanus for the consulship. It may tell by not telling, like the murderous hinting of sly King John to his agent Hubert, the reticence of touchy Coriolanus declining to boast, and the nervous reserved babble of Hamlet after seeing a ghost.

In hundreds of narratives and fragments of narrative, Shakespeare illustrates – and also contemplates and studies – narration, its expression of character, its social and psychic genre, its affective drive, its styles of construction and its dynamic relationships. He always knows who is telling, why, where, when, to whom and with what result. Usually he is making narrative contribute to idiolect (individualized style), but Clarence's dream is an example of his interest in genre and passion rather than character. As a speech it could be adapted to a variety of character interpretations: in this scene Clarence's innocence is local and sketchy, to be filled in performance, though by an actor who can strongly articulate the visualizing and amazed imagination, as he relates his experience.

As Cominius praises Coriolanus, in Act II, scene 2, recommending him for the consulate, he is not strongly psychologized – a soldier, a politician and a trained master of patrician and demotic styles, his exemplary narration displays the skill and power of encomium, no more. It is conspicuously political, like everything in its play, a social narrative, a political testimonial and a praise. The speaker is not complexly characterized, but his act of praise is carefully constructed, in classical Latinate language, compressed, laconic, brilliant in compounds and metaphors. The speech is formal, as befits the occasion, and the speaker introduced, as so often in Shakespeare. Here the cue is 'Proceed', eliciting the immediate response of a conventional rhetorical figure, the disclaimer or apology, modernized in 'Unaccustomed as I am to public speaking':

> I shall lack voice: the deeds of Coriolanus
> Should not be utter'd feebly.

And in the middle of the speech there is that form of *occupatio* (saying something by saying it will not be said) we call the topos of inexpressibility (saying that something cannot be expressed):

> For this last,
> Before and in Corioles, let me say
> I cannot speak him home.

The praise is not uttered feebly, and a combination of the physical and the abstract, like the epic speeches in *Macbeth* and *Hamlet*, make the body of the speech classical, heroic and epic:

> It is held
> That valour is the chiefest virtue and
> Most dignifies the haver: if it be,
> The man I speak of cannot in the world
> Be singly counter-pois'd. At sixteen years,
> When Tarquin made a head for Rome, he fought
> Beyond the mark of others; our then dictator,
> Whom with all praise I point at, saw him fight,
> When with his Amazonian chin he drove
> The bristled lips before him; he bestrid
> An o'erpress'd Roman, and i'th' consul's view
> Slew three opposers; Tarquin's self he met
> And struck him on his knee . . .
> . . . and for his meed
> Was brow-bound with the oak. His pupil age
> Man-enter'd thus, he waxed like a sea,
> And in the brunt of seventeen battles since
> He lurch'd all swords of the garland.
> . . . as weeds before
> A vessel under sail, so men obey'd
> And fell below his stem: his sword, death's stamp,
> Where it did mark, it took; from face to foot
> He was a thing of blood . . .

At the end it startlingly modulates into colloquial bluntness:

> Our spoils he kick'd at,
> And look'd upon things precious as they were
> The common muck of the world.

It is important that one listener is not present: at the beginning of the assembly Coriolanus refuses to stay and hear himself 'monstered'.

The narrative has to be seen in terms of its teller and its audience, as a tactful and manipulative communication made to patricians and plebs, but the psychology of the teller does not really go beyond the immediate situation. It is a superb exercise in political oratory.

But to study his acts of narration is to recognize that Shakespeare is usually shaping speech to an idea or image of personal character. Cassius's narration of his swimming-match with Caesar is characteristic, not only in its jealousy and scorn but in its *ad hominem* argument. The function of the story, invented by Shakespeare, does not only much 'belittle' Caesar (who was actually a good swimmer), as the Arden editor, T.S. Dorsch, suggests in his note, but also characterizes the attitudes and relationship of the teller and listener. It may be an important part of the play's argument against Caesar, but it is certainly also an important part of Cassius's persuasion of Brutus and of Brutus's less than immediate and enthusiastic response. Like Cominius's speech, it is a fine piece of elocution, to swell the actor's part, as it is also part of the characterizing of Cassius. He begins with the – very personal – statement of political hostility and works himself up into a simply worded, fast-moving contemptuous anecdote of Caesar's physical feebleness:

> Well, honour is the subject of my story.
> I cannot tell what you and other men
> Think of this life; but for my single self,
> I had as lief not be as live to be
> In awe of such a thing as I myself.
> I was born free as Caesar; so were you;
> We both have fed as well, and we can both
> Endure the winter's cold as well as he:
> For once, upon a raw and gusty day,
> The troubled Tiber chafing with her shores,
> Caesar said to me, 'Dar'st thou, Cassius, now
> Leap in with me into this angry flood . . .'
>
> (I.2)

It is interesting, I think, that Brutus makes no direct comment on this powerful piece of narrative and may, in performance, give it only a part of his attention, as he also – or instead – listens to the crowd applauding Caesar, 'Another general shout?' The dialogue – or absence of dialogue – contrasts Cassius's personal and jealous motivation with Brutus's more high-minded, rational and abstract republican ideals. Even if a director or actor plays the scene as effective persuasion, Cassius's speech may well strike an audience as peculiarly beside the point, or gracelessly *ad hominem*, in his denigration of Caesar's weakness, the interpretation of cowardice and the self-aggrandizing comparison of himself to Aeneas and Caesar to the feeble old Anchises. There is a significant emphasis on the first person singular, and the uncontrolled excitability and over-personal arguments – repeated in the famous quarrel scene later in the play – find expression in the consistent physical belittling of Caesar: 'As a sick girl', 'this god did shake' and the wittily unfair transferred military image: 'His coward lips did from their colour fly'.

Shakespeare's passionate scenarios for the performance of a story are often programmed by explicit and implicit personal narrative characteristics, like Juliet's Nurse's habit of rambling and circumstantial reminiscence, Othello's spellbinding range of candid and proud speech, rapt particularization, controlled and released passion and Juliet's swings between impetuous imaginative susceptibility and common-sense checks and inspection.

Narrative brings in the old-fashioned concept of character – never old-fashioned in the theatre, in acting – but Shakespeare is not only interested in character. Even as he makes narrative particular, he achieves what we may call the artist's taxonomy. Sensing individualities, we find classification. If we put together all his forgetful characters, for instance, we recognize an actor's and director's interest in verbal memory; and the differences between the forgetfulness of Polonius, Hotspur, Coriolanus, Fluellen (in *Henry V*) and York (in *Richard II*) inform us – as the last example informed Freud* – about slips of memory. Like Freud, Shakespeare is sufficiently interested in memory to be interested in forgetting. He

* *The Psychopathology of Everyday Life: The Standard Edition of the Complete Psychological Works of Sigmund Freud*, vol. VI (London, Hogarth Press and the Institute of Psycho-Analysis, 1901, p. 100 n.).

repeats and varies the particulars, getting at classification through pragmatic, particular and passionate dramatizations.

For instance, if we group some of the long reminiscences – Prospero's, Egeon's, Edgar's, Hamlet's – we see a concern with impassioned acts of memory. It is a concern coming both from a technical need to give actors passionately expressive speeches and from the psychological observation that constructive and deconstructive recall is affective and variable, not fixed and stable. In these cases the sense of a life-narrative goes along with the awareness of art. If we group together his talkative women – and the few garrulous men – we see how he perceives a social construction of gendered narrative. By looking at his liars and slanderers – mostly wicked but a few good – we see his creative interest in self-generative form, his knowledge of rhetorically effective circumstantial detail, apology, the topos of inexpressibility, compression and his acknowledgement of the encouraging, critical, interrupting, prompting and collaborative listener.

Shakespeare does not write naïvely and leave the critic to collect and reconstruct and classify these cases. He draws attention to what he sees by a sophisticated technical vocabulary, not because he is imagining the idiolects of scholars and pedants – when he does, he usually gives them a rough time – but as he imagines queens, kings, princes, dukes, commoners, oppressed women, soldiers, shrews, clowns, cowards, faithful and faithless lovers, spies, runaways, people in disguise. They are given languages that conceptualize acts and arts of storytelling, emphasizing rhetoric, genres, length, timing, realism, surrealism, selection, disorder, order, particularity and passion. Othello, Macbeth, Cymbeline, Edgar, Egeon (in *The Comedy of Errors*), Cordelia and hundreds of others share technical insights. Cassius is aware that stories have themes, Othello knows the difference between listening to a story piecemeal and 'intentively', Macbeth about vacuous tales full of sound and fury, Cymbeline about circumstantial detail and abridgement, Edgar about amplification, Egeon about sequels, Cordelia about hyperbole and understatement. The language of narrative shows Shakespeare's awareness of his subject and his art. The self-reflective language is used simply, ambiguously and metaphorically, but it usually seems to come naturally, not pedantically or abstractly but in the heat of passion. He uses other means of self-conscious direction, too: literary allusion and imitation, comic and satiric heightening, and thematic concentration which promotes technical awareness, like the recitation of Aeneas's Pyrrhus story, reinforced by Hamlet's *aficionado* analyses of acting.

Characteristic of Shakespeare's reflexive narration is the repetition, variation or revision of an event the audience has already seen acted. Multivocalism was not invented by James Joyce, and Shakespeare too tells the same story from different points of view, at different times, in different moods. Edgar tells how he cared for his father, describing Gloucester's eye-sockets in jewel-metaphors that recall to us the terrible scene of the blinding and make us, like Edgar, remember and reflect: in no stage production can we clearly see eyes or sockets, but Edgar's aesthetically distanced and decorative conceit makes us feel we have, as it makes us aware of transformative language. In *Richard III* Richard of Gloucester coaches Buckingham in a slanderous story designed to win the citizens' support, and Buckingham returns to recall the ineffective speech, reporting a cold curt repetition by the unsympathetic Lord Mayor, whose dissociation of himself as he narrates is more eloquent than voiced antipathy: the speech is narrated in three voices, never in direct performance, its quality entirely defined by indirections, in a wonderfully original and apt critique of manipulative political speech-making. In *Henry IV, Pt 2*, Rumour's self-explanatory speech as allegorical Chorus is followed by the particular enactment of everything that was abstractly adumbrated. Pyrrhus's slaughter of Priam is one of Shakespeare's bloodiest stories, an excerpted narrative speech by Aeneas to Dido, brilliantly recited as a 'touch of quality' by the First Player, introduced and applauded by Hamlet, from a play invented by Shakespeare for the occasion, with Virgilian and Marlovian reminders. Shakespeare layers arts and acts of narrative, inviting the audience to compare the shifting revisions of life and art.

At times the play is clearly about narration, thematizing it. In

Othello, *King Lear* and *The Winter's Tale*, for instance, the action, characters and language emphasize the powers of true or false telling, fantasy and report. The dominant acts of telling and listening are constructed in ways that call attention to the theatre, ethics and psychology of lying and speaking the truth. Iago, Othello, Desdemona and Emilia are a quartet of tragic narrators, one liar killing three truth-tellers. *Antony and Cleopatra* and *Macbeth* problematize the politics of hegemony and oppression, in a network of the unreliable, manipulative and dangerous communications of rulers, spies, secret agents and reporters. The process of every play depends on the intricate cellular structure of narrative exchange. Clarence's dream and Othello's story of the handkerchief are exotic, but the stories of everyday life are familiar. In the first scene of *King Lear* Gloucester casually, humorously and callously tells the courteous Kent the story of his illegitimate son's begetting, in that son's presence, indifferent to both his listeners. The disguised Kent invents a brief life-sketch when he asks Lear for a job, pretending candour, mixing truths and lies. Just before taking the Friar's drug, Juliet imagines the worst then talks herself out of her fear. In the Forest of Arden Rosalind–Ganymede invents an uncle and a training in love-therapy for Orlando's ear, tailoring a story for emotional ends. After she has been disinherited, Cordelia asks Lear to put the record straight and tell France she has not been vicious or unchaste. Ophelia is bullied into telling the story of her relationship with Hamlet. Hamlet's father's ghost moves the listeners on and off stage by what he passionately reveals about his death and what he passionately explains he cannot tell about his afterlife. Hermione fondly cajoles and encourages her little boy – 'You're powerful at it' – to tell his winter's tale, which he never finishes, though the play does. Prospero tells Miranda about his earlier years and hers. Desdemona is frightened into telling a silly lie to her husband. The stories we tell to our acquaintances, employers, lovers, parents, children, enemies and ourselves are all there, in formal speeches and casual fragments, composing the natural-seeming flow of character and relationship, inner and outer life.

The nature of narration is compounded structurally, at key points in the plays, by narratives conspicuous in themselves, in their complex layerings or their relation to each other, like shapes and colours in a painter's composition. The play often begins by stressing the act of beginning, and may be matched by the ending. Many dramatic endings recapitulate past action, but Shakespeare often sums up sparingly, mentioning but postponing a final summary as something which will shortly occur, but offstage, after the characters have left. He couples the audience's knowledge with the characters' ignorance, and combines closure with openness.

Narrative and Theatre
'Action's self'

Narrative is a primary act of mind, a way of comprehending and constructing social and psychic life, as inevitable and central a subject of drama as of prose fiction, but there is a sense in which the inset narratives of novels and stories move easily with the grain of the genre, micro-narratives within a larger narrative. The total narrative is conducted and voiced by a dominant narrator or narrators, speaking in the third of the first person. The first person may be fleshed out fully and made central to the story, an autobiographer recalling the past, like David Copperfield, Jane Eyre, Henry Esmond and Proust's Marcel. The narrator may be given a certain amount of identity and history but subordinated to other more important characters, revealing themselves only insofar as they narrate, like Nick Carroway in *The Great Gatsby*, though sometimes the centrality and subordination are teasing, ambiguous and interchangeable, as with the heroes in Henry James's *Roderick Hudson.* A narrator may be a fully or partly informed author or other authority, like the teller of *Persuasion* and *Middlemarch*, using the first person pronoun sparingly or lavishly.

Unlike the novels and stories of prose fiction, drama can dispense with a narrator, and it usually does so: one of its defining properties is the articulation in dialogue, a dialogue of individual and equally privileged voices or characters. Where there is a prominent narrator, as in Greek drama or Brecht, it never dominates all the time. In Shakespeare it may begin but fade out, like the Prologue to *Romeo and Juliet*, after two appearances, developing enough to show purpose, then letting individual voices take over, or alternate with the characters' dialogues, as in *Pericles*, or stay silent between a framing prologue and epilogue, as in several of the histories.

The presence of a narrator in drama is specious or misleading, deliberated to create an undramatic weight before we are released into dramatic freedom. An unusually and heavily weighted narrative introduction, like the beginning of Brecht's *The Caucasian Chalk Circle* or Christopher Hampton's *Tales from Hollywood*, is interesting because it seriously or playfully subverts the norms of its genre, flaunting rule through exception. Something like this happens briefly in *Romeo and Juliet* and more lengthily in *Pericles*.

Dramatic action tends to be active, interactive, extrovert, many-voiced, mobile, gestural and immediate. Narrative tends to be inactive, introvert, single-voiced, quiet, retrospective or prospective. Plays which are all narrative, like some of Beckett's, are brief and impassioned, like lyrics, their monologism expressing moral or psychic states, like the speaker in *Eh Joe*'s obsessed tirade or *Not I's* solipsistic screaming. Working against the generic grain, though – and significantly not at great length – Beckett brilliantly reminds us that narrative's monologism and stasis, like other characteristics, are tendencies and not fixed attributes.

Until about forty years ago prose fiction was expected to be dramatic, and Victorian authorial commentary was usually criticized, or occasionally defended, as 'intrusion'. Since the narrative or diegetic mode has been disparaged or neglected in novel criticism, it is not surprising that it should be disparaged and neglected in theatre criticism. A hard and fast distinction between telling and showing has turned artistic narrative into a poor relation. But the distinction is not properly hard and fast: narrative can show as it tells, as it does in the animated and characterized authorial voices of Thackeray, Dickens and George Eliot and so even more pronouncedly in Shakespeare's plays, where dialogue is the norm.

Outside art too, in those narratives of everyday life, sometimes the action is internal, in memory or fantasy, where it perhaps seems immobile and static to the outward ear and eye, however energized and individualized by emotion and intelligence. Think of the way we repeat to ourselves the narrative of obsessional desire and joy, and the wish-fulfilling or dread-averting anticipation. And sometimes it is external. When we buttonhole our wedding-guests, we do it by the power of passion – usually in the double excitement of reliving and telling the story. The affectivity of our storytelling is content and form. In Coleridge's poem 'The Ancient Mariner' the mariner is excited, as he tells, by his present feelings of horror and moral contrition but also by the feelings of the past, some of which he no longer feels but retrieves, like his old callousness, fear, guilt and horror, some of which blend with the remorse and compulsive elation of the present. The narrative poem blends the two sets of emotions into a third set, in which the teller remembers but as he tells inevitably changes the remembered events, obeying the narrative law of indeterminacy. And of course there is the sheer excitement of the telling, of getting it right and moving the listener.

Memory changes the story of the past not only because it cannot retrieve everything or get everything right but because as it seems to move back from present to inspect past, it does so in a revisionary new mood which – in the words of Coleridge's remarks on imagination in Chapter 13 of the *Biographia Literaria* – dissolves, diffuses and dissipates past experience. Art uses and analyses the life-process as it creates simulacra of real characters and their stories in forms of fiction.

Some of Shakespeare's ways of making narrative theatrical seem simple and obvious: for instance, he activates the storytelling with emotion and breaks up the monologue by interruption and question. But as I have said, these devices are not simply and wholly solutions to staging problems. They also present the nature of narrative outside theatre. Shakespeare does two things at the same time. Passion is form and content: when we tell over our memories, the telling will be shaped and worded by a prevailing emotion. Dialogue is form and content: when we question or interrupt a narrative it will be for intellectual, emotional and social reasons; we stop or tease or collaborate or compete with the storyteller, refusing to stay as mere listeners, because we do not understand, because we are fascinated, hostile, sympathetic, bored or jealous, because narrative prompts more narrative. In Prospero's retrospect in the second scene of *The Tempest*, Shakespeare is the inquiring psychologist, demonstrating the affectivity and waywardness of memory as he realistically renders the distress and sympathy of father and child, and compares Prospero's full, deliberated retrieval with Miranda's involuntary, fragmentary recall. He is also the craftsman in the theatre, making his play lively as he provides chunks of necessary information about the past, making retrospect impassioned and dialogic to relieve and animate monologue and statis. Shakespeare's plays contain many long detailed narratives like Prospero's, which reflect and reflect on the narratives of everyday life while solving the problem for theatricality in a number of vigorous, bold and experimental ways. (For an example of a different response to Prospero's retrospect, see R.A. Foakes's judgement, in his introduction to the Arden *Henry VII* (p. xlii) that it is 'tedious'; Foakes is highly critical of the last plays, and says little about their stage effects or experiments, but he was writing at the end of the 1950s, when the tragi-comedies were still neglected in the theatre.)

In recent productions, these complex narratives are sometimes obscured by the fashion for disguising narration, probably taking a cue, experimentally or facilely, from the cinematic flashback. Prospero's tale to Miranda may be acted out by Antonio and Alonzo and Gonzago as the teller tells his tale. In his film *Othello* (1996) Kenneth Branagh uses flashback shots to break up and visually enliven Othello's long double narrative, in which he tells the Doge and Senate how he won Desdemona by telling her the story of his life. Solving the technical 'problem' which Shakespeare had already solved, endows the scene with fresh life but can obscure the social and psychological analysis of narration. I found Laurence Fishbourne's interesting Othello too crudely powerful because he was not given the time and space for narrative domination like the storytelling Othello in traditional performances.

There is a sense in which the fashionable translation of retrospect into the visual mode seems appropriate, even Shakespearian. It is what happens in *The Murder of Gonzago*, the play within the play in *Hamlet*, where narrative is first mimed in the dumb show then spoken in monologue and dialogue. But there are local reasons for this: Shakespeare wants the initial narrative to be teasingly visual, more opaque than words, giving the actor who plays Claudius two stages of response instead of one, and postponing his 'Lights, lights'. The response to the dumb-show offers a range of interpretations: not attending, not being able to see it, registering some suspicion, getting the message but not breaking down. When Ophelia tells Polonius about Hamlet's distraught visit to her chamber, in a long and detailed account of an encounter the audience does not see, except through her words, a director may use a mimed scene as substitute or as accompaniment. This is bound to shift the emphasis. The motive for Ophelia's total narration is good, because of the silence of everything she narrates and describes. It is all narration, and it engrosses the mind's eye, leading it to dwell on place, business, costume, gesture, expression, behaviour, producing the maximum tension between telling and showing:

> My lord, as I was sewing in my closet,
> Lord Hamlet, with his doublet all unbrac'd,
> No hat upon his head, his stockings foul'd,
> Ungarter'd and down-gyved to his ankle,
> Pale as his shirt, his knees knocking each other,
> And with a look so piteous in purport
> As if he had been loosed out of hell
> To speak of horrors . . .
>
> (II.1)

As she tells how Hamlet acts and behaves, making an entrance and an exit, in a conspicuously disarrayed costume, making faces and gestures for Ophelia to interpret, the essence of acting is joined with the essence of narrating. The listening is political: the woman tells the story of one man's behaviour, which she does not understand, to another, who is manipulating her as he interprets and acts, and may have helped to precipitate the event she relates. It is puzzling, like so many of the events in the play – like the nature of the ghost and its haunting, and the delay, the guilt of Gertrude and the relationship of all the chief characters to each other and to the murder. The action and expression must be silent, because Hamlet's behaviour must remain a mystery. It is impenetrable for Ophelia, tragically excluded as a passive woman, and misread by Polonius, for all his clever politicking: he does not pass on the story to the King and Queen, though it persuades him to tell them his theory of love-madness and show them one of Hamlet's love-letters. It is a little less of a mystery for the audience, because the last time we saw Hamlet, in the scene before the last, he was in communication with horrors, out of hell – 'shall I couple hell?' – or purgatory. (The intervening Polonius–Reynaldo dialogue makes a useful time-lapse.) But it is still not something we feel sure about – one of the many seemings in which the play abounds. However we interpret Hamlet's behaviour here – he may or may not be putting on an antic disposition, he may be registering genuine horror and loss through the antic affectation – the reported scene adds a touch of anguish to the relationship of Hamlet and Ophelia. In terms of the play's history. Hamlet goes straight from his father's ghost to Ophelia, and her report articulates a passionate action through the painful concentration and attentiveness of her sensitive love. Its recitation of passion's behaviour joins extremes in genre-consciousness: all telling but all about showing.

Drama need not apologize when it is narrative but handles narrative in special ways to make it theatrical. At the beginnings of *Henry VIII*, a play teeming with historical awareness, Shakespeare makes Buckingham respond to Norfolk's elaborate story of the magnificent Field of the Cloth of Gold with incredulity, 'O you go far', to provoke Norfolk's insight and disclaimer. The narrator insists that no mere narrative can give you – can match – the actual event:

> . . . the tract of ev'ry thing
> Would by a good discourser lose some life
> Which action's self was tongue to.
>
> (I.1)

That paradox in the last line fixes Shakespeare's clear sense of the difference between telling and showing.

His craft analyses narrative outside the theatre while it dramatizes relationships and passions of telling and listening and shows how he is brilliantly working against the theatrical grain, doing something difficult. It is the kind of demonstration he provides for his virtuoso actors, like the political role reversals and impersonations of Hal and Falstaff, Cleopatra's daring anticipation – designed to be spoken by a boy – of 'her' character played by some squeaking boy – and the crafty, layered gender shifts of Rosalind, Viola and Imogen. Shakespeare loves the theatre's transformations of narration, boldly flaunts method, playfully and seriously flourishes self-analysis. His big narratives and small ones draw attention to genre and cunning, by comment, technical language, satire, reflexive form and theme.

PART ONE

Narrative Constructions

CHAPTER ONE

Self-Conscious Narrative:

'And tell sad stories'

Narrative Allusion

One of Shakespeare's uncompromising narratives is Egeon's speech at the beginning of *The Comedy of Errors.* A strong example of Shakespeare's triumph over disadvantage, it is formal but dynamically passionate. Egeon asks the Duke to 'end woes and all' 'by the doom of death'; the Duke explains the sentence and asks Egeon to explain why he came to Ephesus as an illegal immigrant. Shakespeare likes narrative neatness of question and answer, a dialogic entry to monologue, so Egeon's answer snaps back as spontaneous response, which is also a classical allusion to distressed storytelling. The verse is described by R.A. Foakes in the Arden edition as having a 'measured dignity . . . with its single-moulded lines' which 'finely conveys the present plight of Egeon, and his fantastic story, told with . . . simple gravity' (p. 3). His narrative is a self-analysing model and an affective medium. The storyteller's emotion justifies itself by paying homage to a long tradition.

Homer's Odysseus hears his own story sung by Demodocus in the Phaecian Palace and secretly grieves; later on he asks the blind bard to resume the Troy tale and breaks down. His tears prompt Antinous to solicit his story, so he changes from listener to teller, to continue the professional narrative in the first person. Art becomes conscious autobiography at the beginning of Book IX of the *Odyssey* when Odysseus says the words picked up by Virgil and passed to Shakespeare:

But now you wish to know my cause for sorrow –
and thereby give me cause for more.
(Everyman's Library, 1992, trans. Robert Fitzgerald, p. 145)

For the next four books Odysseus grieves as he recalls pains, fears, desires, hates, loyalties, triumphs, frustrations, and epic adventures with the Cyclops, Scylla and Charybdis, the sirens, Circe, and the ghosts of Hades. The wildest, most fantastic happenings, with the highest proportion of primitive folk-tale material, are related by the self-authenticating witness, distressed narrator of his own distress. Homer knows exactly who is telling and listening, as he tells. An oral poet, he uses the voices of specific speakers, professional and unprofessional, addressed to specific listeners within the poem, within a story told in the impersonal epic poet's voice, Muse-inspired.

Shakespeare is writing for voices too. He did not know the *Odyssey*, but he is keen on Virgil's famous version of Odysseus's story, adapted for his speaker, Aeneas, as another command performance, for Dido. He accepts the narrative burden though it will grieve him to revive the old grief:

Iubes regina infandum renovare dolorem
(*Aeneid*, Bk II, 3)

Shakespeare alludes to this famous line, which editors sometimes dismiss as 'a commonplace', on several occasions. Egeon's version is especially interesting as evidence that Shakespeare could read Virgil in Latin, since he does not follow the English versions but gives an apparently independent translation.*

There is another narrative allusion in Egeon's speech, an imitation of the Prologue to Plautus's *Menaechmi*, in which a comic uncompromising narrative sets out the history of the separated twins. Shakespeare is cunning, crossing his sources, drawing conspicuously on the Virgilian narrative, which contains an important truth about the passions, still paying homage to the Plautine source of his story. In the *Menaechmi*, a comically blunt Prologue is self-

* According to T.W. Baldwin (*Shakespeare's Small Latine and Lesse Greeke*, University of Illinois Press, Urbana, 1944), who acknowledges that the source was spotted by Theobald. Neither Baldwin nor Theobald mentions Homer in this context.

consciously matter-of-fact about exposition, mentioning brevity (recommended by rhetoric books discussing *narratio*) and referring to the theatrical conventions of beginning:

> My business is to call
> Plautus before your . . . ears, not eyes, today
> So please attend to what he has to say.
> And please attend to me, while I unfold,
> Briefly, the tale that here is to be told.
> [. . .]
> Now for the argument – which I present
> In generous measure . . .
> (*The Menaechmus Brothers*, in *The Pot of Gold and Other Plays*, trans. E.F. Watling, London, Penguin Classics, 1965)

Shakespeare's expository narration recalls Plautus by doing something completely different. Egeon's story is told in a personal way, realistically energized in retrospect and length, highly motivated, and also self-conscious and conventional. As so often, the story is being told by a dramatist and a character, in fused collaboration. It is an agonized life-story, a self-generative memory, in which nostalgia for good times is overtaken by grief at bereavement. As the narrative modulates from legal testimony into vivid memory, present dissolves into past. The Virgilian paraphrase instructs the actor to break up the lines, to pause, sigh, gasp, or weep, to appear – almost – overwhelmed:

> A heavier task could not have been impos'd,
> Than I to speak my griefs unspeakable;
> Yet that the world may witness that my end
> Was wrought by nature, not by vile offence,
> I'll utter what my sorrow gives me leave.
> In Syracusa was I born, and wed
> Unto a woman happy but for me,
> And by me, – had not our hap been bad.

The last line's pause, which replaces the pentameter's tenth syllable, is one of the covert emotion-cues in his dignified report, and there are one or two more explicit – an 'alas' before he relates the family's embarkation and a longer break as he comes to their shipwreck, 'O, let me say no more;/Gather the sequel by that went before'. Shakespeare's intense speeches are often marked by a reminder of art; sometimes, like that 'sequel', in a buried metaphor revived by rhetorical context. The Duke insists on the sequel, with a touch of Dido's listening pity, 'we may pity, though not pardon', and there are many cues for Egeon's passion leading to the artistically conscious and emotional winding-up:

> Thus have you heard me sever'd from my bliss,
> That by misfortunes was my life prolong'd
> To tell sad stories of my own mishaps.

The return to Virgilian allusion is answered by the Duke's humane request for more, with another technical term, 'for the sake of them thou sorrowest for,/Do me the favour to dilate at full . . .'; the skilful dilation ends simply, 'here doth end the story of my life'; and the Duke rewards painful narrative with brief remission.

Egeon's long narrative has been adversely contrasted, by Marvin T. Herrick (*Comic Theory in the Sixteenth Century*, Urbana, University of Illinois Press, 1950), with the animated by-play of characters and rapid dialogue in Egeus's exposition at the beginning of *A Midsummer Night's Dream*, but I do not think his condemnation is entirely justified. When we look at the speeches closely we see that Egeon's namesake Egeus has a briefer tale to tell, a motive of fatherly murderous fury, and companions in conflict. I suspect that Shakespeare anticipated the contrast, amusing himself by writing strikingly different expositions for two Greek fathers of similar name and opposite nature, as he varies his time-structure for the two fantasies of *The Winter's Tale* and *The Tempest*.

The tribute to Virgil is recalled at the end of *Titus Andronicus*, when Lucius relieves Marcus in an apologetic speech. This allusion involves retrospect and prospect, in a double reference to Aeneas's telling and Dido's listening. Marcus proposes the younger speaker, his nephew, as more likely to calm the crowd, and his invocation of ancestry is politic, expressive of character and functionally self-conscious, as it prompts monologue to become dialogue:

Speak, Rome's dear friend, as erst our ancestor,
When with his solemn tongue he did discourse
To love-sick Dido's sad-attending ear
The story of that baleful burning night
When subtle Greeks surpris'd King Priam's Troy.
Tell us what Sinon hath bewitch'd our ears . . .
(V.3)

Narrative allusion thickens as lying Sinon and sympathetic Dido join truthful Aeneas and the gullible Trojans, and the telling is passionately self-aware:

My heart is not compact of flint nor steel,
Nor can I utter all our bitter grief,
But floods of tears will drown my oratory,
And break my utt'rance, even in the time
When it should move ye to attend me most,
And force you to commiseration.*
Here's Rome's young captain, let him tell the tale,
While I stand by and weep to hear him speak.

It is the cue for Lucius's speech of political justification, the story of the murder and rape committed by Chinon and Demetrius. He speaks emotionally, drawing attention to truth-telling and modesty, 'I am no vaunter, I', retracts dangerous self-praise, apologizes for digression and hands the story back to Marcus.

Literary Narrators

As they tell personal stories, Marcus and Egeon unconsciously and consciously recall the great narratives of their culture on their author's behalf. Shakespeare's professional storytellers, authors, presenters, choruses, messengers and ambassadors also make demonstrations of narrative as they perform their artistically and politically significant roles.

John Gower, who acts as chorus in *Pericles*, is Shakespeare's

* The Quarto reading, 'Lending your kind commiseration', looks like a feeble first or corrupt version, but the variant brings out the fine detail of Shakespeare's imaginative attention to listening and response.

most sustained and elaborate act of literary mimicry. The reincarnation of a medieval writer, who supplied Shakespeare with his main plot, the author of the romantic and visionary *Confessio Amantis* is a good choice, not simply as a playful image of the source within the play but as a narrative poet writing fantastic moral tales of tragic and untragic love. He tells his stories, drawing, like Shakespeare, on classical and medieval sources, in a relaxed and easy line, uses several narrative voices and makes an amusing cultural bridge between the Elizabethan audience and the classical subject-matter of the play. Shakespeare uses a subdued medieval pastiche for the choric idiolect – his Middle English is tactfully more modern than John Gower's, though he sprinkles the choruses with some fifteenth-century forms and words – and he varies the verse-form, like Gower, with rhyming octosyllabics and pentameter. His narration includes the customary discussion of stage illusion and audience-participation along with a vast coverage of fantastic material which Shakespeare chooses not to dramatize – so vast that it could not be dramatized – compressing and distancing the plot's voluminousness and romantic extravagance. The narration in *Pericles* complements that of the other romances, each of which has an appropriately exaggerated or grotesque use of narrative. The mutual discovery of father and child which is narrated as offstage action in Act IV of *The Winter's Tale* is here totally dramatized, in one of the most solemn and touching scenes in Shakespeare, with a slow gradual process of ecstatic and wondering discovery and union which inspired T.S. Eliot's mysterious poem of love's discovery, 'Marina'. But the meeting of Pericles and Marina is framed by Gower's grotesque though dignified narrative, with local appropriateness, since Gower's similar reconciliation scene is the source for this one. He appears as an ancient, in both senses, speaking a strange ancient language and quoting his ancient sources, narrating more action, and making more appearances, than any other choric narrator in these plays. Like the other romantic tragicomedies, *Pericles* creates appropriately playful and reflexive narration for its fantasy and extravagance, in perfect keeping with the original Gower – a self-conscious, homage-paying, teasingly self-deprecating author whose book is also tragi-comic, standing 'betwene ernest and game' (*Confessio Amantis*, Liber Octavus, l. 3109).

In *Romeo and Juliet* the Chorus takes the form of two expository sonnets, suggested by the three prefatory sonnets in Arthur Brooke's poem 'Romeus and Juliet' (1562; Bullough, vol. I). Shakespeare's preliminary sonnet offers a brief abstract and prospect, telling the story lyrically by picking out past and future passions, 'ancient grudge', 'misadventur'd piteous overthrows' and 'fearful passage of . . . death-mark'd love'. When it makes its next and last appearance at the beginning of the second act, it continues the story of passions in the present tense, 'old desire', 'new affection', 'steal love's sweet bait from fearful hooks' and a final couplet:

> But passion lends them power, time means, to meet,
> Tempering extremities with extreme sweet.

Each poem names feeling as dominant and causal and, as you would expect of a sonnet, articulates involvement of feeling in affective words like 'piteous', 'fearful', 'sweet' and so on.

The second Chorus at the beginning of the second act, left out in the Quarto, was criticized by Dr Johnson for adding nothing to the play. Although he is right about it relating 'what is already known' and adding no 'moral sentiment', the reappearance conforms its narrator's status as impersonal but affected observer and not mere Prologue, and its commentary halts the intense swift action of the first act, dwelling on passions through generality. It intensifies the play's lyricism, and what Coleridge finely called its unity of feeling, by taking the form of a narrative sonnet and a lyrically present-tense narrative, in a crossing of genres which the sonnet–prologue started. The complete, curtailed, regular and irregular sonnets within the play's action respond. So a poet appropriately presides as Prologue over these first acts, then withdraws, his lyric emphasis done, to let tragic intensities gather uninterrupted into action.

The information given at the beginning outlines the action and tells us the end, to ensure tension and stress theme without foretelling any particulars so that, knowing the end, we are free to concentrate on the processes and immediacies of action, propelled by what Coleridge called the play's 'precipitancy', tensed by a threatening and ironic awareness.

These lofty professional narrations are unlike the tradition-conscious but personal and partial speeches of Egeon, Lucius and Marcus in detachment, but like them in passion. They also animate narrative life-modes, as in their different ways they blur the line between narrative and poetry, formal commentaries spoken with feeling, like public narration in its social and political functions. Passion and the presentation of social form preserve these expositions and introductions from mere function.

The complex choric narration in Act II of *Henry V* gives the audience vital information. This Chorus tells us that war is about to start, sets the king on his way to Southampton, advances the action beyond Henry's previous declaration of intent and informs us about the traitors. On its first appearance, before the first act, the choric prologue was unconventionally free from narrative, devolving all the exposition to characters, simply giving the audience a playful warm-up discussion of stage-illusion. The narrative retrospect of the second Chorus is brief and lyrically exalted with patriotic delight in the war – 'all the youth of England are on fire', and exclamations of loyal anger and blame. Shakespeare brilliantly continues and conflates the aesthetic persuasions of the first chorus with the patriotic fervours of the second; each is concerned with drumming up support and enlisting sympathy, one for the theatre, the other for king and country. An effective theatrical device exposes the ends and means of public rhetoric:

> O England! model to thy inward greatness,
> Like little body with a mighty heart,
> What might'st thou do, that honour would thee do,
> Were all thy children kind and natural!
> But see, thy fault France hath in thee found out,
> A nest of hollow bosoms, which he fills
> With treacherous crowns . . .

The narrative looks ahead to the conspiracy to kill Henry, taking us in an affective trajectory of pious patriotic persuasion, reproach and shame to the verge of expectation. Like the personified Expectation in the speech, which sits on air and hides a sword, it is a tense, thrilling and curtailed public narrative. Then the action is comically held up by Nym and Bardolph, picks up where the Chorus left off, to reach the scene where Henry pretends to trust Scroop, Gray and Cambridge before arresting them. It is an elegant construction, varied, teasingly retarded and joining a terse characterized two-line narration – telling us what the Choric narration did not tell, that Henry knows the plot – with a prophetic, though not omniscient, forecast. What is formal, professional and separated from action is joined by the passions of persuasion, neatly dovetailed in narrative collaboration between Chorus and characters.

The Chorus in *Henry IV, Pt 2* illustrates Shakespeare's asymmetry because *Henry IV, Pt 1* has none. This Induction is presented by Rumour, personification of a famous social narrative, who for much of the speech, fascinatingly, does not narrate. We move from Rumour's self-characterization (probably inspired by Virgil and Ovid, but more teasing than their typical figures) which proliferates the type and sets out motivation: 'Rumour is a pipe/ Blown by surmises, jealousies, conjectures'. Shakespeare's playful and subtle Rumour is very different from the straightforward characterizations of Virgil and Ovid. He includes a playful illustration of what Rumour is not, exploiting the difference between his two modes, narrative and dramatic. The figure painted full of tongues idly slips into the truth, moving from description to narration, full of fun:

> I run before King Harry's victory,
> Who in a bloody field by Shrewsbury
> Hath beaten down young Hotspur and his troops,
> Quenching the flame of bold rebellion
> Even with the rebels' blood. But what mean I
> To speak so true at first?

Rumour observes the bad logic of self-characterization, which has led to inconsistency, and goes on charmingly, to tell the truth, about lying. The rumour has gone out that Harry has lost and Hotspur won. Shakespeare tells the story twice, accurately, then inaccurately, but so that the audience knows that the inaccuracy is inaccurate and gets the true report twice. It's a handy device which enlivens historically 'factual' narrative and fixes the unreliability of news and reporting. It can be read as clearing the way to make a true report or as subverting the whole idea of accurate reporting.

When Shakespeare switches from narration to the purely dramatic mode, Rumour performs as promised. In the dialogic and active mode the story is told twice too. The characters first get things wrong, then right, then wrong again; but since we have had the first doubling of accurate report, confusion is unlikely. Or if there is confusion, so much the better for Rumour's demonstration.

So Shakespeare dramatizes problems of transmission, creates the appropriate political and military web of doubt and lies, keeping and revising the traditional figure of Rumour by first narrating and not showing distortions, then showing them, as truths and lies, in action. He is not only demonstrating the corruption of news, as he goes on to do most unnervingly in *Macbeth*, but making an unstable *nuntius* figure, untruly true to life and an impudent travesty of tradition, verging on a narrative satire. Shakespeare is playing an elaborate game with the imitative fallacy, in a teasing model of unreliable communication which is also a disguised exposition, taking its time, and offering different versions, before the clinching irony, 'This is the news at full'.

Public Narrators: Messengers and Ambassadors

Rumour and the characters who spread rumour or get the news right are types of the ancient figure of the messenger.* This conventional and usually minor character carries a charge of political analysis and judgement. The responsibility and the fallibility of communications show themselves in the messenger. The person-

*There are two general discussions of the messenger: Wolfgang Clemen's 'Shakespeare's Use of the Messenger's report', *Shakespeare's Dramatic Art*, London, Methuen, 1972, and Gary Scrimgeour's 'The Messenger as a Dramatic Device in Shakespeare', *Shakespeare Quarterly*, 19, 1968. R.A. Foakes's introduction to the Arden *King Henry VIII* is particularly good on the play's 'gossiping gentlemen'. There is a discussion of the messengers in *Macbeth* in Chapter 10 below.

ality and vitality of Shakespeare's messengers contrasts strikingly with *Gorboduc*'s, where the figure Webster called 'the passionate and weighty *Nuntius*' in the Address to the Reader of *The White Devil*, is ponderous, stiff, formal and dispassionate. Shakespeare makes his messengers and their messages passionate, and they are never merely functional but characters involved in danger, doubt and ambiguity, for instance, in *Henry IV*, *Macbeth* and *Antony and Cleopatra*. He creates rounded and highly individualized parts, as Sophocles and Euripedes did for their messengers, most complexly in *Antigone* and the *Agamemnon*, never forgetting the demands of the audience for character or the hazards and powers and frailties of news and reporting. Like theirs, Shakespeare's messengers are highly individual, lucidly observed and judged as essential means of communications, telltale prompters of high event. They are also politicized, frail or strong instruments and agents of greater powers, signs and symbols of their society.

Sometimes the messenger is a major character, like King Lear's servant Caius, the disguised Duke of Kent. He is contemptuous of Goneril's messenger Oswald, and it is an insult to the king when he is put in the stocks. But the messenger is usually an unnamed character, putting in a brief appearance. *Antony and Cleopatra*, for example, multiplies images of the vulnerable or fearful messenger, the powerless communicating with the powerful, vivid small-part renderings of political forces. The play's Mediterranean map has grand routes busy with messengers. Antony, Cleopatra and Caesar are involved with them in crucial scenes animated and complicated by the tension, humour, politics and psychology of this genre of social communication. The play's geographical spaciousness, with its subjects of civil war and imperial conquest, brings messengers and messages to the forefront of action. After the Roman judgement and amorous dialogue that begin the play, there is 'News' from Rome, Antony demands its 'sum', and is goaded by Cleopatra's 'Call in the messengers', and 'Hear the ambassadors', to postpone receiving the Messenger, action identifying the play's conflicts, decisions and indecisions. Antony leaves for Rome, and Cleopatra's 'twenty several messengers' post off to him, 'He shall have every day a several greeting'. Antony behaves with extreme dignity to the first messengers, in contrast to Cleopatra's hysterical ferocious punishment and jealous interview of the messenger in Act II, scene 5, but Caesar's honourable reception of Antony's schoolmaster in Act III contrasts with Antony's whipping of Caesar's messenger Thidias in Act IV. Messengers from Rome are balanced by the messengers from Egypt. In two scenes messengers come in quick succession, static but urgent narrations reporting the world's action. All these scenes are prolonged, intimate and individualized, and as they regularly punctuate the action – at least one crucial messenger scene for each act – they mark stages in the play's progress.

The relationships between the rulers and the messengers ring changes on the traditional injunction, 'Don't shoot the messenger'. Antony's first messenger knows 'The nature of bad news infects the teller' as he prepares Antony for 'stiff news'. Cleopatra insists that the messenger is the message, 'Though it be honest, it is never good to bring bad news'. She has great comic scenes (II.5 and III.3) with the messenger who announces Antony's marriage, 'I that do bring the news made not the match', and who, after being haled up and down, describes Octavia prudently enough to be employed as Cleopatra's messenger – 'I find thee/Most fit for business'. Such scenes are not merely comic but political reminders of the vulnerable anonymous communicators – usually powerless – on whom kingdoms, councils, battles and alliances depend. Shakespeare's messenger is always an individual, even in his briefest appearance. The agent and the actor are respected.

In this play Shakespeare's interest in the subject is not shown just by the length, number and individuality of his messenger scenes but in their assimilation to the development of the major characters. Antony's degradation, public and private, is marked by the change in his treatment of the messenger, as he loses control and self-respect. It's the other way round with Cleopatra. The ambiguous exchange (III.13), in which she sweet-talks Thidias, 'Most kind messenger', after objecting to his first sudden entrance – 'What, no more ceremony?' – and the more emotional and subtle dialogues with Proculeius and Dolabella (V.2) mark the progress in her control, dignity and 'better life'. Shakespeare gives good parts to the actors playing messengers and involves them in the tragic process.

At the end of *Love's Labour's Lost*, where the announcement of a king's death is minimal and laconic, the messenger, Marcade, interrupts exuberant fun and festivity. His eloquent appearance – he's always in black – makes it unnecessary for him to say more than eight words. He begins, shares, sums up the story, interrupts and is interrupted, in Shakespeare's most abridged narrative:

> *Enter Monsieur MARCADE, a Messenger.*
> *Mar.* God save you, madam!
> *Prin.* Welcome, Marcade,
> But that thou interrupt'st our merriment.
> *Mar.* I am sorry, madam; for the news I bring
> Is heavy in my tongue. The king your father—
> *Prin.* Dead, for my life!
> *Marc.* Even so: my tale is told.
>
> (V.2)

Shakespeare likes to condense, as well as elaborate, and this reduction of theatrical and social conventions of telling and listening to suggestion and inference brings the *nuntius* dangerously close to travesty but dignifies him and the occasion in a brilliantly particular and original animation. It is also perfect for the comic genre, turning levity to gravity as curtly as possible.

Henry VIII is Shakespeare's only history play to concentrate on the purely civic, non-military, events of an England at peace, and its messengers, as Foakes points out in the introduction to his 1957 Arden edition (liv–lv), are a cleverly handled group of anonymous gentlemen, their informed gossip punctuating the play. Shakespeare obviously decided not to make comedy of ill-informed rumour and report, as he had done so successfully and so thoroughly in *Henry IV*, nor to create strong little character parts for the actors, as he had done so often, but to dramatize and personalize, with a kind of brilliant neutrality, the ordinary quotidian media of political and personal court gossip. Its characters are no one in particular, though close enough to the corridors of power to observe and communicate. Its theme is the who's in, who's out of the powerful lords and prelates – Buckingham, Wolsey and Cranmer – and the royals, Queen Katherine and Anne Bullen. He creates, with speed and stylization, a dialogue of thumbnail sketches in what Foakes calls 'the often unappreciated scenes . . . full of quick characterization . . . conveying information or carrying forward the action with a remarkable economy of means', which also 'direct or counterbalance the audience's reaction' and show the public characters, and represent 'a national view' from varying viewpoints. These 'gossiping gentlemen' fill the play's population, joining with the low-life stereotypes in the crowd to show styles of public opinion, all fascinated and powerless as fortunes rise and fall. Persons and styles are drawn with a minimal, subtle, light irony, because this play is directed by a purpose of topical royal compliment, to Princess Elizabeth and James I, and a nostalgic one to the reign of Queen Elizabeth I. Satire on power and high place is tactful and subdued, but the commentaries play an important political part in countering the loyal compliments.

A flowing, easy, conversational verse is the medium from which formal narratives may or may not rise, an iambic metre on which ordinary phatic dialogue is delicately counterpointed, a choric commentary individually voiced. The gentlemen discuss and promote the rumour of a royal separation:

1 Gent. Let me have it;
I do not talk much.
2 Gent. I am confident;
You shall sir: did you not of late days hear
The buzzing of a separation
Between the king and Katherine?
1 Gent. Yes, but it held not . . .

(II.1)

They report the crush at a new royal wedding:

1 Gent. . . . Where have you been broiling?
3 Gent. Among the crowd i'th' abbey, where a finger
Could not be wedg'd in more: I am stifled

With the mere rankness of their joy.
1 Gent. You saw
The ceremony?
3 Gent. That I did.
1 Gent. How was it?
(IV.2)

They talk about a treason trial:

2 Gent. Were you there?
1 Gent. Yes indeed was I.
Pray speak what has happen'd.
2 Gent. You may guess quickly what.
1 Gent. Is he found guilty?
2 Gent. Yes truly is he, and condemn'd upon't.
1 Gent. I am sorry for't.
2 Gent. So are a number more.
(II.1)

It is a fresh and original achievement, individualizing voices of society, straight, fast and simple, without irony, criticism or stereotype, as if Shakespeare had freed himself from a brilliant but simplifying and cruder typology into a realistic and sociologically analytic narrative.

Comic and Satiric

Love's Labour's Lost, a much earlier play, invents what is probably Shakespeare's most exaggerated satire of narrative in Don Armado's letter to the King, telling how he arrested Costard for consorting with a woman.

It is more complex than meets the eye, a self-exposing narrative in the form of a letter designed to be read by a critical and unsympathetic reader, narrating in two voices simultaneously, the writer's and his own. It illustrates what happens when a first-person narrative is read by a second person, with less than total sympathy, and the blend is gorgeously funny as the reader's performance defeats the writer's intent at every breath. It is a comic version of that experience of feeling identity turned into story. The King reads, ironic in his superior, critical and amused voice, impersonating the writer's pomp and circumstance in parody or mixing the styles, incredulously and fastidiously picking his way through the bookish rhetoric:

> So it is, besieged with sable-coloured melancholy, I did commend the black oppressing humour to the most wholesome physic of thy health-giving air; and, as I am a gentleman, betook myself to walk. The time when? About the sixth hour . . . so much for the time when. Now for the ground which? which, I mean, I walked upon . . . Then for the place where? where, I mean, I did encounter that obscene and most preposterous event, that draweth from my snow-white pen the ebon-coloured ink, which here thou viewest, beholdest, surveyest, or seest. But to the place where: it standeth north-north-east and by east . . .
>
> (I.1)

A single-voiced story is turned into a three- or four-voiced one, past transformed into the present, and book compared with reality, as a parody of the rhetorical heads recommended for narrative is transformed into movement and physical immediacy, people doing things on a stage. As he makes fun of the wrong way of learning rhetoric's lessons, Shakespeare demonstrates the right way: after all, what the books recommended for *narratio* were the physical particularities of place and time and person. In 1553 Thomas Wilson in his *Arte of Rhetorique* (ed. G.H. Mair, Oxford University Press, 1909, and quoted in the relevant note by the Arden editor, Richard David) recommends seven heads, but Armado is made to pick out the most physical.

Costard is subject turned listener, in his comic version of the Odyssean experience of finding your life turned into story. Costard's self-delight at identifying himself with the character in a narrator's words makes him one of the most lively of Shakespeare's interruptors, as he laments his early absence from Armado's narrative ('Not a word of Costard yet'), impatiently questions ('Me? . . . Me? . . . Still me?'), eventually enjoys recognition ('O! me'), and finally puts in 'With a wench', to be joined by Dull, echoing his 'Me' because everything in this neat and wild play has a twin, an opposite or a travesty.

The model of narrative particularity makes a comment on rhetorical aridity. The abstraction of Where, When and What, in Don Armado's pedantic application of his rhetoric book, is cheekily put down by the live characters who are reduced and reified in his story, just as the celibate academy is challenged, invaded and then destroyed by stubborn human particulars of sex and politics. The abstracting pedant varies his synonyms but dully and excessively, and the result is a joke, variety is provided by rude teeming life. Life impudently crops up in the dramatist's contrast and counterpoint, as that interrupting 'Me' is repeated and permuted. Narrative is shown in its bare bones and its flesh, comically flattened but only in order to be animated, and the free entertaining interlude turns out to be a sly satirical microcosm of the play, a little play in which a dull scholar's loving labours are lost. The intelligent amused critic's unawareness here that he is like the object of his amusement is one of Shakespeare's finely amusing touches.

Another self-conscious narrative treads a tightrope between gravity and parody in *The Winter's Tale*, where Shakespeare presents an offstage report of Leontes's and Perdita's recognition and reunion. The choice of method may almost seem a breach of decorum, and I have known Shakespeare scholars who dislike it, but I think it works as a stylish flourished economy, a kind of travesty which allows the dramatist to reserve dramatic immediacy for the reunion of Leontes and Hermione. As I have already said, the reported meeting of father and daughter complements the direct and dramatic presentation of the reunited Pericles and Marina: Shakespeare clearly made a decision to do the discovery-scenes in contrasting ways: one is all drama, the other is all narrative. And in both plays there is a marked contrast between offstage and onstage, past and present, tragic and comic.

In the last act, after the action returns to Sicilia, Shakespeare does his worst and his best, as he accumulates self-conscious narrative. The second scene begins with the story of a story, Autolycus hearing by request the first gentleman's brief account of 'the opening of the fardel', and the shepherd's 'relation' of 'the manner how he found it'. The telling is very brief but includes cues for passion,

Autolycus's 'Beseech you', the gentleman's 'a little amazedness', and his rhetorical apology for a 'broken delivery of the business'. He delivers it gracefully, as the convention emphasizes, a story of passionate, and not wholly understood, response, told with elegant balance, strong hyperbole and violent metaphor:

> the changes I perceived in the king and Camillo were very notes of admiration: they seemed almost, with staring on one another, to tear the cases of their eyes: there was speech in their dumbness, language in their very gesture; they looked as they had heard of a world ransomed, or one destroyed: a notable passion of wonder appeared in them; but the wisest beholder, that knew no more but seeing, could not say if th'importance were joy or sorrow . . .
>
> (V.2)

After this contrast of vehicle's pure narration and tenor's pure action, we have the stunningly compressed sentence of the second messenger, who begins where the first gentleman leaves off, having been ordered out: Rogero's report is image, summary, news and topos of inexpressibility in four clauses:

> Nothing but bonfires: the Oracle is fulfilled: the king's daughter is found: such a deal of wonder is broken out within this hour, that ballad-makers cannot be able to express it.

Rogero introduces the third narrator, Paulina's steward, 'he can deliver you more' and 'How goes it now, sir? This news, which is called true, is so like an old tale'; and the third reporter supports its truth with 'circumstance' and 'unity in the proofs' in another extravagant narration of passionate silence: 'casting up of eyes, holding up of hands, with countenance of such distraction, that they were to be known by garment, not by favour', and inexpressibility, 'I never heard of such another encounter, which lames report to follow it, and undoes description to do it.' After more urging from Rogero and the first gentleman, now listeners, he responds, 'Like an old tale still, which will have matter to rehearse, though credit be asleep and not an ear open', completing the story of Antigonus's death, Paulina's mingled grief and joy, and concluding with her invitation to view the statue. The whole story still unfinished, the second gentleman suggests that they join the others, and the first agrees that they must miss nothing: 'Every wink of an eye, some new grace will be born: our absence makes us unthrifty to our knowledge. Let's along.'

They leave Autolycus to wry soliloquy: he could have been the newsgiver and agent of revelation if the lovesick prince had only listened when he told him that the old man and his son had been talking about 'a fardel and I know not what', but he concludes that such benign discovery by him would have been indecorous, out of character for a bad character. It is one more clever self-conscious variation, one more comic reminder of the rhetorical rules and social inhibitions of narrative. The narrative virtuosity of the scene is comic, the storytelling exaggerated and concentrated. There is the contrast between artificially pronounced narrative vehicle and the emotional and performative tenor, the theatrically self-conscious insistence on what hearers missed by hearing and not witnessing, the travesty of messenger function in the rapid succession of nonce narrators, and their perfunctory discrimination – one anonymous, one named, one distinguished by function. Shakespeare is amusedly anticipating the critic's approval of the individuation and variation of sheer function. He makes free with its technical terminology ('ballad-makers' and 'old tale'), and dares us to think of non-verbal language ('speech in . . . dumbness', 'language in . . . gesture', 'dignity of . . . act', 'audience' and 'acted'). Self-consciousness, speed and replication are comical intensifiers, like the zany and farcical piling up of bodies in the famous cabin scene of the Marx Brothers' film *A Night at the Opera*.

There is serious emotion in what is told in this clowning narration, as well as meta-narrative. Through conspicuous rhetoric and exemplary demonstration, telling and showing what narrative can and cannot do, Shakespeare instructs the audience in what he is doing, as he does it. He insists that he is not being crude, that he knows what he is doing. In this scene, as in Ophelia's narration of Hamlet's distracted visit to her closet, the largely performative nature of the story brings out the contrast, and tells what in one way is better told, since these actors tend to speech, not mime, and yet in another way can least easily be told. He is like an expert juggler, prompting an awareness of virtuosity and skill by a daring demonstration of difficulty, not getting it wrong but moving close to the errors of narrative excess. He challenges the critic to object, and the critic has occasionally done so, falling into the cleverly set trap.

As Paulina is torn between the two emotions – grief for losing her husband and joy in finding Perdita – she is echoing the Clown's earlier comic conflict, at the end of Act III. At the mid-point of the play, modulating from tragedy to comedy, Shakespeare uses a naïve and maladroit teller to relate a twofold disaster, overloading his incapacity, blunting the tragic events for a tragi-comic genre. The Clown's story switches from the bear eating Antigonus to the shipwreck, both beyond help, described with instant relish in a fine travesty of present-tense narrative, compounded by the problem of telling two things at once. The event is unactable and has to be narrated, and Shakespeare makes the most of the rhetoric of inexpressibility. But the comic narrator is not patronized: the naïvety of his apt see-saw action adds to the gallows humour, but his narration is neat, balanced and compressed, his idiolect not obtuse but bluntly graphic, his repetitions brilliant, his ordering and selection aware of principles:

> *Clown* I would you did but see how it chafes, how it rages, how it takes up the shore! But that's not to the point. O, the most piteous cry of the poor souls! sometimes to see 'em, and not to see 'em: now the ship boring the moon with her main-mast, and anon swallowed with yest and froth, as you'd thrust a cork into a hogshead. And then for the land-service, to see how the bear tore out his shoulder-bone, how he cried to me for help, and said his name was Antigonus, a nobleman. But to make an end of the ship, to see how the sea flap-dragoned it: but first, how the poor souls roared, and the sea mocked them: and how the poor gentleman roared, and the bear mocked him, both roaring louder than the sea or weather.
> *Shepherd* Name of mercy, when was this, boy?
> *Clown* Now, now: I have not winked since I saw these sights: the men are not yet cold under water, nor the bear half dined on the gentleman: he's at it now.
>
> (III.3)

In *The Taming of the Shrew* Shakespeare's comic demonstration works through a comic listener. Another purely physical action is related in self-assertive narration, in an exaggerated display of narratively democratic dialogue, when Grumio tells his fellow servant Curtis the story of the rough post-wedding ride. This is banter and knockabout, like much in the play, but puns, proverb and farce draw attention to artful narration.

> *Curt.* . . . I pray thee, news.
> *Gru.* First know my horse is tired, my master and mistress fallen out.
> *Curt.* How?
> *Gru.* Out of their saddles into the dirt, and thereby hangs a tale.
> *Curt.* Let's ha't, good Grumio.
> *Gru.* Lend thine ear.
> *Curt.* Here.
> *Gru.* There. [*Strikes him.*]
> *Curt.* This 'tis to feel a tale, not to hear a tale.
> *Gru.* And therefore 'tis called a sensible tale; and this cuff was but to knock at your ear and beseech listening. Now I begin. *Imprimis*, we came down a foul hill, my master riding behind my mistress—
> *Curt.* Both of one horse?
> *Gru.* What's that to thee?
> *Curt.* Why, a horse.
> *Gru.* Tell thou the tale. But hadst thou not crossed me, thou shouldst have heard how her horse fell, and she under her horse; thou shouldst have heard in how miry a place, how she was bemoiled, how he left her with the horse upon her, how he beat me because her horse stumbled, how she waded through the dirt to pluck him off me, how he swore, how she prayed that never prayed before, how I cried, how the horses ran away, how her bridle was burst, how I lost my crupper, with many things of worthy memory, which now shall die in oblivion, and thou return unexperienced to thy grave.
>
> (IV.1)

The comic narrative flaunts narrative extremes, in a parody of narrative formality – the Latin beginning and the *occupatio* – collaborating with the rude dialogue. As often – in the Clown's story and Armado's letter, for instance – Shakespeare turns what looks like comic condescension into political correctness. In a stroke, the question of narrative engrossment – social and artistic – is comically judged and avoided, monologue turned to dialogue, the unactable narrated, compression and speed accomplished, and the point after all taken by the shrewd Curtis, 'By this reckoning he is more shrew than she'.

In *Measure for Measure* Angelo – judge, hypocrite, slanderer and liar – is a more complexly characterized impatient listener, irritated by Pompey, a comic teller less competent than the mode-mastering Grumio. Escalus and Angelo hear Pompey's elaborate attempts to refute Elbow's muddled testimony about his wife's visit to the brothel. Pompey is a prolix narrator, whose style of over-circumstantial garrulousness is more often mocked, sometimes deceptively – by Shakespeare and others – in stereotypes of women. He insists on a detail of crockery: 'a fruit-dish, a dish of some three pence, your honours have seen such dishes, they are not china dishes, but very good dishes —'; Escalus shuts him up, 'no matter for the dish', and he sycophantically but incorrigibly agrees, 'No, indeed, sir, not of a pin; you are therein in the right: but to the point'. He repeats the demotic narrative tags, 'As I said', and 'As I say' six times in one sentence, breaks off to get reinforcement from Froth, over-particularizes, with lavish use of the narrative fillers, 'Indeed', and 'Very well', and makes further excursions, until he is pulled up by Escalus, 'Come, you are a tedious fool. To the purpose'.

Like the cross-purpose ramblings of Dogberry and Verges in *Much Ado About Nothing*, and Mistress Quickly, these rich digressions and specificities of time, place and person challenge the imitative fallacy, boring the audience in the play to delight the audience outside: 'He, sir, sitting, as I say, in a lower chair, sir – 'twas in the Bunch of Grapes, where indeed you have a delight to sit, have you not?' and Froth – whose minutely chronicled close-up prune-cracking could only be narrated – replies 'I have so, because it is an open room and good for winter'. Again like Mistress Quickly and Dogberry, the defendants accumulate circumstantial testimonies ('here be truths') as educated listeners respond, in character. Again, superiorities of lexis and order are ironical, even specious.

The plain prose of critical truthful Escalus is more tolerant than the witty verse of scornful untruthful Angelo, and their treatment of the low-life characters, in an interlude of comic relief, echo and anticipate graver causes, mercy, severity and judgement:

> This will last out a night in Russia
> When nights are longest there. I'll take my leave,
> And leave you to the hearing of the cause;
> Hoping you'll find good cause to whip them all.
> (II.1)

In *Henry IV, Pt 1*, Hotspur's narrative style suits his character, attractive but lacking what Coleridge called 'that prospectiveness of mind, that *surview*' (*Biographia Literaria*, Chapter 18). His story gets out of control as he defends himself for not handing over his prisoners. It begins amusingly and sympathetically, as he parodies the effete perfumed envoy annoying the soldier 'Breathless and faint' from action:

> Came there a certain lord, neat and trimly dress'd,
> Fresh as a bridegroom, and his chin new reap'd
> Show'd like a stubble-land at harvest home . . .
> He question'd me, amongst the rest demanded
> My prisoners in your Majesty's behalf.
> I then, all smarting with my wounds being cold,
> To be so pester'd with a popinjay,
> Out of my grief and my impatience
> Answer'd neglectingly, I know not what,
> He should, or he should not, for he made me mad
> To see him shine so brisk, and smell so sweet,
> And talk so like a waiting-gentlewoman
> Of guns, and drums, and wounds, God save the mark!
> And telling me the sovereignest thing on earth
> Was parmacity for an inward bruise . . .
> (I.3)

There's wit in the contemptuous sharp comparisons and detail, as he remembers the 'bald unjointed chat', and works himself up and into vagueness and looseness: 'I know not what', the clauses slung together with 'ands', and the repetition, 'as I said'. There is a later, better-shaped speech in defence of Mortimer, then he is snubbed by the King and becomes incoherent again in over-elaborated, over-exclamatory, choleric speeches – including the famous one about plucking bright honour from the palefaced moon. His inventive flights of metaphor are put down by Worcester's irony: he 'apprehends a world of figures. . . . But not the form of what he should attend'. Shakespeare allows the exuberant wit to make, then overshoot, his mark, in bluster, bombast and eccentricity, as 'a windy man who rants'.

Hotspur's incompetence in telling is connected with his bad listening. He takes no notice of questions, his self-absorbed impulsive speeches break down, he forgets the name of Berkeley Castle – 'what do you call the place?/A plague upon it, it is in Gloucestershire'. Narrative degenerates into cursing, then peters out, and he hands over the tale to his uncle, having 'done'. Shakespeare strikes a delicate balance with Hotspur, in a dynamic narration which sometimes engages sympathy but finally loses it. It is the right form for a choleric soldier who is eloquent but wild, imaginative but impolitic, the opposite of manipulative, time-biding, cold Prince Hal. And the extravagant narratives are politically appropriate, too, precipitant, irrational, and disorganized, like the Percys' revolt. (This almost gets said in *Henry IV, Pt 2*, I.3, when Lord Bardolph meditates on Hotspur 'eating the air and promise'.) It is appropriate that when one of Hotspur's late speeches – actually brief and to the point – before Shrewsbury, is interrupted, he is glad, 'I thank him that he cuts me from my tale', and that his grandiose dying speech – less controlled – is also cut off:

> And time, that takes survey of all the world,
> Must have a stop. O, I could prophesy,
> But that the earthy and cold hand of death
> Lies on my tongue: no, Percy, thou art dust,
> And food for—
>
> (V.4)

Another narrative joke, a grim one, against this splendid flawed narrator, as he uses the grammatical term 'stop', but is not allowed one. His full stop, like his last word, and like his death, is provided by Hal: 'For worms'.

Generating a Story: Viola's Blank

Shakespeare now and then catches someone in the act of creating a story. There are forms of spontaneous construction in the fluent, uncontrolled narratives of the talkative uneducated women, Mistress Quickly and Juliet's Nurse, the imaginative anticipations of Juliet and Richard of Gloucester, and the improvised hand-to-mouth lying of Edmund and Falstaff, but Viola's case in *Twelfth Night* is a particularly interesting mixture of the impromptu and the deliberated, not part of an idiolect but a striking example of a lie. It acts as a model of self-generating invention.

In Act II, scene 4, her story starts impulsively, and she is forced to go on and finish it. The seeds of invention are sown as she eloquently praises the music: 'It gives a very echo to the seat/ Where love is thron'd', Orsino is moved by her – 'Cesario's' – 'masterly' speech to guess that she has loved, and her answers are ambiguous. After Feste's song 'Come away, come away death', and more talk, Orsino's claim that no woman's love can compare with his, prompts Viola's rash, 'Ay, but I know'. She catches herself up, and stops, or he interrupts to question her, 'What dost thou know?' and after two lines when she plays for time, her story follows:

> Too well what love women to men may owe:
> In faith, they are as true of heart as we.
> My father had a daughter lov'd a man,
> As it might be perhaps, were I a woman,
> I should your lordship.

He asks, 'And what's her history?', and she replies: 'A blank, my lord.' The answer is equivocal, once again she is playing for time. At this stage, we may suppose, the history of her imaginary sister is indeed blank, not yet invented, and the brilliant 'blank' acts both as a prologue and a convenient hesitancy, belonging to tenor and vehicle, theme and construction. It is the blank of creative pause, holding up and then releasing narrative momentum:

> A blank, my lord: she never told her love,
> But let concealment like a worm i' th' bud

> Feed on her damask cheek: she pin'd in thought,
> And with a green and yellow melancholy
> She sat like Patience on a monument,
> Smiling at grief.

The next question, 'But died thy sister of her love, my boy?' is equivocally answered: 'I am all the daughters of my father's house,/ And all the brothers too: and yet I know not.' The tight little story is sandwiched between ambiguities, which keep as close as possible to the truth. It is baroque in ornamentation, padded with two similes, telling as little as possible, forced into being by its impulsive beginning, urged on by Orsino's questioning, which is a rare and significant example of him showing an interest in somebody other than himself.

The laconic story is about not telling. Viola's eloquence is carefully prepared, elegantly expanding within its small compass, filling that blank with an approximate truth, 'she never told her love', to dwell misleadingly but not untruthfully on love-melancholy and patience, then truthfully leave the ending open. As a fiction, it stays close to truths. It is a characterizing story, impulsive, reticent, moral and ingenious. And illustratively self-conscious.

Narrative as Dominant Theme

In *Othello* narrative is a dominant subject, in the foreground of action and character. The demonstration of storytelling is serious, intense and tragic, in a play about the ethics of narrative. Narration is made demonstrative by an intense self-awareness of narrative as a personal and social act, as well as by the usual sense of narrative as craft.

Othello is a narrator, but on two occasions, when he tells the Senate about his wooing and just before he dies, he performs the part of the narrator, acting persuasive or diverting truths. His opposite is Iago, who acts fictions, in grossly abusive report (breaking the news of his daughter's marriage to Brabantio), scurrilous jokes (in sexist chit-chat to Desdemona in Cyprus), persuasive lies and slanders to everyone. Unlike Shakespeare's other destructive liar, Edmund, even at the end he is not allowed to confess, as if truth would be profaned by his utterance.

The play begins in the middle of narration (according to the *ordo artificialis* and not the *ordo naturalis* of medieval rhetoric). Iago arouses our curiosity by protesting ignorance to Roderigo, speaking allusively, then makes his narration more obscure by interrupting himself and turning to his grievances against Othello. We pick up the story of Othello's marriage to Desdemona when Iago brutally and aggressively reveals it to Brabantio, in the grossest bestial terms: the *mauvaise langue* dominates and poisons communication until Othello takes over in the big narration scene when he tells the full story of his courtship. He makes his impact in the context of Iago's filthy telling and the contrast is powerful. Iago is significantly sent offstage, 'Ancient, conduct them', as if purifying the stage for Othello to tell his story 'justly' to the 'grave ears' eagerly waiting for it.

Shakespeare's narrative conventions cluster. Othello's narration is an immediate reply to urgent need. It begins with a formal invitation, 'Say it, Othello'. The act of narration is emphasized by a compounding: it's a layered story, about telling a story. There are technical terms. The narrative is shaped by emotional response. There is a marked psychic and social form: Othello is arguing in personal justification, as we all do as we look back, and he is testifying, defending himself against an official charge of seduction and witchcraft. It is a complex interweaving of telling and listening: he noticed Desdemona listen, took the opportunity to elicit her request to hear more, told her his story, then heard her propose – not marriage, directly – but more storytelling.

This story of a story begins with Brabantio's request for Othello's life-story, to be told in its entirety ('I ran it through, even from my boyish days,/To the very moment that he bade me tell it'), summarizes the travel-tales, goes on to the story of Desdemona's eager piecemeal interrupted listening, fitted in between household duties, 'with a greedy ear' and 'not intentively', to end with his seizure of 'a pliant hour' and 'good means':

> To draw from her a prayer of earnest heart,
> That I would all my pilgrimage dilate,
> Whereof by parcel she had something heard . . .
> She gave me for my pains a world of sighs;
> She swore i' faith 'twas strange, 'twas passing strange;
> 'Twas pitiful, 'twas wondrous pitiful;
> She wish'd she had not heard it, yet she wish'd
> That heaven had made her such a man: she thank'd me,
> And bade me, if I had a friend that lov'd her,
> I should but teach him how to tell my story,
> And that would woo her. Upon this hint I spake . . .
> (I.3)

(The flashback to earlier narrations in Kenneth Branagh's film was a nice reminder of Brabantio's earlier friendliness, though it broke up the spell-binding narrative rerun.)

Othello's storytelling was not witchcraft, his tale would win the Duke's daughter too, and Desdemona comes to corroborate the story. Narrative has been powerful again, in a 'plain unvarnished tale', filled with convolutions and complexities of telling and listening, as it is told and heard.

At the end of the play, when slander and lies have smothered truth, Othello gives an even more thrilling demonstration of the theatrical power of narrative, its capacity to change events, its control and compounding, its passion and its immediacy. Shakespeare knows that final composure – even of remorse – does not come easily or quickly. After the fatal slanders, and Emilia's killing story – 'I speak true' – Othello's first long speech in response is disjointed, strange and incoherent:

> Here is my journey's end, here is my butt,
> And very sea-mark of my utmost sail.
> . . . Where should Othello go?
> Now: how dost thou look now?*

He addresses the dead Desdemona, his cold girl, shifts to Iago, 'O cursed slave!' and breaks down in a wild self-destructive pain which goes beyond words:

*These lines are omitted from the First Quarto.

> Whip me, you devils,
> From the possession of this heavenly sight,
> Blow me about in winds, roast me in sulphur,
> Wash me in steep-down gulfs of liquid fire!
> O Desdemona, Desdemona dead,
> Oh, oh, oh.
>
> (V.2)

He tries to kill Iago, is disarmed, and a few minutes later pulls himself together, extraordinarily, for the famous speech leading to his suicide. As they start to 'bring him away', he collects himself, and in striking contrast with the agonized speech in which he cannot order language into narrative, he makes a formal courteous request and tells a complex reasonable story:

> Soft you, a word or two:
> I have done the state some service, and they know't;
> No more of that: I pray you in your letters,
> When you shall these unlucky deeds relate,
> Speak of them as they are; nothing extenuate,
> Nor set down aught in malice; then must you speak
> Of one that lov'd not wisely, but too well:
> Of one not easily jealous, but being wrought,
> Perplex'd in the extreme; of one whose hand,
> Like the base Indian, threw a pearl away,
> Richer than all his tribe . . .

Othello anticipates becoming part of a story; his request for true report carries a proud pathos as it recalls the distortions of truth in his story and echoes that earlier claim to plain unvarnished telling. Of course there is a valedictory feel about his self-summary, but he is not simply planning a farewell. There are stories within the story, 'the base Indian', as Coleridge brilliantly spotted (*Shakespearean Criticism*, ed. T.M. Raysor, London and New York, Everyman, 1960, vol. I, p. 48), acting as external image for remorse, pity, even colour, and the extenuating and cunningly placed memory of killing the Turk, also externalizing the self and performing what he sees as a civic duty. The retrospect re-enacts, judges, sentences and executes Othello. The speech scans future, then past, and then present, to articulate the bitter sense of self and history, but also to empower and dignify suicide:

> I took by the throat the circumcised dog,
> And smote him thus.

He draws the weapon and stabs himself, violently breaking the security of narrative reminiscence. The climax and conclusion is a final action, shocking the story-lulled listeners in the play and outside it, as the story of a bloody act in the past becomes present violence. His last word, 'thus', is a blunt monosyllable to be released when the actor acts the stab, metamorphosing story to doing, history to immediacy. The course of the play is redetermined, for the last time, by brilliant narration.

The performance of telling is a startling but characteristic act and a paradigm of the dramatist's imagination and control. Lodovico's response uses one of the most astonishing of Shakespeare's technical terms in agony, 'O bloody period!', and Gratiano's 'All that's spoke is marr'd' brings in another self-conscious theatrical reminder. Othello's speech also is highly reflexive, in its compounding, in ways apt for its function, marking a regained control after the actor has moved – in minutes – from the inarticulate to the articulate, in a straight but shocking line of feeling to a last performance. It is a speech which was criticized by T.S. Eliot in 'Shakespeare and the Stoicism of Seneca' (*Selected Essays*, London, Faber, 1934) and F.R. Leavis in *Reading Out Poetry* (published by the Queens University of Belfast, 1979). They concur in judging Othello's language as an over-aestheticized act of self-dramatization which ignores Desdemona, and I believe they not only neglect the dramatic and narrative self-reference in a naïve character-criticism but ignore the force of Othello's terribly willed determination to execute himself, slowly spelled out in the careful planning and playing for time – deceptively self-dramatizing – and culminating in the contempt – which becomes self-contempt – for the circumcised Turk. Shakespeare wonderfully joins self-consciousness and violently perfected passion.*

*A.V. Nuttall sees this speech as more spontaneous and less artful, than I do: also disagreeing with Eliot and Leavis, he proposes that in the last speech Othello reverts to the heroic vaunt of a primitive shame-culture, nobly and professionally recovering 'himself': 'he has a job to do – like the jobs he did before – and he knows how to do it well' (*A New Mimesis: Shakespeare and the Representation of Reality*, London, Methuen, 1983, p. 141).

An earlier powerful narrative performance is Othello's story of the handkerchief, after Iago has told his lie about seeing Cassio wipe his beard with it. Halfway through his speech, as Othello warns Desdemona to make it her 'darling' – to lose it will be perdition – she exclaims 'Is't possible?' and his answer rushes to satisfy her terrified question:

> 'Tis true, there's magic in the web of it;
> A sibyl, that had number'd in the world
> The sun to make two hundred compasses,
> In her prophetic fury sew'd the work;
> The worms were hallow'd that did breed the silk,
> And it was dyed in mummy, which the skilful
> Conserve of maidens' hearts.
>
> (III.4)

And she asks again, 'I' faith, is't true?'

Apart from his last speech, this is the only other instance of a direct, strong, unmediated act of telling by Othello. Also frightening, it is less self-conscious and less complicated than the last speech. There seems no ground to distrust his claim that it is 'true', and 'veritable', though I can see that it could be played as dishonestly manipulative, and it is true that he has never told it before and has just been lied to by Iago. It is an amazing, fantastic and exotic story, and its telling achieves a second, fatal domination of Desdemona. It terrifies her and makes sure she will lie; before his story she has told the whiter lie, 'I have it not about me', but after it she says, 'It is not lost, but what an if it were?'

It compounds narrative and symbolism: as he tells his mother's story about the handkerchief's history of sibylline fury, hallowed worms and maidenheart mummy. The telling is solemnized, its performance a hieratic ritual, letting us feel the power we only heard of, indirectly, in his abridged account of the courtship-stories, and only feel again at the end. This magical story about magic, which casts its own spell, puts us in direct touch with his power, which seems to speak from another culture. (Though eclectically mixing east and west in the sibyls and mummy.) As it relates a talismanic history it makes the handkerchief a sacred object. And as Othello terrifies Desdemona, the actor should hypnotize the audience. Perhaps this is why it doesn't matter whether the story's 'true' or not. It intensifies the irony of his susceptibility to Iago's lies and slanders, and perhaps helps to elucidate it, but, above all, it is an incantatory speech for ritualized performance. Like a charm or curse, the story's articulated strangeness and solemnity are designed to make us feel the fear and pity of tragedy through a teller's and an actor's power.

CHAPTER TWO

Some Narrative Beginnings

'It was upon this fashion'

Narrative begins most of the plays, and the exceptions – most conspicuously the first active scenes in *The Tempest* and *Macbeth* – prove the rule, and create an urge to know more of the story that is beginning – in Hamlet's words, looking before and after. The narrative of Shakespeare's beginnings is usually highly time-conscious, compounding the sense of beginning, looking back in exposition, and looking ahead to the end. Like the beginning, the end is also time-conscious, compounding conclusion, and also looking back and – less expectedly – ahead.

There are many time-conscious first narratives, anticipating the end, in likeness and difference. *Hamlet* begins and ends with the clock, 'your hour', ''Tis now struck twelve' the repeated 'goodnights', and the story of the previous night, with a martial emphasis and with the dominance of Horatio, good listener and trusted teller; its initial uncertainty has turned by the end to bitter knowing. Rumour's Prologue to *Henry IV, Pt 2* is time-conscious, in 'acts commenced', 'from the Orient to the drooping West', and speaking 'at first'. Its Morality Play personifications start off the illustrative characters and debates of the play, like the Lord Chief Justice's conflict with Falstaff, and the proliferation of riot, weapon and body images; the Prologue contrasts with the Dancer's epilogue which is unlike brash Rumour in its cautious and intimate predictions of theatrical sequel containing more Falstaff. *A Midsummer Night's Dream* begins with dialogue about time, starting clock and calendar details, marriage and night, and its subjects and symbols are recapitulated in the final scene between Theseus and Hippolita, which repeats the themes and images of time, night, solemnity, sleep and dream and marriage. The only image not repeated, that of the moon, appears in Puck's nocturnal. *Love's Labour's Lost* begins and ends with the narration of young men's vows, emphasizing time, and the clash between ideal and real, all repeated at the end, which also makes a reversal as art is forced into the suffering and mortal heart of the real world, remote from the academy. *Troilus and Cressida* has Prologue and Epilogue, the first an anti-romantic narration by an armed man, audience-persuading and going back to the war's beginning, the second an equally anti-romantic narrative by Pandarus, and the future calendar, 'live aye with thy name', 'some two months hence' and 'at that time'.

The Sonnet–Prologue to *Romeo and Juliet* has the characteristic marks of Shakespeare's beginnings. Time-conscious and theme-conscious, its overture starts the play's clock and imagery with 'two hours traffic', 'star-cross'd', and 'passage'. Time is also stressed in its discussion of theatrical conditions, starting a transition from an audience's cool self-awareness to a measure of self-suspension. It is an initiating narrative which makes preparations and meets a response in the last narration of the play.

It is a sonnet, not a traditional narrative form, repeated before the second act and varied in the play. It is not formally repeated at the end, but it is recalled in the Prince's final six-line address:

> A glooming peace this morning with it brings:
> The sun for sorrow will not show his head.
> Go hence to have more talk of these sad things.
> Some shall be pardon'd, and some punished,
> For never was a story of more woe
> Than this of Juliet and her Romeo.
>
> (V.3)

It is like a sonnet's sestet, answering the fathers' earlier nine lines, which are like a sonnet's octave with one extra line. A deregulating of the sonnet seems appropriate: the fathers have rapidly made peace, promising somewhat competitively gold statues of the lovers. But their balm is not allowed to heal the pain of the play, and the Prologue is recalled in the imagery of light, dark and cosmos. Another link is the rhyme: the Prologue's 'misadventur'd piteous overthrows' born of 'foes' is echoed in the last couplet's 'Romeo' and 'woe'. The first conventional persuasion of audience by the Prologue–Narrator gives way to the Prince's command to his audience within the play: aesthetic address is displayed by an urgent imperative that subverts reconciliation and ends as it began, with tragic feeling.

Orlando's formal but integrated exposition in *As You Like It* is a good example of straightforward, time-conscious exposition – someone telling someone something he knows, to enlighten the audience and establish a time-frame:

> As I remember, Adam, it was upon this fashion bequeathed me by will but poor a thousand crowns, and, as thou sayst, charged my brother on his blessing to breed me well . . . for my part, he keeps me rustically at home . . . call you that keeping for a gentleman of my birth, that differs not from the stalling of an ox? His horses are bred better . . . This is it, Adam that grieves me . . .
>
> (I.1)

The first sentence looks back, the last sentence looks ahead: 'I will no longer endure it.' The speech is a matrix, with pastoral animal images, and though it is formal in rhetoric and syntax, its emotional drive makes dialogue and address seem natural, showing itself in the contemptuous animal images and the repetitions. The superficially redundant reminders are plausible forms of aggrieved questioning, Orlando telling Adam what he knows perfectly well, not to inform him but to get support and reassurance. The beginning is a match with the narrative at the end of the play, which tells the story of the brother's repentance and retreat, a return to the subject and another blunt – even blunter – expository narrative.

Closely packed narratives begin *Timon of Athens*. There is no formally labelled prologue or induction, but the dialogue in Act I, scene 1 between two characters, though integrated with the main action, is set off as a formal introduction; it is highly self-conscious, with its Poet and Painter speaking as representative and prophetic artists. They and their work are corrupted and reified by market-values, even though they criticize these values. Shakespeare refuses to privilege the artist by drawing a line between creative intelligence and transactional dealing, so he makes his prominent artist-figures speak with genuine sensibility and intelligence. Involved like nearly everyone in the play (and like the speaker in some of Shakespeare's sonnets) in competition and acquisition, they are superior to other sycophants only in their wisdom. They know, as the tragically romantic Timon does not, that no one can stand outside society.

Shakespeare imagines them producing a poem and a painting which are both time-conscious prologues and emblems of the play's theme and plot, and artworks for sale at the best price. Later on the satiric Apemantus calls the Poet a liar and flatterer, but the Poet knows this, and images art expressing itself in a painted lip. Shakespeare knows the artist cannot rise above the market, and has his themes determined by it. But those themes are not simple acts of flattery; they take on the question of patronage truthfully and morally, in a good hard creative insight: art may analyse politics but is still determined by politics. Their poem and painting image the course of the play, but if Timon completely attended to the art he buys, which tells his story in full, the course of the play would be different. The buyer of art is corrupted, as well as the sellers.

The sycophantic salesman-poet is a real poet, allowed not only to give his version of Shakespeare's play, about Timon's downfall, but also to articulate a rare access to Shakespeare's insight into generative power. His style is a fashionably affected shrug of self-deprecation but analytic as well. Shakespeare's only elaborate character of a poet is marvellously clear and complex. He is created out of a deeply ironic but humane sense of poetic fellowship, in weakness and strengths. It isn't accidental that he speaks of 'Our poesy':

> A thing slipp'd idly from me.
> Our poesy is as a gum which oozes
> From whence 'tis nourish'd; the fire i'the flint
> Shows not till it be struck: our gentle flame
> Provokes itself, and like the current flies
> Each bound it chases.

The other common prologue-features of clock, image-matrix, and of course – in the Poet's narrative and analysis – aesthetic awareness are all present in this extraordinary beginning of Shakespeare's most extraordinary play, from the authorship of which generations of scholars have argued, unconvincingly, to extricate him.

Especially marked in the play is the match of beginning and end, working through narrative asymmetry and symmetry. The Poet and Painter turn up in Act V, where their dishonesty and complicity are plain, but theirs is not the last image or the last word. The subject of art, reflective and reflexive, returns in Timon's encomium:

> These well express in thee thy latter spirits.
> Though thou abhorr'dst, in us our human griefs,
> Scorn'dst our brains' flow and those our droplets . . .
> . . . yet rich conceit
> Taught thee to make vast Neptune weep for aye
> On thy low grave . . .
>
> (V.4)

The tribute to his 'conceit' – his imagination – does not refer to the words of his bitterly cursing epitaph but to the inspired inventive symbolism which makes him choose the shore for a grave.

These are narrative expositions, but Shakespeare evades narration for *Macbeth* and *The Tempest*, where the audience is presented with a musically and pictorially incisive scene, with minimum or absence of exposition. As in the expository beginnings, each first scene is marked by time awareness, time-imagery and a match with the narrative at the end.

The witches' lyrical incantation in the brief opening scene of *Macbeth* is a form of narrative question-and-answer which tells little: two cryptic lines say the weird sisters will meet after the battle's lost or won, with Macbeth on the heath. There is no detail as they make the assignation, and most of the lines are 'sound and fury' signifying evil: 'In thunder, lightning, or in rain', 'When the hurlyburly's done', 'Paddock's' call and 'Fair is foul, and foul is fair:/Hover through the fog and filthy air'. It is an atmospheric overture, to be reversed and remembered at the end in Malcolm's pious promise:

> . . . this, and what needful else
> That calls upon us, by the grace of Grace
> We will perform in measure, time, and place.
> (V.9)

The speech is a ritual undoing the unholy prophecy – as it turns out – and black magic of the beginning, completing a sense of blessing in that promise to 'perform' and in measure, time and place. The verse-narration changes the trochaic dance-time rhythm of the witches' chant to the slower speech-rhythm of iambic pentameter but keeps the rhyme, as it exorcizes the witches' 'measure' of dance and verse. It repeats an appointment in time and place, but substitutes a benign for an unwholesome sense of community. This is the traditional and simple view of the relationship of beginning and conclusion, but a sense of apparently settled end has been unsettled by some interpreters, for example, Polanski in his film of the play. Malcolm's revising echoes of the witches' enigmatic and questioning lyric 'When shall we three meet again?. . . Where the place?' in his calm narration, 'in measure, time, and place', can be played as secure or insecure, his imaginative recapitulation functioning in a straight or a subversive interpretation. A Donalbain or a Macduff sneaking off to find the witches again is permitted by the last anticipation because of its ironic match with the play's beginning. A pious ordering in confirmed by the invocation of grace and the insistence on proper measure, due time and hallowed place.

In *The Tempest* the shipwreck in the first scene is a fine example of the *ordo artificialis*, plunging the audience into the middle of events without preliminary or explanation, giving moral hints, stressing action, almost eliminating narrative but intensifying time-consciousness in the prospect of death. The musical atmospheric beginning of *Macbeth* is followed by the contrast of a strong narration, the initial scene deferring disclosure, the witches' song and dance followed by the Bleeding Sergeant's agonized epic report. In *The Tempest* the storm is succeeded by the long three-part narration in which Prospero tells the story of the past separately to Miranda, Ariel and Caliban, answering another question urgently raised by not telling the audience the beginning of the story.

In this play there is the match of beginning and end. *The Tempest* has an epilogue by Prospero, which minimizes narration, in a conventional request for applause. This echoes the play's beginning, but its return is to ordinary human powers – of acting rather than elemental forces. Stormy winds and the boatswain blowing till he bursts his wind are replaced by the audience's 'gentle breath', which must fill, not wreck, their wind and his sails. There is the structural recall of that absence of story in the enigmatic tempest scene, and another contrast with narration, because Prospero ends by promising to elucidate remaining mysteries.

CHAPTER THREE

The Story at the End: Narrative Injunction

'This fierce abridgment'

In their forms, Shakespeare's beginnings are not strikingly different from those in other Elizabethan plays, except perhaps in their complexity and technical versatility, but his endings carry an individual imprint, a sharpened awareness of the over-arching narrative of the play and usually in a way appropriate to the genre, whether tragic, comic, tragi-comic or historical. This takes the form of a demand or request or invitation, at the end, for someone to recall and relate the story of the play.*

*Shakespeare seems to have originated the figure of total future recapitulation, but John Lyly's *Gallathea*, c.1595, has a sub-plot character, Dicke, who intends to make his 'Father laugh at these tales'; Dipsa at the end of his *Endimion*, c.1591, will 'hereafter recite the cause of my first follies' to Geron; and at the end of *The Maides Metamorphosis*, c.1600, once doubtfully attributed to Lyly, Phoebus anticipates a couple boasting that he provided the music for their wedding. (Lyly is known to have influenced Shakespeare in many ways.) After Shakespeare, there is John Ford's *'Tis Pity She's a Whore*, which ends with a full Shakespearian narrative prospect: 'We shall have time to talk at large of all' (Ford is Shakespeare's most conspicuous disciple). I first noticed the projection in Victorian fiction, at the end of Dickens's *A Tale of Two Cities*, George Eliot's *Silas Marner*, Thomas Hardy's *Under the Greenwood Tree* and *The Return of the Native*, then in Shakespeare: these novelists knew Shakespeare well. I have just found, from Clifford Leech's note in his Arden *Two Gentlemen of Verona* (1969) that J.C. Maxwell noted the figure in his New Cambridge *Pericles* (1969) as 'a typical Shakespeare ending', referring to *Pericles*, *Two Gentlemen*, *Measure for Measure*, *Merchant of Venice*, *All's Well* and *Winter's Tale*. J.H. Pafford, in his Arden *Winter's Tale*, says 'retirement for exchange of experience is

At the end, or near the end,† of a majority of the plays, the narrative injunction appears. In the tragedies it makes a tragic intensification. *Romeo and Juliet* ends by ordering the surviving characters of the play, who have been listening to the story as it emerges from the confession of the Friar, to go on attending: 'Go hence to have more talk of these sad things'. The moral is spoken; the tragedy refuses to end cheerfully. In a way, it refuses to end at all, ignoring – like the Prince – the recompense, reconciliation and ending offered by the rich fathers. So the gravity of a moral tragedy is compounded.

Hamlet articulates a need to have his story told fully and truthfully. *Hamlet* ends with an apparent reconciliation, a change of regime instead of a threatened anarchy. Hamlet's and Horatio's insistence on narrative as a healing force can have a touch of irony, however, brought out in post-Fascist productions which subvert any suggestion of stability and health in Fortinbras's succession. *Othello* undermines the sense of narrative as a stable and ordering act: Gratiano says 'all that's spoke is marr'd', Iago says nothing, and Othello chooses and controls narrative performance to disguise and facilitate suicide. This does not mean that he is merely acting; to adapt George Eliot's comment on Rosamond in *Middlemarch*, he is acting himself. The narrative requested at the end of the tragedy of *Hamlet* and *Othello* is itself tragic, a tragic prolongation or compounding, like the ending of *The Spanish Tragedy*, which after all the bloody revenges of the action, can contemplate even more revenges in Hades, and thus 'an endless tragedy'. In Shakespeare this sense of intensified continuation is cast in technical, self-referential terms. But *Hamlet* and *Othello* also suggest a common need to understand and judge the culpable tragic heroes and to justify the genre of tragedy.

In comedy, the happy and healthy characters do not have to anticipate the telling of their story after death. Instead they ask for

common at the close of Shakespeare's plays, particularly of those which end happily', but this makes the figure more restricted than it is, in content and genre.

†In *Troilus and Cressida* it appears in Act III, scene 2, and in *Henry VIII* – sometimes thought not to be by Shakespeare – in Act IV, scene 2.

more of the story, and more of the kind of story in which they have played a part, in a telling which will make for festivity and fun. Marvin Spevack has passed on to me Brownell Salomon's suggestion that the festive departure at the end of Shakespeare's comedies may originate in Plautus and Terence, where there is frequently a sense of continuing the play offstage, with a final *komos* or feast.* There is a good English example at the end of Ben Jonson's *Bartholemew Fayre*, where Overdo's general invitation to supper clinches the conclusion and seems to hold both players and audience in a hospitable embrace: 'We'll ha' the rest of the play at home'. This may well have derived from Shakespeare as well as from Roman comedy. What Shakespeare does is to make the *komos* feature storytelling, especially in its favourite public form of gossip, among its pleasures. So he makes a dual emphasis for his happy ending. It is an ending which the surviving comic characters of the play, like the survivors of tragedy, do not yet know, because they do not all know everything that has gone before. At the end of *The Comedy of Errors* the characters are all invited to 'a gossips' feast'; here two meanings of 'gossip' ('friend' and 'godparent') are fused in a proposal for a ritual recapitulation in good company, and a new christening as the lost family is reunited. The promised narrative pleasures are communal and domestic, in contrast to the political reports and encomiums and platform speeches of tragedy, and emphasis is placed on talk, entertainment, food and drink.

The invitation in this play comes from a dignified hostess, the Abbess, also wife and mother, compounding social functions:

> . . . vouchsafe to take the pains
> To go with us into the abbey here,
> And hear at large discoursed all our fortunes. . . .
> Go to a gossips' feast, and joy with me,
> After so long grief, such festivity.
>
> (V.1)

**Love's Labour's Lost* is the comic exception, its festivity and its story interrupted, its conclusion postponed.

She emphasizes a longed-for elucidation and completion, and the hospitable ceremonies of harmony, community and healing joy. This is not just the conventional happy ending of a story but storytelling conceived as happy ending.

In Act V, scene 5 of *The Merry Wives of Windsor* there is a similar proposal, appropriately less pious, ceremonial, and formal, and on a smaller domestic scale, to clear up misunderstanding and make friends. It is also a comic and narrative nemesis, a mischievous invitation to prolong the joke they have played at Falstaff's expense, appropriately by a woman, their disingenuous hostess Mistress Page, who invites them home pointedly addressing the husband to whom she has been faithful:

> Good husband, let us every one go home,
> And laugh this sport o'er by a country fire . . .

There is reconciliation as well as revenge: 'Sir John and all.'

At the end of *The Two Gentlemen of Verona* the nemesis and narrative injunction is less good-tempered, responding to a harsher comedy of betrayal, infidelity and threatened rape. The story to be told after the play ends will forgive but not forget. The Duke looks forward to 'triumphs, mirth, and rare solemnity', but as Valentine assents he also makes a qualification: 'And as we walk along, I dare be bold/With our discourse to make your Grace to smile'. His joke, 'What think you of this page?', provokes the Duke's 'What mean you by that saying?', providing Shakespeare's favourite form of inspiring question, which insists on an answer and gets it:

> Please you, I'll tell you, as we pass along,
> That you will wonder what has fortuned.
> Come, Proteus, 'tis your penance but to hear
> The story of your loves discovered.
> That done, our day of marriage shall be yours,
> One feast, one house, one mutual happiness.
> (V.4)

The comic happy ending is true to the whole story, and insists on harmony by including discord. Like Falstaff, but more painfully, Proteus is a listener who will not only be enlightened by the full story but punished by hearing his own sorry part as part of story, and from another's point of view. Becoming part of the story has different implications in each play. The idea is Homeric, the variations Shakespearian. In comedy, the narrative completion will free the company for festivity, like a catharsis, but not glibly or generally. The implications of the narrative summing-up are different for each play, sometimes even for each character.

All's Well that Ends Well also ends with an ethical emphasis.

> Let us from point to point this story know
> To make the even truth in pleasure flow.
> [*To Diana*] If thou beest yet a fresh uncropped flower
> Choose thou thy husband and I'll give thy dower;
> For I can guess that by thy honest aid
> Thou kept'st a wife herself, thyself a maid.
> Of that and all the progress more and less
> Resolvedly more leisure shall express.
> All yet seems well, and if it end so meet,
> The bitter past, more welcome is the sweet.
>
> (V.3)

The King's proposal to hear the story is made in the interests of knowing the full particulars of truth, which will give 'pleasure'. His phrase 'from point to point' is probably proverbial or traditional (Gower uses the phrase, in the same way, in *Confessio Amantis*). There is a brief suggestion of uncertainty in 'if', but 'guess' sounds confident and matches the audience's knowledge.

In *Twelfth Night* the narrative injunction is less comprehensive, because the final scene makes so many disclosures of identity and plot. After the disclosures of the romantic 'upper' plot, there follows Malvolio's indignant but reasonable story and Olivia's amused, apologetic response. She postpones judgement but is forestalled by Fabian's equally reasonable confession, and Malvolio leaves, unplacated, after hearing his part in the story. One loose end, which shows the piecemeal narrative still incomplete, is brought out as the Duke suggests pursuit of Malvolio, not to make peace (though this may be implied) but to complete the story, offstage: 'He hath not told us of the captain yet':

> When that is known, and golden time convents,
> A solemn combination shall be made
> Of our dear souls.
>
> (V.1)

Though truth is not mentioned, the harmonious union depends on full disclosure, as the structural word 'combination' confirms, so the tying in of the loose end is a necessary reminder.

Twelfth Night is a play where disclosure and harmony are not complete. Malvolio's dignified letter and spoken narrative have expanded sympathy, and his isolation at the end is reinforced by his opposite, rival and fellow alien, the Fool. The Fool is outside the love-comedy's happy ending, too, appending a story we may guess but have not heard, unsettling Orsino's image of golden time with his melancholy, 'the rain it raineth every day'.

As You Like It more strongly folds the sense of story into a final harmony, as narrative disclosure is completed, sweetened and compounded by music, poetry, dance and myth. The final ceremony is staged, not deferred, and the main matter postponed is ethical, to be taught by the convertite Duke to Jacques: 'There is much matter to be heard and learn'd'. Before this projection Hymen proposes future disclosure, with a fear of confusion rather like Paulina's fear of too much 'relation' at the end of *The Winter's Tale*, but also appropriately avoiding discord.

Everyone is invited to tell their story, in civilized informality, during the ceremonial music. Like the Abbess, Hymen invokes rites of good gossip, a hint of satisfying wonder linking the plot complications with the strangeness of the romances, as conclusion joins artistic and social self-awareness:

> Peace ho! I bar confusion.
> 'Tis I must make conclusion
> Of these most strange events.

and

> Whiles a wedlock hymn we sing,
> Feed yourselves with questioning,
> That reason wonder may diminish

How thus we met, and these things finish.
(V.4)

In the genial, lyrical close to *The Merchant of Venice* Shakespeare cheekily makes Portia abridge the good news which makes the ending happy, referring to a letter from Bellario about the trial, another for Antonio (sealed but known to Portia) about his ships. She casually dismisses causality, 'You shall not know by what strange accident/I chanced upon this letter', and uses amusingly apt legal language to defer narrative closure which sits well on the frivolous and unsympathetic Portia of recent pro-Shylock interpretations:

It is almost morning,
And yet I am sure you are not satisfied
Of these events at full. Let us go in,
And charge us there upon inter'gatories,
And we will answer all things faithfully.
(V.1)

One of the fullest dramatizations of narrative summary and deferral comes at the end of *A Midsummer Night's Dream*, where a reflective backwards look, appropriate to the subject of ordering and disordering dream, is spread over several scenes. The lovers wake on midsummer morning to have the telling of their story plausibly deferred by Theseus, out hunting:

Fair lovers you are fortunately met;
Of this discourse we more will hear anon.
(IV.1)

Once more the telling is postponed for a feast, to be held 'in great solemnity', but the lovers also plan to talk over their experiences informally, 'by the way . . . recount our dreams'. In the next scene, Theseus and Hippolita marvel at the way these dreams confirm each other, making it clear that in the scenes' interval, they have heard the story of the night. The audience is spared repetition, the feast, almost always unacted, is taken as completed, the 'three hours/Between . . . after-supper and bed-time' to be filled by the mechanicals' play.

At the end of Act IV, scene 1, Bottom lets his telling extend into that future, after the play, and compounds deferral, echoing title and theme, as he projects the story of his untellable dream, his topos of inexpressibility insisting on amazement: 'I will get Peter Quince to write a ballad of this dream: it shall be called "Bottom's dream", because it has no bottom; and I will sing it in the latter end of a play . . .'

This is the only play by Shakespeare in which narrative completion is handed over – at least in project – by a character to a professional teller – and director, poet and joiner. Actually, the epilogue is not sung at the latter end of the play, the Duke conveniently refusing epilogue, 'your play needs no excuse'. The audience is spared, and the dream is left dreamily unfathomed, without bottom, in an endless comic deferral. Narrative is self-conscious in a way which keeps faith with play, characters and genre, and title.

Measure for Measure deals briefly with the deferred telling. In his final speech, as he deals out measure for measure, the Duke hints 'There's more behind that is more gratulate', promising to tell all that 'is meet' for them to know (V.1). The future telling is associated with his last hinted proposal to Isabel, to be repeated offstage. In his cursory, and not festive, proposal there is a reflection of the play's sour unpleasantness, particularly apt for productions which show Isabel's final reluctance or rejection. There is also a touch of the Duke's manipulative power, in that pompous, restrictive, firm 'meet you all should know'.

These endings are responsive to their plays. The self-conscious narrative invocations at the ends of the comedies are less emotional, more aesthetically assertive and more formal than in the tragedies, suggesting that Shakespeare is deploying narrative ellipsis or deferral for a kind of generic flouting or subversion, not only to avoid detailed recapitulation of a story the audience knows but to avoid glib jolly traditional tying up of loose ends in happy ending. What happens at the end of *Love's Labour's Lost*, where the chief wit is instructed to practise on the sick and dying and where Jack does not get Joan, makes the point explicitly, but it is subtly made in most of Shakespeare's comic conclusions.

A Midsummer Night's Dream and several of the romantic comedies explicitly mention wonder as they contemplate their own story. This awareness is invariably present in the late tragi-comedies, which we call romances, and which use supernatural and fantastic materials. When the final narrative promise is made, the characters remark the amazing nature of their own story. Strangeness is brought into the open and motivates the longing for the story to be clearly and completely told and made plausible. The incredible material will be made credible to characters, as it has been – it is implied – to the audience, who have seen it all. At the same time the unrealistic nature of the genre is declared.

In *The Winter's Tale*, extraordinary stories make up the plot; there is a multiplication of story, and awareness of story at every turn ('Like an old tale') and at the end, after layers of narrated recapitulation (already discussed in Chapter 1), a complicated deferral of narrative. Wonder is stressed, and it is left for Paulina, privileged plot-maker and teller, to initiate the injunction. As Hermione begins to recount her survival to Perdita, Paulina stops her story to make space for the joy of reunion:

> There's time enough for that;
> Lest they desire (upon this push) to trouble
> Your joys with like relation. Go together,
> You precious winners all . . .
> (V.3)

What she is talking about applies to the characters' reunion, and to the play's conclusion: neither needs to say too much about the past. A similar decorous evasion marks Leontes's anticipation of retrospect, which stresses wonder, not remorse, as he responds to Paulina:

> Thou has found mine;
> But how, is to be question'd; for I saw her,
> As I thought, dead . . .

In a fascinating playing-down of self-blame, with the significant passive form 'We were dissever'd', Leontes anticipates a leisurely collaborative telling, after the hasty exit. Narrative injunction runs into the last line to join future, past and immediate present, keeping the romantic tragi-comedy and this spring myth unshadowed by the past.

This proposal to hear the story offstage also makes clear the convenient motive for exit in all the curtainless conclusions:

> Lead us from hence, where we may leisurely
> Each one demand, and answer to his part
> Perform'd in this wide gap of time, since first
> We were dissever'd: hastily lead away.
>
> (V.2)

The end of *Pericles* is a strong closure, after Gower makes his last commentary, in an Epilogue formally specifying the 'due and just' punishment' of 'monstrous lust' and the rewards of virtues, as didactically as though less generally than the original author, Gower, in his own *Confession*, where the lover bids farewell to earthly love. The last line of *Pericles* looks forwards for the audience 'New joy wait on you!', and simply states the present 'our play hath ending.' Before Gower's Epilogue, Pericles, like Leontes, announces the exit into more storytelling: 'Lord Cerimon, we do our longing stay/To hear the rest untold: sir, lead's the way' (V.3), having already asked for Thaisa's story:

> Now do I long to hear how you were found,
> How possibly preserv'd, and who to thank,
> Besides the gods, for this great miracle.

Begging Cerimon, 'Will you deliver/How this great queen re-lives?', he has been promised that everything will be told, and everything found with her shown, like relics, in Cerimon's house. Once more, the characters' sense of wonder and mystery declares the nature of the play, forestalling objections to its improbabilities and fantasy. The word 'miracle' originates in Gower, with his narrative device and frame of the confessional, with a confessor and a lover, using the language of religious wonder and with an interesting hint of narrative summary, 'For every man this tale hath told/As for miracle, and were glade' (Liber Octavus, l, 1867).

The end of *Cymbeline* is exaggeratedly reflexive. Aware of genre, ancestry and particular craft, it voices an amusing refusal to tell, through Cymbeline's insistence on hearing all the particulars of all the intricate plots. Given one of the longest retrospective explanations in any of the plays, he still asks for more. He has listened in horror to an animated piecemeal account of the events of which he has been ignorant – the preservation of his sons, the evil of his Queen, the suffering and survival of his daughter – and asks:

> When shall I hear all through? This fierce abridgement
> Hath to it circumstantial branches, which
> Distinction should be rich in.
>
> (V.5)

Not one of Shakespeare's brightest kings, his words appreciate the role of the passions in narration: 'fierce' used of 'abridgement' works like an oxymoron, brilliantly linking cold technical term and emotional adjective. Its transferred epithet reminds us of the violence of the events related – battle, poisoning, attempted rape, lies, kidnapping, revenge and death – while also describing the rush and vehemence (Samuel Johnson's word) of the summary telling. For character and audience, it suggests violent content and violent medium.

The story is pieced together by the sufferers, panting and stricken by the events they recount. Cymbeline's questioning is also intense, though perhaps it should be played as less stricken. Always the questioner ('Nursing of my sons?'; 'How? my issue?'), his questions and responses are piled up in the last concentrated narrative scene. He laments a lack of tidings of his rescuer (Posthumus in disguise), asks his other allies where they come from ('Report it'), hears the messengers who bring blunt and businesslike reports of the Queen's perfidy, with interruptions and urgings ('delicate fiend' and 'Proceed'), and ends with brief self-forgiveness and pious trust. His accumulation and his curtness take us to the brink of the comic. As he interrogates those 'circumstantial branches' under the heads Shakespeare ridicules in *Love's Labour's Lost*, the speed and compression of his questioning approach parody:

> Where? how lived you?
> And when came you to serve our Roman captive?

> How parted with your brothers? how first met them?
> Why fled you from the court? and whither? These,
> And your three motives to the battle, with
> I not know how much more, should be demanded
> And all the other by-dependances,
> From chance to chance. But nor the time nor place
> Will serve our long inter'gatories.
>
> (V.5)

After Cymbeline talks, aside, to Imogen, in a clever narrative elision like the talk during *Twelfth Night*'s music, he questions Iachimo with eager imperatives ('strive, man'), eliciting a full but morally ambiguous confession, which seems parodic in its self-interruptions and repeated roved-over headings of time and place. The mimed interruptions and qualifications are so regular and conventional – by the book – as to register an automatized villainous hypocrisy on Iachimo's part:

> Upon a time, unhappy was the clock
> That struck the hour: it was in Rome, accurst
> The mansion where: 'twas at a feast, O, would
> Our viands had been poison'd . . .
>
> (V.5)

After the traditional rhetorical heads have been heaved into position, Iachimo's lengthy narrative moves into new rapid mode, to summarize the men's group boast-and-wager that sent Iachimo to Imogen's bed. This storytelling is technically aware ('to be brief'), and its apostrophe, 'Methinks I see him now', is the cue for Posthumus, like Othello, to turn past into present, narrative into action: 'Ay, so thou dost/Italian fiend.' What begins as comic or grotesque turns into tragic passion and physical threat.

In all this Shakespeare walks a tight-rope between the tragic and the comic. He combines seriously impassioned question-and-answer and a travesty of question-and-answer. Self-conscious exaggerated curiosity makes an ironic parody of Shakespeare's narrative injunction, though it still makes a space for the audience's restrospect. There is individuality as well as comedy in this fervent quest for enlightenment. The speeches bristling with demands and requests ironically underline Cymbeline's passiveness and political impotence. Shakespeare remembers character as he serves the needs of ending. (He makes narrative injunction express Hamlet's sense of political responsibility, Horatio's morality, Othello's pride and the Prince's combination of personal guilt with disdain for Capulet and Montagu.) In *Cymbeline* the interrogation springs further revelations, comically but gravely too. The play makes its tragi-comic demand for elucidation to criticize Cymbeline but also to elicit serious, passionate and vivid recapitulations, like the confessions of Posthumus that follow.

At the end of *The Tempest* there is no exaggeration or parody, and the requests for Prospero's story, which the audience has heard at such length, are made with gravity and wonder. In Act V, scene 1, Prospero briefly tells his story but to listeners whose 'fancy' is still 'unsettled'. Even when he changes his strange clothing for the old garments of 'sometime Milan', they are still incredulous. Alonso is not sure if he is dreaming, and if not, 'this must crave . . . a most strange story.' He continues, amazed: 'But how should Prospero /Be living and be here?' Gonzalo is afraid and doubtful, and Prospero gently explains that the 'subtleties' of the isle are still making him feel uncertain. He assures the villains Sebastian and Antonio, whose new treachery he has prevented, that for the moment he will 'tell no tales', and Sebastian's offensive 'The devil speaks in him' meets his curt grave 'No'. Alonso's continued incredulity is insistent ('If thou be'st Prospero,/Give us particulars), but he is only told briefly, 'I am Prospero, and that very duke/Which was thrust forth of Milan; who most strangely/Upon this shore . . . was landed.' And Prospero postpones the rest of the story:

> For 'tis a chronicle of day by day,
> Not a relation for a breakfast, nor
> Befitting this first meeting.

After meeting Ferdinand and Miranda, and finding the Master and Boatswain alive, Alonso is still amazed ('These are not natural events; they strengthen/From strange to stranger . . .' and 'This is as strange a maze as e'er men trod;/And there is in this business more than nature/Was ever conduct of: some oracle/Must rectify our knowledge'), but Prospero still keeps him waiting:

> Sir, my liege,
> Do not infest your mind with beating on
> The strangeness of this business; at pick'd leisure
> Which shall be shortly single, I'll resolve you,
> Which to you shall seem probable, of every
> These happen'd accidents . . .

He invites Alonso and his 'train/To my poor cell' promising the usual advantages of circumstantial detail, elucidation of mysteries, and time-absorbing narrative: he will make the night 'Go quick away' by telling 'the story of my life,/And the particular accidents gone by'.

At the very end we hear that Prospero's meditation on death solemnizes Alonso's sharp curiosity, as he completes the Duke's line:

> *Pros.* Every third thought shall be my grave.
> *Alon.* I long
> To hear the story of your life, which must
> Take the ear strangely.
> (V.1)

Then Prospero's resonant 'I'll deliver all' is the cue for exeunt, and his last half-line, 'Please you, draw near', enfolds and promises marriage, happiness, smooth seas and the retelling of the story in the near future. The anticipation of retrospect matches the beginning, and any hint of the grotesque disappears in the gravity of poetic justice, the repeated sense of strangeness and death as the common ending for all life-stories.

Three of the English histories – Parts 1 and 3 of the three-part *Henry VI*, the two-part *Henry IV* and *Henry V* – provide the chief exceptions to this form or figure of narrative self-consciousness at the ending. The historically serial structure means there is no need to ask for more, since this is going to be supplied anyway, for instance, as tactful recapitulation in the prologues or beginnings of a sequel. There is no need for authentication, since this is history and supposedly true. There is no point in recapitulation to mark ending, since the action is continuous. There is no need to open out action at the end of the play, since it is open anyway, to the next play in the sequence, as when we are promised a sequel to Falstaff's story at the end of *Henry IV, Pt 2* and when at the end of *Henry V* we are referred to a historically later play, *Henry VI*, already written and often played. But the classical histories, except for *Titus*, include the injunction, in a way which blends prospect and retrospect, and one or two of the English histories hint at it,* reminding us of the genre of history, though not always right at the end.

Henry VIII ends with a particularly closed triumphant conclusion, in a hindsight vision of Jacobean glory and peace, with no space for a narrative injunction. But in Act IV, just before Katherine of Aragon's death, there is a trace of narrative foresight, which movingly highlights the ethic of narrative in a way congenial to the play's prevailing sense of tolerance and patience. Griffith, the good narrator, has persuaded the divorced queen to let him supplement and answer her compassionate, charitable but naturally critical obituary of Cardinal Wolsey – who has been her enemy – with this survey of the man's 'good'. His long, imaginative and reasonable narrative begins:

> From his cradle
> He was a scholar, and a ripe and good one . . .

and ends:

> His overthrow heap'd happiness upon him,
> For then, and not till then, he felt himself,
> And found the blessedness of being little;
> And to add greater honours to his age
> Than man could give him, he died fearing God.

His fair-speaking follows her critique, modifying it and impress-

**Henry VI*, *Pt 2* ends with Warwick's anticipation that the battle of St Albans 'Shall be eterniz'd in all age to come', and *Richard II* has Bolingbroke recognizing a 'deed of slander'.

ing her, then dynamically invoking her sense of her own story. Narrative begets narrative. Katherine moves, softened but isolated and stricken, to imagine becoming part of history – as of course she has become – in her own imagined present and the dramatic present in which the audience observes – and having justice done to her. After so much malign report, which has cost her her marriage, crown, reputation and identity, she has told Wolsey, 'Ye turn me into nothing' (III.1). She finally asserts herself – indeed develops herself – in a dignified and naturally wishful anticipation of posthumous good report. Like Othello she wants honest chronicling, like Hamlet she'd like to pick her close, informed and honest chronicler, and in a way she has, in Shakespeare, who has after all invented Griffith as a model narrator:

> After my death I wish no other herald,
> No other speaker of my living actions
> To keep mine honour from corruption;
> But such an honest chronicler as Griffith.
> Whom I most hated living, thou hast made me,
> With thy religious truth and modesty,
> Now in his ashes honour: peace be with him.
> (IV.2)

The narrative self-consciousness is there, as muted as possible, in one of Shakespeare's most complex, yet easy-seeming, dialogues of story, a gem of art. He develops his historical character most subtly, allowing the cast-off queen that benign entry into chronicle she is too modest and too realistic to articulate except as a wish, as she imagines and becomes part of the narrative of history whose shifts and powers her author is demonstrating. Shakespeare most tactfully lets her personal wish appear, then give way to her formal wish for Wolsey's rest. Historical narrative deconstructs its own genre, form and medium in an impressive and unshowy passage, whose quietness and subtlety is characteristic of the two dramatic speakers and of Shakespeare's most interestingly neglected play. As usual, looking towards life and art, Shakespeare creates a sense of two times, the past imagining the future, a present imagining its past.

Before the end of *Antony and Cleopatra*, at the end of Enobarbus's story, Enobarbus claims 'a place i' the story' – amusingly, since he is Shakespeare's fiction, and perhaps this is what he is saying. (Enobarbus is developed from Domitius, an uncharacterized figure in Plutarch, who leaves Antony, is treated magnanimously by him, and repents.) At the play's end, partly though not wholly invented by Shakespeare, Octavius Caesar anticipates the Augustan future in which the lovers' story will become part of his glory. The play's marked interest in the power-structure of historical narrative may well be the result of the dramatist's research and revision. As he made close studies of the historical sources, both keeping and changing material, he seems to have developed an interest both in power-narrative and blends of fiction and factuality. He was observing the powers of narrative authorship and authority, and exercizing his own, looking at life and art, and at the overlap between the two – especially blurred, uncertain and fascinating – in the narratives of history.

At the end of *Julius Caesar*, in his last sentence, Brutus says 'Brutus's tongue/Hath almost ended his life's history.' Enobarbus reminds us that the self-conscious invocation of story is not confined to the end of plays, and one of the most famous examples of Shakespeare's narrative self-reference is the genre-conscious proposal by the doomed Richard II (*Richard II*, III.2) that he and his friends should sit upon the ground and tell sad stories of the deaths of kings. His proposal – expressively indulgent and structurally proleptic – is successfully rebuked by Carlisle, who sees it as inactive. Two scenes later it is Richard's Queen – in another episode teeming with artistic self-consciousness – who proposes to 'tell tales': she cannot decide if they should be of joy or sorrow, and both would be saddening in different ways. There is no narrative injunction at the end of the play, when all the news has been told, and the story made clear, but there is an interesting moment of awareness on the part of Exton, one of Richard's murderers. He sees himself become part of a damned story, 'this deed is chronicled in hell.' The present tense, 'is chronicled', makes a generic recognition, the play is proving that the murder has become unwholesome history, and the idea is repeated at the end in

Bolingbroke's 'A deed of slander'. The histories conclude with an awareness of the transformation of characters and events into history. The characters themselves do not need, or even seem, to be authenticated by the suggestion of offstage telling, because they are already authenticated, as history.

A similar point is made in *Troilus and Cressida*, but in the middle not the end, as the lovers make their vows by daring history to mythologize their characters. The characters are defiantly prescient – in strong contrast to the tentatively wishful Katherine of Aragon – and as their ignorance of the future is measured by the audience's knowledge of it as past, the ironies and illusions of 'reality' are powerful: 'let all constant men be Troiluses, all false women Cressids, and all brokers-between Pandars! Say "Amen"' (III.2). The characters think they are fantasizing about the way they will turn into story, and the audience knows they are not. The projection into a future when they will become part of story cannot wait for the end. At this point in the play Troilus, Cressida and Pandarus can imagine and articulate the future and the truth only as a horrid and incredible negation of what they believe; it is the not unfamiliar act of averting the future by imagining the worst it can bring – and getting it horribly right.

At the end of the play there is no space for such bravado of imagination. It is too late: we are left remembering Thersites's bitter repeated compounding of wars and lechery, refracted through Troilus's 'Stay yet', as he refuses to end with his praise of Hector, and 'there is no more to say'. There is more, in his blended sexual jealousy and military violence, his rejection of Pandarus, and Pandarus's disgusted version of love and death. We are left with these extreme images of the play's action, confirming all those worst fears of the lovers' challenge to a future.

In *Macbeth* and *Lear*, the offstage telling would be redundant. Malcolm's summary bluntness, 'This dead butcher, and his fiend-like Queen', does rough justice and emphasizes the exclusion of the survivors from an audience's intimate knowledge. At the end of *Lear* everyone left on stage knows the story, Edgar's last narrative having told them all they did not know. In *Titus* the political need for the kind of restorative story which *Hamlet* articulates can't be postponed, because the turmoil has not reached even a temporary solution, and must be resolved within the play, before the end. But even though its story is summed up before it ends, *Titus* is a play where the terminal sense of story is so prominent and reflexive that if we knew more about the chronology of the plays, it might prove to be the play which suggested Shakespeare's concept of offstage telling.

That proposal to tell, fictionalizing characters who do not know they are characters in a story, gives the cue for exeunt. It reminds the audience of the completion of the story, their own access to it, and the fact of fiction. It also reminds them of the characters' relative ignorance and the illusory lifelikeness of the characters. As the participants speak of hearing their story, they internalize it and so make it and themselves sound real. By reminding the audience of their privileged access and knowledge, through their own exclusion, they make clear the difference between the occluded viewpoint of the characters, ignorant of everything that happens outside their scenes (as Tom Stoppard's Rosencrantz and Guildenstern make clear) but for whom the story is real, and the real audience to whom the players have told all, for whom it is fictitious. The end is closed, in a sense, as the demand for the story indicates that it is all over. It is opened, in another sense, as recapitulation is requested or promised, and postponed. In a weird way, the action is prolonged to a fictitious future beyond the play's final word.

The characters' anticipated story is the audience's memory, projected into the fictitious future. It shadows our own summarizing grasp of the story, as we anticipate remembering. Its concluding reminders of the construction of story, the access to story, the instability of story and the illusion of story bring about an oscillation between the sense of fiction and the sense of reality. The narrative injunction ritualizes a transition from the end of the play to the life outside, especially prominent and valuable for Shakespeare's curtainless stage, as first the actors and then the audience leave, but it is still relevant to modern audiences as the performed story starts to become stage-memory.

CHAPTER FOUR

Shakespeare Reading Narrative

'As erst our ancestor'

Some of Shakespeare's characters listen to stories. 'A dismal treaties' (an oral or written story) used to make Macbeth's 'fell of hair . . . rouse and stir'; Lady Macbeth disdains 'A woman's story at a winter's fire'; Hermione encourages her son's story – 'you're powerful at it' – about the man who lived by a churchyard; Desdemona is spellbound by Othello's travel tales; Hamlet loves Aeneas's story to Dido, from a play too good for the public. A few of his characters are readers: Marcus and his nephew Lucius have read Virgil's *Aeneid*; Titus, his daughter Lavinia, and his grandson young Lucius read Ovid; Lucius and Lavinia read Cicero; Imogen, after reading for three hours by candlelight, turns down the leaf at the relevant story of Tereus, in an unspecified book which could be Ovid, Chaucer, Gower or Painter; Brutus, another night-reader like Imogen, mislays and finds a book with another leaf (anachronistically) turned down; Richard of Bordeaux knows the Gospels; Bolingbroke mentions a ballad, 'The Beggar and the King'. There are far more images drawn from the experiences of listening and reading than there are named authors and books, but Shakespeare is clearly interested in responses to oral and written narrative.

Behind Shakespeare's writing lies his own response to narrative forms, old wives' tales, ballad, epic, prose and verse romance and of course drama. Much work has been done on his written sources, understandably concentrating on subject-matter and theme, though also influenced by the popular critical topics of character and imagery. It has tended to direct itself, again understandably, to particular sources for particular plays.

What is the interest of the narrative sources for the student of his own narrative? – narrative made theatrical and affective, narrative which is self-conscious, narrative which implicitly analyses the constructions of memory, fantasy, gossip, lies, news? Most obviously, reading his non-dramatic sources clarifies the way the dramatist made narrative theatrical, since we see the actual process of changing genre. To read some of his major subject-sources, such as North, Holinshed, Gower, Virgil, Ovid or Arthur Brooke, is to see chronicle and narrative verse made into a language for actor, stage, action and passion. As I have said, Shakespeare is not only shaping his invention into dramatic narrative but often showing within the play a distinguishing awareness of narrative meant for a reader and narrative meant for an audience.

The revisionary process must have sharpened genre-consciousness. Its collations must also have sharpened self-consciousness. Moreover, some of the sophisticated authors he read – Virgil, Gower and Sidney, for example – were self-conscious themselves, brilliantly reflecting on genre, tradition and craft as they wrote. Shakespeare was reading literary criticism as well as narrative. And his authors are, like him, not only interested in art but using art to make psychological and sociological inquiries into narrative life-forms.

If we read a few of the vast number of narratives he read, as openly as possible, looking at their handling and awareness of narrative rather than seeking particular thematic origins, we find occasional signs of Shakespeare's response, not as a magpie or mimic but as a good reader. Of course we see the profit for the writer, what he keeps or uses, omits or changes and joins together. But from time to time we see something less obvious. We come across insights and inquiries, or failures of insight and inquiry, into the craft and structure, as well as the themes and content, of art-narrative and life-narrative – insights and inquiries that Shakespeare may have noticed, not always consciously but not always unconsciously either. Some of the ideas or examples he seems to perceive are not from the obvious play sources. A lie or a distraught memory or a silence may echo a narrative 'source' which has no obvious or immediate connection with his text.

But I begin with some clear responses to well-known narrative sources. Reading North's translation of Plutarch's *Life of Antonius* (from his *Lives of the Noble Grecians and Romanes*, 1579), the source of *Antony and Cleopatra*, we find Shakespeare often keeping close to North's prose, while adapting it to the direct speech of his inverted and historical characters. The play's most fictitious character, Enobarbus, is given one of its dazzling speeches, the story of Antony's meeting with Cleopatra on the river Cydnus. It was revised by Dryden (in *All for Love*) and T.S. Eliot (in *The Waste Land*), and like Odysseus's anguished memory of Troy it is a key narrative recycled for new centuries and new voices.

For Enobarbus the dramatist takes North's generalized and impersonal narrative voice, not so much adapting it to a character as enlarging and deepening that character by using his voice for the narrative. The adopted style, faithful to North, fits Enobarbus's character, in gusto, sensuality, humour and detachment. North's story is slightly adapted to impress it with Enobarbus's humour, and though nothing in the passage is changed to bring in his critical irony, that quality, in performance, modifies and complicates the simpler appreciation of North, both checking and authenticating Enobarbus's praise and enthusiasm.

In Enobarbus's narration, Antony's susceptibility to Cleopatra is appreciated by a man who comprehends him – and her – but not uncritically, so the story can keep North's ring of detachment and authority. Unlike North's narrator, Enobarbus is engaged in the higher masculine gossip, and his story of the meeting on the river Cydnus is instigated, encouraged and eagerly heard by Agrippa and Maecenas, Romans fascinated by the high jinks in Egypt: 'You stay'd well by't in Egypt'; 'Eight wild-boars roasted whole . . . is this true?'; 'She's a most triumphant lady, if report be square to her.' Their questions prompt the formal introduction, 'I will tell you' (II.2), and their interjections ('O, rare, for Antony!' and 'Now Antony must leave her utterly') keep narration dialogic. Like the particularizing chronicler, Enobarbus provides the physical details his friends are keen to have, and his narrative animates North's rich visual imagery with Shakespeare's rhetorical and psychological dynamism. That traditional sociolect or genderlect of the Roman (or modern) locker-room – knowing and sexually stimulating male talk – plays a part in fitting the highly wrought descriptive prose into the characterizations of a verse play:

> I will tell you.
> The barge she sat in, like a burnish'd throne
> Burn'd on the water: the poop was beaten gold;
> Purple the sails, and so perfumed that
> The winds were love-sick with them; the oars were silver,
> Which to the tune of flutes kept stroke, and made
> The water which they beat to follow faster,
> As amorous of their strokes. For her own person,
> It beggar'd all description: she did lie
> In her pavilion – cloth of gold, of tissue –
> O'er-picturing that Venus where we see
> The fancy outwork nature. On each side her,
> Stood pretty dimpled boys, like smiling Cupids . . .

and some lines later:

> A strange invisible perfume hits the sense
> Of the adjacent wharfs. The city cast
> Her people out upon her; and Antony,
> Enthron'd i' the market-place, did sit alone,
> Whistling to the air; which, but for vacancy,
> Had gone to gaze on Cleopatra too,
> And made a gap in nature.
>
> (II.2)

You feel Enobarbus's spoken appreciation of Cleopatra's magnificent show, in description which takes nearly all visual detail, and many actual words, from the source:

> [She took] her barge in the river of Cydnus, the poope whereof was of gold, the sailes of purple, and the owers of silver, which

> kept stroke in rowing after the sounde of the musicke of flutes, howboyes, citherns, violls . . . she was layed under a pavillion of cloth of gold of tissue, apparelled and attired like the goddese Venus . . . prettie faire boyes apparalled as painters doe set forth god Cupide, with little fannes in their hands . . . the barge . . . out of which there came a wonderful passing sweete savor of perfumes, that perfumed the wharfe's side . . . there ranne such multitudes of people . . . to see her that Antonius was left post alone in the market place.
>
> (Bullough, *Shakespeare's Narrative and Dramatic Sources*, vol. V, p. 274)

Shakespeare animates North's brilliant static scene by metaphor, simile and personification: 'Burn'd', 'like a burnish'd throne', 'the waves were lovesick', 'hits the sense'. A topos of inexpressibility, 'beggar'd all description', replaces North's painting analogy, perhaps as a dramatic narrator's joke about description not being enough. Shakespeare's narrative is more solidly specific than North, as he dramatizes the details of gorgeous and excessive expense and develops an erotic sub-text, beating gold and dimpling 'prettie faire boys'. North mentions the presiding images of Venus and Cupid; Shakespeare goes one better, and makes the whole natural and man-made world aphrodisiac, salaciously titillating and amusing his male listeners with the slightly corrupt sensuality of boys' flesh and those 'strokes' of which the waves are 'amorous'. As Shakespeare rewrites the last sentence in the extract I quote from North, Enobarbus's diffused humour is given a say in the joke about nature abhorring a vacuum, 'And made a gap in nature'. North's decorative scene is reshaped and characterized, for an actor's imaginative but also knowingly man-to-man communication. There is a kind of friction between irony and compliment in the speech, like that in Octavius Caesar's speech recalling the past achievement of Antony, which is close to the same source. They make a pair of striking narrations, both filling in important details of the play's past and of Antony's, both individualized versions of a narrative more blandly voiced in North's indirect style. In both speeches Shakespeare changes North's words, which he admires enough to imitate, to suit the character and style of the speaker, to make the monologue impassioned and dialogic, as it does not need to be in North – or Amyot, whom North translated, or Plutarch, whom Amyot translated – and to integrate the speeches into the play's argument, motion and structure. These narrations are like great arias, opportunities for performance, structurally balanced in antithesis. Each speech brings out an opposite aspect of Antony, the lover and the soldier; they voice opposite viewpoints, of ally and antagonist; one is all Roman, the other all Egyptian; one contemplates the body's toughness and suffering and endurance, the other its softness and sweetness and indulgence. Each is a psychologically and sociologically typed narrative; each an engrossing, sensuous and lyrical script for theatrical elocution.

Octavius Caesar is a stern critic and suspicious ally, and his reminiscences of Antony's past glory come as he is battered by bad news. He has read a letter, 'the news', about Antony in Alexandria, heard one messenger report Pompey's popularity and another bring news of the pirates, Menas and Menecrates. His narration is spoken in the presence of Lepidus – a listener too feeble for much interaction – but addressed as an urgent apostrophe to the absent Antony, summoning him back to Rome and the man he once was:

> Antony,
> Leave thy lascivious wassails. When thou once
> Was beaten from Modena, where thou slew'st
> Hirtius and Pansa, consuls, at thy heel
> Did famine follow, whom thou fought'st against,
> Though daintily brought up, with patience more
> Than savages could suffer.
>
> (I.4)

This is close to the relevant passage in North, a brief fairly factual account of the Consuls' expulsion of Antony and victory at Modena, but it animates the famine (interestingly leaving out Caesar's part), and makes language less abstract, for instance in substituting the last two lines for North's 'by pacience he would overcome any adversitie'. North's account – twice as long as Shakespeare's, with some moralizing which Shakespeare cuts – contains one vivid particularized sentence, which Shakespeare spots and uses:

> It was a wonderful example to the soldiers, to see Antonius that was brought up in all fineness and superfluitie . . . to drinke puddle water, and to eate wild frutes and rootes: and . . . it is reported, that . . . they did eat the barcks of trees, and such beasts, as never man tasted of their flesh before.
>
> (Bullough, vol. V, pp. 267–8)

Shakespeare goes one better, to voice Caesar's fastidious and ironic contemplation of Antony drinking 'The stale of horses and the gilded puddle/Which beasts would cough at': 'gilded' is a finely nuanced image for scum, or urine, suggesting appreciative repulsion. Like it, other details are made more specific and lively for the story in which Caesar's mind's eye keenly scrutinizes Antony's past, sometimes by a small change, like the strengthening of 'such beasts, as man never tasted' to 'thou didst eat strange flesh,/Which some did die to look on.' Caesar and the impersonal fact-collecting historian share the scrupulous 'it is reported', because Shakespeare is dramatizing Caesar's attention and his ambivalence. The generalized chronicle style, clear and competent, can be kept for Caesar, its facts compressed, its sources mentioned, its baldness giving way to a few circumstantial details and cues for emotion. As with the Cleopatra scene, a powerful chronicle is heightened, exaggerated and characterized.

The narrative acts are solidly placed in social context, and they are introverted, dramatically rapt memories and meditations. Shakespeare's poetry, complexly in character, is expressive both of the subject (the narrator) and object (the person discussed). Enobarbus's rapturous hyperbole characterizes a sensualist with imagination and humour, shaping for other men a sensual woman also with imagination and humour, staging a scene. Caesar's bitter savouring of austerity and endurance speaks the politician's – and the general's – ambivalent wry admission of need, as he remembers and condemns Antony through praise. The emotional charge of each narrative is a blend of irony and appreciation. There is something stronger too, a kind of wonder, diffused through Enobarbus's speech, but concentrated at its end, and appearing only at the end of Caesar's speech in that image of strange flesh, contemplated in disgust and fascination. Each narration is given a strong beginning – Enobarbus facing his listeners, Caesar turning from Lepidus to Antony – and a strong climax at the end. North's vivid but somewhat rambling chronicle is mined and shaped.

The play needs these speeches to complicate characters and conflict, in Enobarbus's controlled rhapsody and intelligent prediction, and Caesar's scornful admiration or admiring scorn for his 'great competitor', each heroizing its object, in a reflective fashion. The speeches match and answer each other, as they prosecute and defend lascivious Antony, their combination further complicating their individual mixed judgements, to suit the ironic judgement of the play, which problematizes a decision in favour of either Rome or Egypt.

Charles and Michelle Martindale, in *Shakespeare and the Uses of Antiquity: An Introductory Essay* (London, Routledge, 1970), suggest that Plutarch is congenial to Shakespeare in his interest in personality and society. The generic difference must also have been highly stimulating. Nowhere else does Shakespeare have such fun with a close verse imitation of rhythmical vivid prose. Iambic phrases, like 'the barks of trees' and the 'the owers of silver' are kept, or nearly kept, by Shakespeare's line, as he improves the prose for passionate, individualizing, self-savouring poetry. Writing his play he pays a poet's homage to his prose source, in delighted collaboration. To compare North's Antony with *Antony and Cleopatra* is to share a writer's enjoyment of language.

Another striking example of a poet's tribute to language and character, in the conversion of genre, came in his reading of Arthur Brooke's *Romeus and Juliet*. The Brooke poem begins with a narrative sonnet, 'The Argument', which gave Shakespeare the idea for the sonnet-prologue I mentioned in Chapter 1. He keeps Brooke's form but totally changes the narrative, replacing Brooke's precise outline of events, which includes the friar's 'counsell', 'Tybalt's rage', 'New mariage' and a five-line specification of the drug and stabbing, with an abstract of tragic situation and plot that leaves the particulars to take us by surprise. Shakespeare turns Brooke's method on its head.

Even more interesting is the way the source's skilled characterization is used but made theatrical and also psychologically more complex. Shakespeare changes Brooke's comic and lubricious Nurse in two ways.* Unlike North, Brooke is a dramatic storyteller, a creator of character and relationship, using direct speech, idiolect and dialogue. In Brooke's poem the Nurse's rambling reminiscences of Juliet's infancy, 'a tedious long discourse', include details of pretty prating and a 'buttocke soft', which she kisses, 'gladder . . . Then I had been to have a kisse of some olde lechers mouth', and are solicitously addressed to an incredulous Romeus, bored by the garrulous 'beldam' but politely giving gold crowns as 'a slight reward'.

Shakespeare replaces Romeus in this scene with the intimate company of a fairly tolerant Lady Capulet and a more reserved or diffident Juliet. The deliberately lubricious anecdote is transferred – and made more humorous and affectionate and less pornographic – to the Nurse's 'merry' dead husband who joins Susan, the dead daughter ('she was too good for me') in fleshing out and dignifying the Nurse's story: Shakespeare knows precisely how the amusing old retainer came to be a wet-nurse. As a narrator she is presented in the play without Brooke's traditional misogynistic judgement of the unreliable talkative woman, her amusing garrulousness extended in feeling and subject-matter. She is sentimental but not sentimentalized – at least not by Shakespeare – and the old servant's tactless rambling particularities, as she chats to her exasperated social superiors, prepare us for her cheery callous opportunism – a link with Brooke – and Juliet's moral rejection. Shakespeare appreciates Brooke's cleverly created comic character but reimagines a woman with a freshly sympathetic and warmly particular narrative style.

*Geoffrey Bullough, in *Narrative and Dramatic Sources of Shakespeare*, says in his commentary on *Romeo and Juliet*, in vol. 1, that Brooke's Nurse lacks comedy, but in his Conclusion, vol. VIII, he praises Brooke's comic power, which is considerable and which obviously struck Shakespeare.

A less certain instance of Shakespeare's response to narrative concerns a possible source for Katherina's last speech in *The Taming of the Shrew*. Shakespeare may have read Erasmus's Latin colloquy *Senatulus*, as was pointed out to Kenneth Muir by J.C. Maxwell (Arden edn, p. 87), and Erasmus has a detailed defence – by a woman speaker – of men's rights and arduous duties:

> they . . . endeavouring to get a Maintenance for their Families, scamper thro all the Parts of the Earth by Land and Sea. In times of War they are call'd up by the sound of the Trumpet, stand in Armour in the front of the Battle; while we sit at home in Safety.
> (trans. N. Bailey, 1725)

Brian Morris points out that Katherina's speech is close to this, in emphasizing a husband's care for 'maintenance' and the woman 'warm at home, secure and safe' (Arden edn, p. 87). It cannot be proved that Shakespeare read the book, but – as I have mentioned – it has long been known that his fools draw on Erasmus's Moria in *In Praise of Folly*, and there are other suggestions of Erasmus in *The Shrew* and other plays. It seems to me significant that Shakespeare's version uses the two words 'Maintenance' and 'safe' but in the same passage inserts two other important items of man's duty and woman's advantage which are conspicuously absent from Erasmus. One is a man's hard work and exposure, as the converted Kate praises and pities him for performing 'painful labour both by sea and land', and for watching 'the night in storms, the day in cold'. The other is a man's lack of mercenary motive: 'And craves no other tribute at thy hands/But love, fair looks, and true obedience'. These emphases which are not in Erasmus are precisely the ones which make Katherina's speech (which I discuss more fully in Chapter 7) ironically inapplicable – and easily performed as ironically inapplicable – to the three newly married men sitting at the feast, whom she is addressing, and who conspicuously represent, and replicate, idleness, shelter, comfort and mercenary motive.

If Shakespeare read the colloquy, as is possible, we can see him supplying these vital political additions, just as when – or if – he read the play *The Taming of A Shrew*, which some scholars believe to be earlier than his own play, he conspicuously cut down its misogyny. (If we believe that *A Shrew* is not an earlier play but written after *The Shrew* and deriving from it, then the revision made it more misogynous.) So we can see him – our sight sharpened by the feminism of our time – amending and extending a narrative written by a man, and impersonating a woman, for his own purposes of irony or interpretative flexibility. The additions may have been prompted by spotting precisely what Erasmus's extensive range of male duties left out. At least, a significant difference is brought out by reading Shakespeare and Erasmus on the same subject.

Titus Andronicus is both Shakespeare's most violent play and his most literary play, and it contains more readers than any other play. Various authors are mentioned, but two narrative poets dominate, Virgil and Ovid. Apart from the Virgilian conclusion, discussed in Chapter 3, there is an earlier Virgilian reference, also to Aeneas's anguished tale to Dido. Titus has lost a hand, and his raped daughter has lost two and her tongue. He is maddened by being unable to get away from the word 'hands', tactlessly if metaphorically introduced by Marcus's familiar phrase, 'teach her not thus to lay/ Such violent hands upon her tender life.' As he protests he too gets grotesquely entangled in the language of persistent metaphor:

> What violent hands can she lay on her life?
> Ah, wherefore dost thou urge the name of hands,
> To bid Aeneas tell the tale twice o'er,
> How Troy was burnt and he made miserable?
> O, handle not the theme, to talk of hands,
> Lest we remember still that we have none.
> Fie, fie, how frantically I square my talk,
> As if we should forget we had no hands
> If Marcus did not name the word of hands!
>
> (III.2)

This painfully playful literary meditation on the power and the impertinence of words and metaphors ends with the bookish child Lucius proposing the traditional solace of storytelling, 'Make my aunt merry with some pleasing tale'. And after an episode of symbolic fly-killing, the distracted Titus agrees to console Lavinia with

'Sad stories chanced in the times of old' but asks Lucius to come and take over the reading when his older eyes 'begin to dazzle'. This reading, in her closet, is never shown, and in the next scene (IV.1) the boy runs away from his aunt, Marcus reminds him how she used to read him 'Sweet poetry and Tully's orator', he defends his fright with another literary reference to Hecuba's madness ('I have read'), and Lavinia grotesquely mimes her desire 'to see' one of the books he has dropped.

There follows another of the play's blends of the macabre and the literary as Lavinia is offered the freedom of Titus's library and mimes her story, lifting up her handless arms 'in sequence' and 'tossing' a book, identified in a fine pentameter, 'Grandsire, 'tis Ovid's Metamorphosis'. She 'quotes', that is, turns the leaves to the telltale story of Philomel, one of the Ovidian sources for the play. It turns up again in the last act when it is morbidly imitated by Titus, who finally blends the literary and the bloody as he varies Procne's role, to serve up – not his child, as Procne did to her husband, who raped her sister Philomela – but Tamora's rapist-sons, Chiron and Demetrius, in the pasties he has cooked for their mother to eat.

In *Titus* Shakespeare displays and discusses his narrative sources within the action of his play. He makes his bookish characters read the books he read, Virgil and Ovid, enjoy them, allude to them, discuss them and use them in coded communication and as models for action. Titus wants to outdo Ovid's characters:

> For worse than Philomel you us'd my daughter,
> And worse than Progne I will be reveng'd.
>
> (V.2)

The influence of literature on other literature, the book as source for another book, is a subject the play assimilates to the gruesome and fascinating question of the influence of literature on life, the book as source for life. The question is also raised in the *Aeneid*, when Virgil makes Aeneas feel his narrative burden – useful in the epic – as painful memory. Shakespeare's response to Virgil – and to Ovid too, with his complexity of source material in the

Metamorphoses – is not simply imaged in the play, but meditated as a problem and a puzzle, especially for the artist engaged in that imitation which Renaissance theory approved as part of learning and practising the creative process. Virgil was a source for Ovid, so there is the sense of layered tradition, of which Marcus reminds us when he invokes Aeneas as ancestor in that final Virgilian allusion. In the play the source-resonances are accompanied both by the physical presence of the book and a diffused Ovidian allusion. The book is more of a stage-property than any other book in Shakespeare, as it is carried, dropped, leafed through, pointed at and read. The allusion to the style of the *Metamorphoses* is made generally, by the play's decorative, fantastic, wildly impassioned, bloody and violent action and language. *Titus* is a physically horrifying play, its narrative constantly using rhetoric to intensify morbid details we cannot see in close-up, not distancing but bringing them intimately close, in specifications permitted, but not blurred, by playfulness. This is Ovid's method too, and the play is a deliberated imitation, a witty metamorphosis in another genre, as Joyce's prose *Ulysses* is a deliberated imitation of Homer's poetic epic. Shakespeare blends Ovid with the dignified melancholy politics of Virgil, as Joyce blends Homer with Shakespeare. It is his most literary play, most totally aware of narrative texts, their style, effects and relationships.

As I said at the beginning of the chapter, there are smaller, less conspicuous, examples which intimately link our reading with Shakespeare's. They are the traces and tracks of his response to the text, as well as his imaginative reconstructions. To read Holinshed and *Macbeth* is to notice small things as well as big ones. Act IV, scene 3 of *Macbeth* is a virtuoso narration-scene, with long formal narrative speeches, a central example of large-scale political lying and subtle insights into relationship between teller and listener. Following Holinshed and other historians, Shakespeare makes a good man, Malcolm, Duncan's son, lie to another good man, Macduff. The lie is one where the end justifies the means, a test of Macduff's honour by Malcolm, who is wary because he has already been solicited by Macbeth's *agents provocateurs* and doubtful of a man who has come to England and left his family behind in dangerous Scotland.

Unlike the shapely imaginative narratives of Iago, Falstaff and Viola, whose generative form and circumstantial detail fascinate Shakespeare, Malcolm's lies are long lists of generalized examples. He begins by clearly stating his suspicions: 'something/You may deserve of him [Macbeth] through me, and wisdom/To offer up a weak, poor, innocent lamb.' After more preliminaries he paints his own picture, thickly laying on villainous colours in a long, graduated narration which is hyperbolic and highly generalized:

> It is myself I mean; in whom I know
> All the particulars of vice so grafted,
> That, when they shall be open'd, black Macbeth
> Will seem as pure as snow . . .

and

> . . . your wives, your daughters,
> Your matrons, and your maids, could not fill up
> The cistern of my lust. . . .

and

> I should cut off the nobles for their lands;
> Desire his jewels, and this other's house:
> And my more-having would be as a sauce . . .

The narration becomes more accumulative:

> . . . the king-becoming graces,
> As Justice, Verity, Temp'rance, Stableness,
> Bounty, Perseverance, Mercy, Lowliness,
> Devotion, Patience, Courage, Fortitude,
> I have no relish of them . . .

Exaggeration, abstraction and inventory characterize Malcolm as the deliberating liar and make plausible his final disclosure of virtue; but they convince Macduff, who eventually admits his despair of finding a decent ally and leader: 'Fit to govern?/No, not to live.'

What fascinates Shakespeare - and us – in this narrative is not just the lie itself but the effect of lying and being lied to. Lies are corruptions of storytelling, and we catch corruption in the act. Macduff endures multiple stress, and Shakespeare takes his time to show the pressures. Shocked by the piled-up listings of vice, Macduff tries to tolerate Malcolm for political reasons, but in the end rejects him in disgust, only to hear after all that he is an honest man, lying to test his own integrity ('my first false speaking/ Was this upon myself') and eager to form the alliance. In Holinshed's *Chronicle*, the chief source for this scene, Malcolm lies, makes his confession, the men embrace, then move on at once to plan their alliance. It is different in Shakespeare. He read Holinshed's description of the immediate embrace, marking no transition from doubt, disgust and dismay to acceptance and alliance, and decided to rewrite it. Holinshed's narrative acts as a negative stimulus, like that of Erasmus's *Senatalus*. This is Holinshed's reconciliation:

> Incontinentlie heereupon they embraced ech other, and promising to be faithful the one to the other, they fell in consultation.*

Shakespeare reimagines the scene for a speechless Macduff who shows no enthusiasm but wryly explains, when the surprised Malcolm asks him why he is silent:

> Such welcome and unwelcome things at once,
> 'Tis hard to reconcile.

After these words, Shakespeare's dramatic tact brings on the Doctor, whose entrance allows Malcolm to say 'Well, more anon' and the benign story of the King's healing follows. Shakespeare imagines the depressing effect of Malcolm's narration, as it is slowly but surely accepted as an admission of vice and villainy, and because, even when retracted, it is still a lie. Macduff has been deceived, his morale lowered. The lie is like the logical teaser about Cretan liars: Malcolm is not a seducer, a tyrant and a liar, but he is a liar when he says he is. In the third section of Malcolm's lying narration he includes a long list of the virtues he does not possess, including 'verity', but when he admits he has been lying he picks

*Bullough, vol. VII, pp. 503–4. I have also discussed this scene in Chapter 10.

out only the vice of lying, as if it had been the sole theme of his last speech. And so makes it the theme. His words, accusing by excusing, draw attention to the moral lie: 'my first false speaking/ Was this upon myself.'

So Shakespeare significantly emphasizes the lie, the political, moral and psychological category of narrative which he is constructing for scrutiny, in the dialogic medium of theatre. He is interested in the relationship of the teller and the listener. He shows Macduff unable to recover immediately from the experience. He cannot jump into amity as the knowing Malcolm, in control, expects: 'Now we'll together.' He has cooled towards him. Perhaps Holinshed's superficiality or inattentiveness sharpened Shakespeare's sense of a lie's destabilizing effects. Unconvinced by Holinshed, he sees what is wrong and so what is right. It is only a matter of inserting a line, but it makes Holinshed's already subtle scene even more subtle. We read with Shakespeare and feel the twitch of the revisionary pen, rewriting the psychology and politics of lies and lying, disbelieving and believing.

When you think of it, it is like the suspension of disbelief when we are moved by acting. (Shakespeare's lies are narrations, and also performances, illusions and impersonations.) We know it is not so, but the emotions of pity and fear say otherwise. Perhaps it is also like the effect of acting on the actor, which can create antagonism or bonding after acting stops. (French actors in the nineteenth century used to be paid extra for acting villains.) The insight may have a source in Shakespeare's stage experience, but it may have been stimulated, or reinforced, by Holinshed's implausible narration, especially conspicuous to someone reading or revising with performance in mind.

Interestingly, another probable source for this scene, according to Bullough (vol. VII) and other scholars, is a Latin history, *Rerum Scoticarum Historia* (1582), by George Buchanan, from which Shakespeare could have taken a suggestion for one of the most famous speeches in *Macbeth*. If Shakespeare read Buchanan, he found a sceptical and sophisticated historian, conscious of historiography, dismissing certain versions of the Macbeth material as 'like Milesian

Fables, and fitter for the Stage, than an History'. I like to speculate that Shakespeare, a man of the stage, who had written about braggart soldiers, was amused by this superior attitude and recalled it when he wrote Macbeth's speech about narrating and acting and converted Buchanan's negations to his own wry imagery, in the 'tale told by an idiot' and the 'poor player'. Even if he didn't read Buchanan, the irony is there, and enjoyable.

His revision of Holinshed for Malcolm's lie to Macduff could also have been positively inspired or endorsed by a passage in Sidney's *New Arcadia*, a striking episode in the story of Parthenia and Argalus (*The Countess of Pembroke's Arcadia*, ed. Victor Skretkowics, Oxford, Clarendon Press, 1987, pp. 30, 44). The situation and the characters are different from those in *Macbeth* but there are several correspondences. There is a lie told by a good character, as a trial of honour, accepted by the listener, then denied in a revelation which cannot be immediately accepted. Parthenia has had her beauty maliciously disfigured, leaves her lover for his sake, and is later cured. She visits him, but when he greets her as his lost love she pretends she is not Parthenia but just looks very like her. Then she tells a complex lie, saying that Parthenia – still disfigured – has suggested that she and Argalus should make a match. True to his love, he refuses with 'hearty sighs' and she reveals herself as the true Parthenia after all. Like Malcolm with Macduff, she expects him to feel instant and delighted relief and runs to embrace him, 'Why then . . . take thy Parthenia.' His feelings have been established as sorrowful by those hearty sighs, and we have been told that he experiences 'sudden changes of joy into sorrow'. Like Macduff, he cannot suddenly switch off sorrow; as the third-person narrator explains, 'sorrow forbad him too soon to believe'. Parthenia has to convince him by telling the whole story in detail: she 'told him the truth with some circumstances'. If this didn't give Shakespeare a fresh insight, it was a prompting or a confirmation. What is important is a similar interest in the psychology and relationships of lying.

Shakespeare's reading of the *Arcadia* is well known, because he took the sub-plot of *King Lear* from it, changing the names of characters. One narrative in that sub-plot, Edgar's impassioned report of his father's death, may owe one of its rhetorical features to Sidney's style. This is the use of parenthesis as a marker of emotional speech. 'The parenthesis is the most obvious feature of Sydney's style', according to Jean Robertson's Introduction to the Oxford edition of the *Old Arcadia* (p. xxix). A good example – from numerous episodes, not all of which are excited speech – is the narration of one of the book's heroines, Philoclea, in which she tells Pyrocles how she and her sister Pamela were tortured, she was shown a faked spectacle of her sister's death and had to put her head through a hole in a scaffold to stage her own death. Not only the story of Philoclea's torment but the lengthy sentences of the indirect narrative, and the excited responses of Pyrocles, are branched and broken by parenthesis, marked by brackets or set off from the main clause by commas and dashes (*The Countess of Pembroke's Arcadia*, pp. 436–7).

In *King Lear* Edgar's parenthesis marks stress rather than disorder, punctuating his narrative with compressed and characteristic moral exclamation ('O fault', and 'O! our lives sweetness/That we the pain of death would hourly die/Rather than die at once!'). The stylized parentheses in Iachimo's confessional narrative, already mentioned, are suggestive and probably sinister, and there are other examples in the long speeches of *Cymbeline*, including some by Posthumus. *Henry VIII* is full of interestingly localized uses of parenthesis, to mark various passions in Katharine, Wolsey, the King, the Old Lady, Norfolk and Buckingham. For example, Buckingham's disturbed diatribe against 'the holy fox' Wolsey is narrative pressed, contorted and speeded up by self-interruptions, its contemptuous phrases or images prominently voiced in the bracketing: '(Whom from the flow of gall I name not, but/From sincere notions)'; '(for he is equal rav'nous/As he is subtle, and as prone to mischief/As able to perform't)', and:

> for worthy Wolsey
> (Who cannot err) he did it. Now this follows
> (Which as I take it, is a kind of puppy
> To th'old dam treason) . . .
>
> (I.1)

The language of such examples may derive, consciously or not, from Sidney. But the use of parenthesis is only one prominent example of their shared interest in affective narration.

Sidney's readers are not left to notice his rhetorical notation of passion unaided, because he is an intensely self-conscious stylist. Shakespeare must have noticed Sidney's elegant and sustained artistic self-reference, as conspicuous in the *Arcadia* as in his sonnets. The narrative speeches, though written for the page and not the stage, are designed to express character and passion, in direct speech, and Sidney – whose *Defence of Poesie* (written in the early 1580s but not published until 1595) has a claim to be the first English work of criticism – clearly draws attention, not indirectly like Virgil and Shakespeare but explicitly and analytically, to the affective shaping of language. For example, Zelmane, disguised as Pyrocles, is desperate, torn and confused, 'her conceit darkened with a mist of desire' and other emotions (*The Countess of Pembroke's Arcadia*, p. 428). When she visits the tormented Philoclea both women are speechless, and Sidney's narrator elegantly joins synecdoche, personification and oxymoron in the rhetoric of silence:

> then began first the eyes to speak and the hearts to cry out. Sorrow a while would needs speak his own language, without using their tongues to be his interpreters. At last, Zelmane brake silence, but spake with the only eloquence of amazement, for all her long methodized oration was inherited only by such kind of speeches: 'Dear lady, in extreme necessities we must not –'; 'But alas! unfortunate wretch that I am, that I live to see this day!'; 'And I take heaven and earth to witness that nothing –'; and with that, her breast swelled so with spite and grief that her breath had not leisure to turn herself into words.
>
> (p. 429)

We may hear Cordelia in the first scene of *King Lear*, in that 'nothing' and perhaps in the idea of turning herself into words – 'I cannot heave/My heart into my mouth' – but I am not claiming this remarkable passage as a source for specific passages in *King Lear*, only showing how Sidney anticipates Shakespeare's combination of sophisticated analysis with strong narrative passion. For Sidney it is an easier linking, because the self-conscious comment is made by a third-person narrator and the passion expressed in the first-person idiolect of a character within a story. Shakespeare is not linking but blending and doing something most difficult and strange when he makes Egeon, Hamlet and Edgar articulate an awareness of rhetoric in the throes of grief.

Another link between the two authors is the subject of inhibited narrative, shown in breakdown and silence. Sidney makes Zelmane first keep quiet, then speak in broken distracted language. Shakespeare invents the incoherent narrations of Hotspur's comic bluster, Othello's hysterical breakdown, and Leontes's crazy asyndeton. In Act V, scene 2 of *Richard II* the Duchess of York asks her husband to resume the story of Richard and Bolingbroke, 'our two cousins, coming into London', brought to a stop by his weeping. Shakespeare invents the striking silences of Cordelia's reticence, Virgilia's habitual quiet, Morton unable to report Hotspur's death to Northumberland, his 'brow, like to a title-leaf' foretelling 'the nature of a tragic volume', Perdita reunited to Leontes offstage, Hermione reunited to Leontes onstage and King John tempting Hubert. In none of them is silence 'Sorrow's own language', but silence speaks for many passions.

John's motive for telling and not telling is sly murderous ambition. He wants to ask Hubert to kill Arthur but cannot put it into words. (There is no source in Holinshed, who baldly reports that other councillors carried out the murder.) It is an emotional and deliberated narrative absence, a narration that is silent on one subject. John feels an unattractive cowardly fastidiousness, rather like Macbeth's, about naming something he is not too fastidious to desire:

> Come hither, Hubert. O my gentle Hubert,
> We owe thee much! within this wall of flesh
> There is a soul counts thee her creditor,
> And with advantage means to pay thy love:
> And, my good friend, thy voluntary oath
> Lives in this bosom, dearly cherished.
> Give me thy hand. I had a thing to say,

> But I will fit it with some better tune.
> By heaven, Hubert, I am almost asham'd
> To say what good respect I have of thee.
> (III.2)

Hubert's reply is restrained: 'I am much bounden', and John continues flattery, bribery, hint and evasion, edging towards disclosure:

> Good friend, thou hast no cause to say so yet,
> But thou shalt have; and creep time ne'er so slow,
> Yet it shall come for me to do thee good.
> I had a thing to say, but let it go:
> The sun is in the heaven, and the proud day,
> Attended with the pleasures of the world,
> Is all too wanton and too full of gauds
> To give me audience: if the midnight bell
> Did, with his iron tongue and brazen mouth,
> Sound on into the drowsy race of night . . .

After the negative clues in imagery of light and pleasure, he finds an appropriate setting and objective correlatives for what he is trying to tell and not to tell, in darkness, iron and brazenness. He imagines his ideal listener, a Hubert filled with animosity and grievance. He wishes narrative could jump communication and tries to make it do so, first eliminating a subject and then breaking off. At last, after all his elegant beating about the bush, there is a violent jump to laconic narrative, verbless, just two telling substantives: 'Death' and 'A grave'.

This example suggests another connection with Sidney, noticed by Ernst Honigmann who quotes a 'similar' passage from *Arcadia* in which Cecropia tries to persuade by conspicuous evasion:

> 'I had a thing to say to you, but it is no matter' . . . [she] stayed indeede, thinking Philoclea would have had a female inquisitiveness of the matter.
> (Arden edn, 1954, p. 76)

Cecropia and John are made more despicable by dodging the discomfort of telling. This connection takes on more importance if we connect it with the Zelmane story, where Sidney is eloquently discussing affective silence. It is one more link – perhaps an affinity of insight rather than an influence – between these two narrative artists who have so much in common, despite differences in genre. When Shakespeare read Sidney, he was reading a storyteller using a contemporary language, congenially pondering the passions and voices of storytelling in art and in life outside art.

PART TWO

Themes

CHAPTER FIVE

Arts and Acts of Memory

'In the dark backward and abysm of time'

Memorial is an act and art of memory, in art, and in life outside art, on which Shakespeare's imagination dwells. Contemplating memorials, he considers the subjects of artistic faith and inspiration, impulses and purposes, the blend of personal with compositional passions, genre and readers. He imagines the survival of his own passionate language, himself as lover and artist becoming a memory and others becoming memories in him and through him. He reflects and reflects on the nature of memory, seeing the awareness of past, present and future, as neither chronological nor linear but a mesh of narrative motions. We look before and after, look before at looking after and after at looking before. The temporal standpoint – where we are – qualifies the passions of prospect and recall and is qualified by them. There are historical and personal preferences for certain time-stances and tenses. The Anglo-Saxon elegiac poets, Jane Austen, Wordsworth, Proust, Yeats, and even the reluctant and resisting James Joyce, all use retrospect as imaginative source, impulse, form and material. Shakespeare is more like Blake, who banished the daughters of memory. His imagination leans forward, its harkings back often need to be projected into the future. As he imagines memorial, he looks ahead to contemplate recall. As the sonnets discover and discuss memorial – its aesthetic, personal and social features – the speakers anticipate remembering the present feeling time and writing time, as a past recovered or recoverable in a future. They entertain prospects of retrospective passion and affection, and of being remembered by posterity. Metaphors and metonymies for memorial in the sonnets (often traditional – such as monument, lines, black lines, pen, gentle verse, poor rhyme and powerful rhyme) register the foldings and unfoldings of anticipation and memory as the poems inspect the passionate orderings of our time sense, in passionate essays at ordering.

The time of each poem is a new present, renewing feeling. The memorial Sonnet 107 may suggest the political context of James I's accession in 1603, perhaps even the change of fortune for Shakespeare's lover, but its emphasis is placed on the matching of social and personal feeling and their conversion into the memorial senses of future:

> Now with the drops of this most balmy time
> My love looks fresh, and Death to me subscribes,
> Since, spite of him, I'll live in this poor rhyme,
> While he insults o'er dull and speechless tribes.
> And thou in this shalt find thy monument,
> When tyrants' crests and tombs of brass are spent.*

The classical commonplace of perennial bronze (remade in Shakespearian materials of brass, gilt and marble) is set against the typographical, prosodic and affective images of black line, poor, powerful rhyme and gentle verse. All the moods of the memorial projects vary – confident, relieved, defiant, blissful, time-wearily tentative, 'And yet to times in hope my verse shall stand' (60). Their sensuousness varies also. The social and poetic projection to a time when memory has gone public, and all readers are strangers, is highly particularized and physical, in Sonnet 81:

> Or I shall live your epitaph to make,
> Or you survive when I in earth am rotten,
> From hence your memory death cannot take,

***The Sonnets and A Lover's Complaint*, ed. John Kerrigan (Harmondsworth, Penguin, 1986).

> Although in me each part will be forgotten.
> Your name from hence immortal life shall have,
> Though I, once gone, to all the world must die.
> The earth can yield me but a common grave
> When you entombèd in men's eyes shall lie.
> Your monument shall be my gentle verse,
> Which eyes not yet created shall o'er-read,
> And tongues to be your being shall rehearse
> When all the breathers of this world are dead.
> You still shall live – such virtue hath my pen –
> Where breath most breathes, even in the mouths of men.

The competition of sculptured monument versus poetry is easily won by poetry, presented as bringing the 'whole soul of man' – senses, imagination, historical memory and powers of forecast – 'into activity'. Scanning eye, shaping tongue and uttering breath will co-operate to rehearse – to tell, practise and perform the funeral rites again. This is a message sent by poet to readers, a message in a sonnet, less of a gamble than a message in a bottle, a kind of no-lose dare, since we see it as dare or gamble only when it succeeds, which up to now it has done. As the reader reads and rereads, aloud, or silently in our day of silent reading, but with the auditory imagination encouraged and stimulated by being so precisely articulated, Shakespeare speaks straight to the speaking and reading mind and body, imagining being remembered, as shaping poet, actor and expert in elocution would imagine, refreshing the conventional epitaph-address as those words about breath breathed in the mouth remind the still-but-not-forever-breathing living of the once-and-no-longer-breathing-dead, poets and lovers. As so often, Shakespeare brings together the most technical references with a sense of common experience. Here it is our common sense of past, present, future and terminus.

This sensuous and affective imagining of time and mortality, this avoidance of a simple backward look, this hot line to a future reader, this insistence on making affection, fidelity and admiration canny, keeps the artistic preoccupation with writing from sounding proud and vain. Still, Shakespeare knows the risk of imagining posterity's response. He plays with it many times, thrillingly in

Troilus and Cressida, a play in which he is much concerned with rewriting and reimagining story, mythology and history, which have been much worked over by other writers, such as Virgil and Chaucer, whom he remembers. Troilus, Cressida and Pandarus reverse the stance of the sonneteer, hoping that they will not become, what they did become, images of fidelity, infidelity and pimping. They speak from a historical, innocent, present-tense confidence designed to be read ironically and sadly by a knowing future:

> If I be false, or swerve a hair from truth,
> When time is old and hath forgot itself,
> When water-drops have worn the stones of Troy,
> And blind oblivion swallow'd cities up,
> And mighty states characterless are grated
> To dusty nothing – yet let memory,
> From false to false, among false maids in love,
> Upbraid my falsehood.
>
> (III.2)

Cressida's incredulous enunciation of the commonplace simile, 'As false as Cressid', is revised by our memory, as we use it imaginatively to contemplate the process through which events and persons are turned into story, comparing literary, mythological and historical knowledge with a sense of particular persons existing in their present. Shakespeare makes Troilus and Cressida send dangerous dares to the future. Hamlet and Othello are more imaginative characters, wisely anxious about wounded names, edited records and damaged memorials. Neither speaks with innocence and irony. Hamlet urges Horatio to tell his story even though it means absenting himself from felicity a while. Horatio's brief abstract narrated to Fortinbras and the English ambassadors is reassuring, up to a point. Othello asks Lodovico to write his report to the Venetian senate, neither extenuating nor setting down anything in malice. These dying articulations of the dangers of becoming memory and story strengthen the audience's double sense of the play's fictitious 'reality' and real fictitiousness. It reinforces, too, our sense of privileged access, and our memory of the play. Hamlet and Othello, in their anxiety, represent the play of memory, and provoke the play of our memory, which so quickly moves away from the drama's engrossment of the present, once the play is over. It needs all the reinforcements it can get, and Shakespeare gives it many.

The memorial anticipations of political heroes interested Shakespeare, who employed much tact in imagining their tactful oratory. He subsumes private boast to patriotic occasion, as Henry V imagines the memorial of St Crispin's Day, in a still topically politic displacement of king to country, leader to army, governor to governed, prospect to retrospect, offering the slogan of memorial. The enemy's memorial of hero or heroine may be set in competition with the memory of the audience, as in *Macbeth*, where Malcolm's memorial is cunningly constructed to make us feel that our memory would not sum up the story in the terms of his restricted memorial of 'dead butcher' and 'fiendlike queen', though of course we see – and have seen – what he means. We may be importing a modern political critique if we cast a cold eye on that golden monument competitively set up by the rich old men Montague and Capulet in memory of Romeo and Juliet, but there is less ambiguity in Caesar's memorializing of Antony and Cleopatra, as he transmutes obituary praise for the great dead lovers into self-laudation. (His memory of Antony's prowess as a soldier in I.4 is an earlier demonstration of his political manipulation and use of apparently magnanimous praise.) He can afford politic compliment for the graceful vitality of Cleopatra's corpse (lying in politic arrangement) as he speaks of glory and empire. His granted memorial of a grave for dead enemies, 'No grave upon the earth shall clip in it/A pair so famous', is also inexpensive since as a pair they offer neither threat nor competition, as far as he knows. He exploits obituary style for patronizing pity and generalized, third-person, delicate but unmistakable self-advertisement:

high events as these
Strike those that make them: and their story is
No less in pity than his glory which
Brought them to be lamented.

(V.2)

(The telling match of their story with his glory is tactfully tucked away as an internal rhyme.) A model of politic praise and claim, the speech underlines the distinctiveness of the play's conflicting values and victories, and keeps the conflict going. Knowing from Plutarch that Caesar, deprived of Cleopatra's prized person, carried her effigy, with asp, in triumph, Shakespeare converted the event into a narrative. It enacts and judges Caesar's prospects of retrospect. Character's expectation of memorial is in character, designed to alert the audience's sense of history and its memory of the play. We may not provide and divide pity and admiration quite as Caesar expects.

Like memorial, the desirous act of memory we call nostalgia involves two times. It retrieves, by reliving, the past. It is absent from the sonnets. Sonnet 104 harks back to the pleasure of a first meeting, 'as you were when first your eye I eyed', but though the playfulness is affectionate, intimate and sexily knowing, the cheeky wit is too cool and assertive to bring the past close and linger. And the sense of intimacy places language in the present. Shakespeare does not dwell on the happy past, and the sonnets contain no Proustian revivals. Of course, Sonnet 30 was appropriated by C.K. Scott Moncrieff to give name, novel epigraph and book epigraphs for Proust's Bergsonian novel *A la recherche du temps perdu*, so that the first couplet is repeatedly memorialized, torn from context:

> When to the sessions of sweet silent thought
> I summon up remembrance of things past . . .

The ineptness of this borrowing has often been lamented. Shakespeare's 'remembrance' suggests neither search nor research, and the poem has nothing to say about involuntary memory. The imaged act of summoning to sessions is not merely deliberated but downright peremptory. Even if the legal connotations of 'sessions' are sweetened and silenced, and seem to be moving to contemplate the nature of reverie, the rapid reappearance of the law in 'I summon' makes 'the sessions of sweet silent thought' look more like oxymoron than qualification. Sweetness and silence are held fast by preceding 'sessions' and succeeding 'summons'. And the past things that are summoned up are not sweet, nor is recollection silent. The poem is clamorous with sounds of woe:

> I sigh the lack of many a thing I sought,
> And with old woes new wail my dear time's waste;
> Then can I drown an eye, unused to flow,
> For precious friends hid in death's dateless night,
> And weep afresh love's long since cancelled woe,
> And moan th'expense of many a vanished sight;
> Then can I grieve at grievances foregone,
> And heavily from woe to woe tell o'er
> The sad account of fore-bemoanèd moan,
> Which I new pay as if not paid before.

'Precious' is an unspecific epithet, and precious friends are generalized and relegated to a remote past, 'hid' not found again, trebly blacked out by death, datelessness and night. The other positive, 'many a vanished sight', is also plural and also generalized. Everything else remembered is grief, much of it re-remembered, Virgilianly compounding new sorrow in new telling: 'new wail', 'weep afresh', 'new pay' and the wailing repetitive and alliterative fluidities of 'grieve at grievances foregone' and 'fore-bemoanèd moan' (which must have schooled Gerard Manley Hopkins's 'pangs . . . schooled at forepangs' and 'tormented mind/With this tormented mind tormenting yet'). But the poem is not entirely given up to retrospect; sorrow is played again to release a sense of happy present. Few final couplets seem to make such a clean sweep of previous quatrains:

> But if the while I think on thee, dear friend,
> All losses are restored and sorrows end.

Perhaps that is what the brief sweetness and silence were preparing. The repeated weeping and wailing formed an *occupatio*, a temporary negative occupation, waiting for a positive, monotonously piling sorrow on sorrow to release the engrossment of present passion by a powerful spring. Wallace Stevens's 'Mozart, 1935' asks the poet to 'Play the present, its hoo-hoo-hoo'. Shakespeare did not need this advice. Like Stevens he is engrossed by the present, entranced by its immediacy, its experiences and images, freed or as freed as possible from category and the rotted words of retrospect. *Occupatio* is not a cancellation but a way of having two times, one much more specific – 'thee, dear friend' – and much advantaged by having the last words. Shakespeare may have had good personal reasons for hating to look back. He may have been a phenomenologist before his time. And his chosen genre of drama, in which all narratives must be rooted in the present tense of performance and audience, may have played its part, as cause or effect, in this absorption in the present. It was there in that breathtaking sense of the reader's breathing. It is a force which inhibits nostalgia.

The characters in the plays constantly look back, but they incline to remember pain and losses. Hamlet and Macbeth are deepened by being given slivers of pre-tragic free reminiscence, but Hamlet's illustration of drama he loved is Aeneas's sorrowful and grim narrative to Dido, re-imagined in an imaginary play, and Macbeth's only tragedy-free recollection is of his hair standing on end at 'a dismal treatise'. Helena, in *All's Well That Ends Well*, does not compliment Bertram when she remembers being in bed with him, 'O my good lord, when I was like this maid/I found you wondrous kind'.* Irony outweighs gratitude, and the bed trick, though a convention, is deconventionalized to allow Helena humiliating memory, which she sharpens into pointed reminder, of being deflowered by her husband because he thought she was another woman. All may be well that ends well, but this end does not simplify memory of the past for character or audience. Helena is interiorized, convention piercingly made particular. Othello remembers the pomp and circumstance of the big wars, but after his 'occupation' has gone, meaning is so lost that the recollection is indeed a rare instance of sorrow's crown of sorrow remembering happier days, though that is scarcely the primary impression that

*For a different view, see Barbara Everett's introduction to the New Penguin *All's Well That Ends Well* (1970): she recognizes the irony but sees Helena as 'able' to suggest that Bertram's sexual instincts are not only natural, but humane and generous. G.K. Hunter, in the Arden edition, ignores Helena's irony when he says 'there was little sense amongst Shakespeare's contemporaries that [the bed trick] was a degrading and unsatisfactory way of getting a husband'.

it makes: the medium of present passion makes past professional and sexual pride lose all their delight.

When characters look back nostalgically, the audience should scent danger. In *The Winter's Tale* Polixenes, prompted by Hermione, relates the golden age of boyhood he shared with Leontes, just before jealousy pounces to attack innocence, love, childhood and memory. Cleopatra is most indulgently and vivaciously engaged with erotic and sporting memories when nostalgia is rudely interrupted by the news that Antony is married to Octavia. Shakespeare shows nostalgia's invitations to travel dangerously far from present events, passions, imperatives and its selective, simplifying propaganda. When the Nurse remembers Juliet's childhood, Shakespeare makes it plain that she loses all sense of present occasion and of the person being remembered. She is stuck in the past. Shakespeare criticizes sentimentality before it is given a name. Meredith's wonderful if somewhat opaque definition (in *Richard Feverel*, famously quoted in Joyce's *Ulysses*) of a sentimentalist as one 'who would enjoy without incurring the immense debtorship for a thing done' is scrupulously elucidated by the Nurse's retrospect. Her memory is the most prolix, expansive, digressive and compulsive in Shakespeare, in repetitiveness outdoing her predecessor, the Wife of Bath, and later man-made talkative women in Dickens:

> And since that time it is eleven years.
> For then she could stand high-lone, nay by th'rood,
> She could have run and waddled all about;
> For even the day before she broke her brow,
> And then my husband – God be with his soul,
> A was a merry man – took up the child,
> 'Yea', quoth he, 'dost thou fall upon thy face?
> Thou wilt fall backward when thou hast more wit,
> Wilt thou not not, Jule?' And by my holidame,
> The pretty wretch left crying and said 'Ay'.
> To see now how a jest shall come about.
> I warrant, and I should live a thousand years
> I never should forget it. 'Wilt thou not, Jule?' quoth he,
> And, pretty fool, it stinted, and said 'Ay'.
>
> (I.3)

Her rambling and circumstantial memory is so beguiling that critics have inaccurately compared it with Lady Capulet's, saying that the Nurse remembers Juliet's age and the mother does not.* The reading might have amused Shakespeare, who works to give the Nurse great nostalgic charm: she remembers suckling, weaning, infantile innocence, the natural world, and death, making Susan, her daughter, live and die in a couple of moving lines, and creating her husband, 'A was a merry man', as she retells three times his joke about Jule falling on her back when she grows up, hilariously completed by the infant's innocent punchline 'Ay'. With such stuff are family albums stuffed. Though warm and amusing, the reminiscences are not moral signs or guarantees of rootedness, like the tender archivism of Fanny Price or Maggie Tulliver's faithful backward reach. Or Prospero's earnest revisions. The Nurse is not an expert in that form of memory we call fidelity, but an opportunist adviser to her charge, to whom she lightly recommends switching to Paris, 'Romeo's a dishclout to him', forgetting what she has previously said about Romeo, and leaving Juliet to feel a desolate moral solitude. The Nurse's nostalgic one-tone dwellings on the past are particularized and sensuous but also enclosed and shallow. She belongs with Thackeray's Barry Lyndon and James Joyce's Simon Dedalus in *Portrait of the Artist as a Young Man*, as a soft image, an indictment of retrospect without renewal.

Sir Andrew Aguecheek's 'I was adored once too' rounds out his grotesque angularity and makes him more lovable. Like the Nurse, he brings out the softie in us. But though the pathetic moment is created to give memory, and a past, to folly and affectation, the invention works in two ways and does not exalt wistful lamentation for past love.

The other nostalgic episodes, like that of the Nurse, are highly circumstantial, also eddying rather than flowing, and presenting memory in one mood, desire to be back in the golden old days. There is plenty of solid specification in the memories of Justice

*Lisa Jardine in *Still Harping on Daughters: Women and Drama in the Age of Shakespeare* (Brighton, Harvester, 1983) agreeing with Laurence Stone, *The Family, Sex and Marriage in England 1500–1800* (Harmondsworth, Penguin, 1979).

Shallow, in *Henry IV, Pt 2*, as he plays thin-man sentimentalist to Falstaff's fat-man cynic. The Nurse excites our susceptibility to tales of childhood and summer, Shallow offers the more robust appeal of rioting, sporting, drinking, whoring and fighting in student days: 'The same Sir John, the very same. I saw him break Scoggin's head at the court gate . . . Jesu, Jesu, the mad days that I have spent!' (III.2) and 'And is Jane Nightwork alive? . . . she must be old, she cannot choose but be old, certain she's old' and 'Ha, cousin Silence, that thou hadst seen that that this knight and I have seen!' (III.2). There are the added halo effects of reflections on friendship and death, 'the mad days that I have spent! And to see how many of my old acquaintance are dead!', the pious tone of 'Jesu, Jesu', the solemn commonplace 'Death, as the Psalmist saith, is certain to all, all shall die' and the nostalgic roll-call of nonce characters with placename support:

> There was I, and little John Doit of Staffordshire, and black George Barnes, and Francis Pickbone, and Will Squele, a Cotsole man. . . .
> (III.2)

Shallow is an endearing sentimentalist, his recall of golden days punctuated and earthed by questions about the market price of bullocks and ewes. But the outside world of farming and recruiting shows nostalgia sealed off in tone. Its gratifications cost Shallow dear, as Falstaff milks his memory of the dear dead past for all he's worth, letting the audience know that young Shallow looked like a forked radish when he was naked and was a lecherous monkey. Falstaff not only deromanticizes nostalgia, but perfectly fakes it in one of Shakespeare's most nostalgically extracted recalls, 'We have heard the chimes at midnight'.

Sentimentality is exposed as the memory telling lies, by enclosure, simplification and selection. It is also something we seem to need and love. If Shakespeare's maturity was too toughminded and wise to let him imagine it except through unimaginative, shallow and simple-minded minds, those minds, made dramatic, do allow him to create these desirous dwellings in the past, cut off, cut out, and making no demands on the present. Cleopatra is made to revise nostalgia, after she flatters herself by remembering the attention of Julius Caesar and Pompey, with the famous line which puts the dear dead days in their place, 'My salad days,/When I was green in judgment, cold in blood' (I.5) In these 'black lines' Shakespeare did not insist on keeping memory green, but as he takes a cool look at greenness, imagining Cleopatra (like Falstaff) as an opportunist, not a sentimentalist, he also takes a cool look at the dismissal of nostalgia. To have absolutely no sympathy with nostalgia is to be not cool but cold.

Cleopatra can switch nostalgia on and off, which does not mean that she is not imagined as never feeling it. (After all, Enobarbus says she has infinite variety.) There is a dignified staging of recall when she bids farewell to Antony, with the brief 'Sir, you and I have lov'd'. Its brevity is permitted by the pretence of reality of wanting to say something else and forgetting:

> Courteous lord, one word:
> Sir, you and I must part, but that's not it:
> Sir, you and I have lov'd, but there's not it;
> That you know well, something it is I would, –
> O, my oblivion is a very Antony,
> And I am all forgotten.
>
> (I.3)

Occupatio, hyperbole and humour are splendid, though Antony dismisses them as idleness, and we are never quite sure what, if anything, was forgotten.

Forgetting is an act of memory – lapse, mistake, failure, absence, disorder – which interested Shakespeare as much as it interested William James or Freud* or Beckett. His theatrical experience of the memorial efforts of performance occasionally comes into this, but his concern goes far beyond the actor's arts and trials. Shakespeare creates a psychopathology of everyday (and everynight) life which not only contributes to his mimesis (which is a means if not an end) but invents, collects, observes, compares, analyses – and in short, studies – the workings of the conscious

*See p. 20.

and unconscious mind. He creates an effortless, almost inconspicuous taxonomy. (Perhaps a means and an end.)

'Proust', said Samuel Beckett, 'had a bad memory', dissolving our sense of paradox by adding, 'The man with a good memory does not remember anything because he does not forget anything.'* To wake, you must sleep. To disinter the past uncorrupted, you must bury it deep. For Proust's *madeleine* in the *tisane* to open the past, its taste must have been, like Cleopatra, all forgotten. Proust's analysis of involuntary memory includes the study and demonstration of voluntary memory and of forgetting. The stimulants which so invigorate memory, like the cake and the uneven paving stone, are guaranteed, in power and mysteriousness, by their neighborhood to a stimulant which does not work, the group of trees. Edward Thomas's memory-poem 'Old Man' would imagine the unconscious mind less profoundly, if its narrator did not fail to remember, as well as remember. Shakespeare suggests something of the gains of forgetfulness, in Sonnet 77, which encourages the receiver of a memorandum book to put in it what memory cannot retain, not, as has been suggested, simply because he is interested in the written record as reliable memory – though he is – but also because the memory will be freshly retrievable. Lost, it can be found. An old note in a notebook may not be as glamorous an example of past's revival as Proust's *madeleine* or D.H. Lawrence's piano, in 'Piano', but it is an example:

> Look what thy memory cannot contain
> Commit to these waste blanks, and thou shalt find
> Those children nursed, delivered from thy brain,
> To take a new acquaintance of thy mind.

Forgetful characters are legion. Hotspur forgets, or thinks he forgets, a map, an essential document for a military meeting where the agenda is the carving up of the kingdom, and also forgets the name of the place where he first met the future Henry IV, Berkeley Castle. Psychologists would expect Hotspur to forget: he is said

Proust (London, Chatto and Windus, 1931).

and shown to be harebrained, impetuous and is the worst listener in Shakespeare. He never attends, so of course cannot remember. Shakespeare puts his flustered brain-racking into the idiolect:

> In Richard's time – what do you call the place?
> A plague upon it, it is in Gloucestershire –
> 'Twas where the mad-cap Duke his uncle kept,
> His uncle York –
>
> (I.3)

That madcap York, in *Richard II*, is himself an example of bad memory, making an early Freudian slip, when he called Queen Isabel, his cousin, 'sister' and extra-metrically corrects himself, 'Come, sister – cousin, I would say, pray pardon me'. (II.2) It has been proposed, I think implausibly, that he mistakes the Queen for his sister (sister-in-law), the Duchess of Gloucester, of whose death he has just been told.* It has also been observed, rightly, by Lois Potter in her lecture 'Nobody's Perfect', (*Shakespeare Survey* 42, 1990) that this is the kind of slip actors constantly make. It is more than this, I think – a true Freudian slip of the tongue, thoroughly, indeed generously, motivated, by York's comic, impetuous and bumbling old age. He is under stress: he's been left to govern in Richard's absence, Bolingbroke has landed, his sister-in-law, last link with brother Gloucester, has just died, and he had intended to ask her for a thousand pounds for the war: his memory fails because stress is compounded and at a time when he needs to compose himself. His forgetting is part of a local pattern, a cluster of forgettings. The dead sister-in-law (Duchess of Gloucester) herself forgot what she wanted John of Gaunt to tell York, on her last appearance: she too is old, distressed, trying to collect herself and failing. Shakespeare completes a little triad of controlled experiment with the forgetfulness of York's servant, who reports the departure of York's son but forgets to tell him about his sister-in-law's death until told to go to Plashy to ask her for money. Two lapses on the part of distressed old people, one on the part of a messenger who can only hold one message in his head at a time.

* *Richard II*, ed. Andrew Gurr, New Cambridge edition (1984).

Shakespeare's important source, Holinshed, chronicling York's tolerance of Richard II, says: 'and did forget as well as he might', and may have brought forgetting to mind. Hotspur and York both forget under stress of war, and help to make a pattern of military lapse, which may lend support to those who believe that Shakespeare saw active service. The most famous forgetful fighter is Coriolanus, hot and bleeding after Corioli, wanting to free one of the prisoners in whose house he has stayed, forgetting his name and making his own diagnosis: 'My memory's fatigued'.* Another absent-minded warrier is Fluellen in *Henry V*. He is passionate and voluble, and his racing tongue outruns his mobilizing memory: he forgets the name of the city where Alexander the Great was born, and the name of its river, his retrievals from the story of memory showing a Welsh national preference, since he does remember Monmouth and the Wye: 'it is out of my prains what is the name of the other river; but 'tis all one, 'tis alike as my fingers is to my fingers', adding, of course, the great line 'there is salmons in both'. Fluellen is not perturbed by his forgetfulness. His third lapse is the best: he forgets the name of one of the best-known characters in Shakespeare, only recently killed off in this same play, 'Sir John Falstaff', and before Gower supplies the name which is on the tip of Fluellen's too-nimble tongue, the audience is given the description of 'the fat knight with the great-belly doublet: he was full of jests, and gipes, and knaveries' and gets there first. Making historical and dramatic characters forget each other's names makes a good theatrical in-joke, helps realize and fictionalize the audience's response to persons, time and the history plays' serial structure and provides a sub-text on the selections and indirections of memory. Fluellen's forgetting of Falstaff's name also suggests, to the attentive, a Welsh vengeance, because Falstaff himself, in *Henry IV, Pt 1*, has forgotten the great Welsh name, Owen Glendower.

*A.V. Nuttall interprets Coriolanus' memory slip as typically 'shallow' aristocratic negligence following typically 'large' aristocratic magnanimity (*A New Mimesis: Shakespeare and the Representation of Reality*, London, Methuen, 1983, p. 119).

The psychopathology of Shakespearean drama should include Polonius, Hamlet and the Duke of Gloucester in *Henry VI, Pt 1*, who tells of a dream and realistically forgets part of it. Macbeth asks the doctor if he can pluck from the memory a rooted sorrow; Lady Macbeth's problem is remembering too well, perhaps only in her bad dreams. Iachimo in *Cymbeline* pretends to forget the silver Cupid andirons in Imogen's room, to act his lie and retard the inventory with which he torments Posthumous, who praises his memory, in confidence or effort. Iachimo's pretended lapse must be put beside his retention of one thing he sees in Imogen's bedroom, the crimson mole on her breast, which he says he does not need to put in his notebook, because it is 'riveted,/Screw'd' to his memory. Miranda has been taken as forgetful; John Kerrigan in the introduction to his edition of *The Sonnets and A Lover's Complaint* uses her to illustrate the idea that for Shakespeare 'recollection is always sadly flawed'. Only certain kinds of recollection are flawed: Miranda's memory, which impresses the not easily impressed Prospero, not only goes back to the age of three but far from not 'grappling', in Kerrigan's words, 'from the "dark backward and abysm of time" those childhood affairs which most concern her on the magic island', she retrieves as a gleam from that dark memory just what is conspicuously absent in her gender-solitude on the patriarchal island. 'Had I not/Four or five women once that tended me?' It is a memory of her own sex, and a memory of mothering.

Two forgetful characters, Desdemona and Prospero, have excellent memories, and their lapses are shown as exceptional breakdowns. Desdemona gives us another Freudian slip in Shakespeare when she sings the willow song and forgets the order of verses. Deeply fearful and stressed, watching Emilia lay the wedding sheets on the murder bed, trying like the Duke of York to pull herself together, with a control sometimes misread by scholars ('This Lodovico is a proper man'), she is obsessed with poor mad betrayed Barbary's song, which 'express'd her fortune'. She eventually gives in to pressing memory, sings it, gets its order wrong, and observes her own error, '*Let nobody blame him, his scorn I approve*, –/Nay, that's not next.' After a pause, she goes back to the verse, '*If I court moe women, you'll couch with moe men*' (IV.3), which is not so central to her situation, or so proleptic. The lines she anticipates, anticipate and so emphasize her dying lie. This also involves a correction: asked who killed her she says, 'Nobody' and with presence of mind revises it to 'I myself' (V.2), so contributing to the study of mind under stress.

Desdemona's breakdown is a failing in one who has a strong hold on the past, whose memory is faithful. Prospero has learnt to be attentive and to review and revise the past: his lapse also marks strong feeling. He is distracted by the distraction closest to Shakespeare's heart and mind, the theatre. The most proficient performance within a play, the masque acted by spirit-actors, make him forget 'that foul conspiracy' of Caliban, Stefano and Trinculo. It is another beautiful theatrical in-joke and a crisis of feeling. Ferdinand notices his disturbance. Miranda has never seen him 'so distempered', and he apologizes for his old troubled brain, excuses himself to take a turn and soothe his beating heart and meets Ariel just in time. Ariel tells him that he had thought of reminding him when 'presenting Ceres' but was afraid. It can be embarrassing to remind the forgetful. And only human beings forget, spirits never.

Prospero's lapse is also in character. Charmed by his books, he forgot a kingdom; charmed by his play, he nearly forgets it again. He is, however, one of Shakespeare's most remarkable narrators, and his memory is the vehicle and the tenor of narration. In the first act, after the inexplicable storm, he performs a threefold reminiscence, telling the story of their past to Miranda, Caliban and Ariel, who need to be told or retold, and to the audience, who need the exposition. His story is told with anguish, bitterness and self-reproach. His memory is not nostalgic but revisionary, the kind approved by Shakespeare, open, thinking, self-aware, imaginative:

> *Pros.* Thou attend'st not?
> *Mir.* O, good sir, I do.
> *Pros.* I pray thee, mark me.
> I, thus neglecting worldly ends, all dedicated
> To closeness and the bettering of my mind
> With that which, but by being so retir'd,

O'er-priz'd all popular rate, in my false brother
Awak'd an evil nature; and my trust,
Like a good parent, did beget of him
A falsehood in its contrary, as great
As my trust was; which had indeed no limit,
A confidence sans bound. He being thus lorded,
Not only with what my revenue yielded,
But what my power might else exact, like one
Who having into truth, by telling of it,
Made such a sinner of his memory,
To credit his own lie, he did believe
He was indeed the duke . . .

(I.2)

His narrated memory, authoritarian and coercive though it is, ramming recollection into Miranda's ear, is open. He is not lost in the past. Unlike the Nurse, he is aware of listeners, and the course of his feelings, re-felt in the telling, is punctuated and qualified by Miranda's amazement (admiration), self-reproach, horror and pity. He reflects on memory while remembering, listening as Miranda comments that her memory seems unreliable, no more authoritative than a dream, in a comment which makes us aware of the overlap between memory and dream, both often fragmentary and shadowy. Prospero asks, jogging her memory, if she can remember 'any other house or person?/Of any thing the image tell me, that/Hath kept with thy remembrance' (I.2); and when she responds he suggests that, since she has remembered something from before they came to the island, she may remember how they came. But memory is discontinuous, not linear, and she does not.

Shakespeare's other long narrated acts of remembering are like Prospero's, impassioned, combining the feelings of the past with feelings of the present, and self-aware. They are usually more enclosed, not interactive, though even a listener who does not speak or speak much is felt as a sympathetic presence, when Egeon, the Ghost in Hamlet, the First Player, Othello in his two memory speeches and Edgar in *King Lear* look back and tell their stories. The model is Virgilian, Aeneas's story to Dido.

Prospero's image of 'the dark backward and abysm of time' is that most subtle and Shakespearian figure, hendiadys, which forces the mind to shuttle to and fro, assessing and reordering category and connection, fitting together the jigsaw of parts to make a whole. The dark backward and abysm of time contains histories, memorials, nostalgia, forgettings and affective memories. But it is not only time in the abstract, it is the conscious and unconscious mind and inside our heads.

CHAPTER SIX

Forecasts and Fantasies

'What's to come is still unsure'

> Sure he that made us with such large discourse,
> Looking before and after, gave us not
> That capability and godlike reason
> To fust in us unus'd.
>
> (*Hamlet* IV.4)

Hamlet is an expert on mind who anticipates Heisenberg as well as Freud. He is made to reflect on the motions of mind, and as he scrutinizes ways in which scrutiny shapes the scrutinizer he uses an uncertainty principle. He calls reason 'godlike' but recognizes that thinking too precisely about events may be inhibiting, so he is praising and deprecating what mind can do. Master psychologist, he is the coward slave of his brilliance. He fixes prolepsis and analepsis as features of what Lukács calls intellectual physiognomy: 'Looking before and after', and I want to suggest that his formulation of prospect and retrospect is shadowed by a kind of ambiguity. Accompanying his perfectly clear sentence, which uses the adverb 'before' about looking ahead, and 'after' about looking back, flickers the possibility of an alternatively composed and completed sentence in which the adverbs face in reversed directions, 'before' suggesting future and 'after' suggesting past, as they would in the phrases 'to look at what happened before', or to recall, and 'to look at what will happen after', or to anticipate. This subdued ambiguity in the adverbs strikes me as functional, apt for Shakespeare's often demonstrated sense that there is no simple backward and forward movement in our consciousness but a complex weave of memory and anticipation. The ambiguity arrests our contemplation, if not in the theatre then in reading the text, sending our mind backwards and forwards to scan and sort out the sentence. We perform the complex act as Hamlet speaks about it.

Shakespeare brings us close to Hamlet's intellectual performance, in this speech and also at many places in the rest of the play, which turns on a past action dominating the present and determining the future. He is jamming recall and anticipation together as a performed indicator of the way consciousness works. To reflect on what is not present is hardly ever, if ever, just to look back or ahead, before or after. Memory and anticipation are confused and interfused, in the present, but we should remember William James's remark that the present is 'specious', not really present at all, more of a saddle-back than a razor-edge. From the saddle-back we look before and after. Living in the present is barely possible for humanity, and the word 'godlike', a cautious hyperbole, distinguishes the human creature as it praises the capability and scope of its 'discourse', a word referring to reasoning and speech. Hamlet admires powers and admits problems, and both powers and problems are busily demonstrated in acts of memory and anticipation, in *Hamlet* and Hamlet. They are especially prominent here, in a speech that weighs the cause and effect of the inactivity of Hamlet and the activity of Fortinbras and his army. Hamlet's 'before and after' denies a simple polarity of recall and anticipation. As the memorial sonnets show, Shakespeare sees the mind's motion as a complex act of weaving. We remember anticipation and anticipate remembering, remember anticipating memory and so on through all the possible permutations. Proust's *A la recherche du temps perdu* is a novel of memory whose narrative cuts through this multiple action, imagining a direct line of involuntary memory with access to a simple past. Hence Samuel Beckett's perception that Proust was a man with a bad memory – he could remember so much only because he had forgotten so much. Hamlet's unattached prepositions insist on the intricacy of discourse, and the intricacy demonstrates itself as Hamlet desperately tries to extricate himself from memory and simply look ahead. He hopes to take resolution into action: 'from this time forth/My thoughts be bloody or be nothing worth'. The effort is self-defeating. It sounds resolute and bloody but really only decides to think bloodily. Action is only anticipated, and the anticipation of action is at a remove even from the name of action. (To be valued or criticized.) In his comparison of his 'failure' with Fortinbras's 'success' he articulates his 'flaw' of thinking too precisely on the event, but the very recognition depends on the close scrutiny. It is a double bind, the inhibiting product of that rational surview he values. (It may be a strength, not a flaw.) His admiration of Fortinbras is not expressed as admiration for a man of action who short-circuits the retrospect and prospect: on the contrary, he knows Fortinbras is energized by 'fantasy' and the desire for fame, and there is a qualifying doubt as hendiadys hesitates, 'for a fantasy and trick of fame'. Doubting the excesses of prospect and retrospect in fantasy and nostalgia, Shakespeare creates acts of mind that demonstrate and articulate the falsifying inventions of looking before and after. (The demonstration allows us to prefer Hamlet's inhibition to Fortinbras's energy, though Hamlet himself may not.)

These narrative meditations on time dramatize the specious present, never faking a direct line to past and future. Shakespeare's method is revised by Beckett who prolongs the sense of presentness, not only by the intricate permutation of shuttling mind but also by bringing into consciousness a flatness, an avoidance of teleology, an unshaped anecdotalizing of narrative, to produce the sense that looking ahead and looking back are unreliable. *In Waiting for Godot* Estragon and Vladimir sublimely undermine and avoid time-shapes by routines, games and repetitions. They try to avoid sequences and successes of memory and anticipation. When they do look behind and ahead they are frustrated and disappointed by the time-sequence in which they find themselves, and the audience also participate in the disfigured time-experiences the characters enact, admit, resist and succumb to.

When we read Shakespeare's sonnets about black ink, black lines, rehearsing tongues and dead and live breathing, our sense of the passed present and the passing present is a sense of the past's anticipation of a future which is our present and of our present's sense of that past's anticipation. Shakespeare and Beckett create this unnerving conjunction of narrator's time and listener's or reader's time. The sense of a once live dead artist thinking about a now living but equally mortal live spectator is thrillingly present in *The Winter's Tale*, when the Chorus speaking as abstract Time is fully conscious of the audience's existence in particular time. Shakespeare imagined this Chorus as a – not too serious – apologist for his high-handed treatment of the unities and assimilates the apologist to the author. In doing this he projects a consciousness of theatrical time and non-theatrical time. This is like Beckett too, whose characters in *Godot* and *Krapp's Last Tape* experience discontinuities and frustrations of time in fictionalized memory while the audience feels them in theatrical experience. We do not just see characters waiting for an end which does not turn up but ourselves wait for an end which does not turn up. (This is why Godot can no more be turned into a referend than Henry James's figure in the carpet, both being designed as absences and evasions.) In *The Winter's Tale*, however, Shakespeare teases our time-sense not through parallelism but through enlargement. The Chorus addresses the technical questions of the unities, the rules of drama and the structure of its play but alarmingly breaks away from the subject of the stage's two-hour traffic to insist on our seven-decade traffic of a life. Shakespeare reaches out to the individual in the theatre in a way that shows you do not need to plant actors in the audience to get that audience where it lives. Distance is suddenly dissolved, and touch becomes unbearably intimate. Shakespeare, as so often, is both reflexive and emotionally shattering:

> I witness to
> The times that brought them in; so shall I do
> To th' freshest things now reigning, and make stale
> The glistering of this present, as my tale
> Now seems to it.
>
> (IV.1)

This address to persons, and to the personal life and death outside the theatre and the fiction, disturbs the audience's complicity and complacency. Theatre is expert at creating such complicity, for instance, through the dramatic ironies as dramatist signals to audience over the heads of the innocent characters. Romeo and Juliet look at the future optimistically and pessimistically, Troilus and Cressida offer dares to their futures in, and as, history and myth, while dramatist and audience share superior knowledge. In *The Winter's Tale*, a play vibrantly aware of fictions and fantasies, the dramatist leaves the audience in the lurch. He breaks the rules of the game, as well as the unities of time and place, to remind us of our tale, our personal time-scheme, our winter. That sense of theatrical enclosure, comfort and security is a product of our willing submission to the entertainer's control, but it can be broken. In the middle of *The Winter's Tale* a collectively concentrated audience breaks into disturbed, self-conscious, separately mortal individuals, as it does at the end of Genet's *The Balcony*. Fiction's declaration that it is not wholly fictitious deals a rough blow. Personified Time is of course fulfilling humbler functions too and quickly moves us back from self-awareness into the role of collectively safe and responsive members of an audience, reminded of Florizel, and Act I, while pedants are (or were) reminded that the laws of drama are not absolute but historically contingent. Startling us out of theatre's concentration on the present, breaking the fragile illusion and unity of theatrical time, deconstructing and demonstrating the specious stage-time, Shakespeare licenses his way of handling time in drama. Why not jump over sixteen years? Time can and will pass more quickly than we realize, outside the theatre, and inside it is child's play. Made to imagine our time's unimaginable or better-not-imagined passage, we are shocked as scholarly argument addresses our mutability. No wonder Time speaks with authorial authority for Act I and the early mention of Florizel: Time is, after all, the authority on change and death.

What the audience is sometimes directly forced to feel, Shakespeare's characters often feel, as their author makes them aware of anticipation. In *The Winter's Tale* the time-gap forces the audience into an acute awareness of rapid movement, but the characters are not especially given to detailed forecast, though the plot turns on an oracle. Oracular forecast, here as in Sophocles's *Oedipus Rex*, is the least psychologically interesting form of forecast, because it is guaranteed by the fiction of religious authority and by the author's authority which disguises hindsight as prophecy. (Dreams often work like oracles, as in *Richard III* and *Julius Caesar*.) But Shakespeare is interested in the ways the ignorant imagination blunders as it sees its future. Romeo and Juliet part after the traditional time-protest of the aubade, in which lovers try to deny the future day and prolong the passing present of night, but dawn, as usual, refuses to be annihilated. This aubade is a tragic one, like Faustus's, in which departure will be prolonged. The lovers look at the end of more than one night of love. Juliet asks Romeo about the future and he reassures her by imagining one which contains the bitter present as experienced discourse: 'all these woes shall serve/For sweet discourses in our times to come'. The mind's shuttling energy is doubled in a duet: Juliet counters Romeo's conversion of her anxious anticipation to happy reminiscence with a different fantasy:

> O God, I have an ill-divining soul!
> Methinks I see thee, now thou art so low,
> As one dead in the bottom of a tomb.
> Either my eyesight fails, or thou look'st pale.
> (III.5)

Her foreboding is a true prediction, faked by the dramatist, since fictitious characters are not allowed to be totally aware of the future. But it is faked cleverly. It is an instance of that visual fantasy recommended by Longinus and illustrated by Orestes's apostrophe to the Furies (Aeschylus), but it is rationalized by Juliet: she explains her flash of foresight, 'now thou art so low', justifying her pessimism and relating it pragmatically to the present, 'Either my eyesight fails, or thou look'st pale.' This is fantasy which creates a shocking moment and a look ahead, but it is made part of Juliet's intellectual physiognomy. Structure and character are both served. Shakespeare imagines Juliet imagining consistently, in vivid visual imagery, in gusts of shaping desire or fear, and always reasoning about the action and contexts of fantasy. Her forecasts are always grounded in her (fictitious) reality. Just as memory is individualized, so is the narrative of future time. Although the concept of dramatic character is unfashionable, it is still entertained by many actors and psychologists, and to examine categories of mind in Shakespeare is to be convinced that he was not indifferent to individual variations, but what seems also pronounced is his interest in intelligence and intellect. Juliet is unrealistically in touch with Shakespeare's predetermined future, and part of her function is to energize, lead and mislead the audience's anticipation, initiated and instructed by the choric Prologue, then moving along a trajectory of freshly enlightening action. Character is structural. But her mind is individualized: she imagines in a way no one else in the play imagines. From the beginning, she is shown as rational, neither stupidly engrossed by the present nor indulgently lost in desirous fantasies of the future.

The play contains Mercutio's long brilliant speech about Queen Mab, in which he sets out, in a free play of image and anecdote, the theory of wish-fulfilment. Never was dream-psychologist so aptly laid back: his improvised Queen Mab presides over dreams and fantasies, constructs answers to wishes and moves

> O'er courtiers' knees, that dream on curtsies straight;
> O'er lawyers' fingers who straight dream on fees;
> O'er ladies' lips, who straight on kisses dream . . .
>
> (I.4)

His companion-fictions sometimes illustrate his theory, engagingly called a 'nothing': Romeo's anticipation of future recall of the parting is blatantly wish-fulfilling. But the theory draws attention to a more rational and less dreamy forecast. Juliet's vision of the tomb is not noticeably more realistic than Romeo's reassurance, but it is presented with more attention to what is going on in the present. Her fantasies are of course not immune to shaping wishes, and her great speech of sexual longing as she anticipates the wedding night is ecstatic and amorously playful, aphrodisiac in fantasy. But as she imagines consummation her fantasy is not fantastic: she looks ahead to what will happen, the coming of night, the passionate loving of two virgins, pleasure and climax. Where her imagination is tried, by pain, not pricked by desire, where she hesitates before taking the narcotic, her sense of reason and reality is strong. That brilliant matter-of-factness which made her alert to Romeo's dangers in the orchard is under stress, but not stifled. Her speech is punctuated by a regular checking of fantasy against likelihood and fact. She begins with the possibility that the drug will not work, then turns back from anticipation to action, sensibly putting a dagger handy just in case. This flow and ebb sets the pattern of the whole speech, which is powered and shaped by a desperate fear of the drug, coma and awakening and an equally desperate determination not to be married to Paris. Passion heats fantasy, and fantasy becomes more particular and more grotesque, but each stage of the narration, except the last, is controlled by common sense. After taking the precaution of the alternative action of suicide, Juliet exchanges the first fear for a second, imagining the drug may work too well, as poison not anaesthetic. She shapes an elaborate little fantasy about the Friar:

> What if it be a poison which the Friar
> Subtly hath minister'd to have me dead,
> Lest in this marriage he should be dishonour'd,
> Because he married me before to Romeo?
> I fear it is.
>
> (IV.3)

Like the first anticipation, it is fired by fear, the passion announced at the beginning of the speech, 'I have a faint cold fear thrills through my veins', and like the first it gives way to her sense of reality:

> I fear it is. And yet methinks it should not,
> For he hath still been tried a holy man.

(In Quarto I, 'I will not entertain so bad a thought' follows.) The fear-formed narratives are hard to suppress, and the next one is nearer the bone:

How if, when I am laid into the tomb,
I wake before the time that Romeo
Come to redeem me? There's a fearful point!

Fantasy becomes more particularized and physical, first anticipating the killing foul air of the tomb, then telling the alternative story of being driven mad by ancestral bones, the corpse of Tybalt, ghosts, smells and all. The final stage of fantasy is entertained and elaborated, to generate extravagance and confusion:

O, if I wake, shall I not be distraught,
Environed with all these hideous fears,
And madly play with my forefathers' joints,
And pluck the mangled Tybalt from his shroud,
And, in this rage, with some great kinsman's bone
As with a club dash out my desperate brains?

The imagery becomes more and more fantastic until future tense becomes present, and imagined horror becomes hallucination:

O look, methinks I see my cousin's ghost
Seeking out Romeo . . .

Fantasy moves through desperate fear to the invocation of Romeo and impels her to action: 'Romeo, Romeo, Romeo, here's drink! I drink to thee!' Fear has worked itself up, and out, and into love, which does the trick.

The rational testing of each product of fearful narration is characteristic of the individual mind Shakespeare designs for Juliet. It stamps her psychological idiolect. She tells her mother coolly that she has not dreamt of marriage, she begs Romeo not to swear lasting love, she thinks practically and undreamily about marriage after meeting Romeo and about sexual consummation. Even her grisly anticipations of death and the tomb have a certain realism and are constructed as revisions of the first impulsive narrative in which she tells the Friar she'd go into a charnel-house or share a shroud rather than marry Paris. Shakespeare makes her impulse into a creative fiat, one which has to be scanned and rewritten, with art's control of passion. So she is made to reimagine the charnel-house, to particularize what she first impetuously outlined. Still, that first outline made the scenario. She creates not one revision but several versions of the story about waking in a tomb. Of course her anticipations are attempts to guess the future, and she is allowed to get close to the actual tragic conclusion to the play's story, to approximate and anticipate the tragic awakening, the tragic mistiming, the tragic miscalculation of the Friar, the suicide, the final *Liebestod*. It is a pretty accurate forecast, as forecasts go, and its fantastic element scarcely exaggerates the play's grotesque fantasy. What she is wrong about is instructive – the physical horrors of the tomb are nothing compared with finding Romeo dead instead of alive, so a comparison of her version with the play's version makes that point too. Like Edgar, she cannot imagine the worst, though she tries.

The tragic ending has been put in the minds of the audience, but only in the most general way, by the choric Prologue: Juliet's frenzied anticipations contribute to the particularized story we accumulate, looking before and after, as we follow the play. It is a story that is also in some ways right and in some ways wrong. It is a story that moves us, as Coleridge knew, to expectation and surprise. Juliet contributes to the total trajectory of dramatic narrative, as well as to Shakespeare's implicit analysis of passionate but rational narration, in and outside art. Juliet cannot get the future right but she is made to imagine almost as well, and in the same way, as her author and is close, as no other character is, to his ending. Like his, hers is an intelligence driven by passion but able to correct and control that drive. She is the artist but also the frightened human being, desperately scanning future likelihoods, rationally, to cope with what may come, and superstitiously, to prevent it coming, since what we imagine cannot happen in exactly the way we imagine it. We play at fantasizing about undesirable futures to prevent the worst. Juliet's imagination also generates energy for decision and action – unlike Hamlet's. She goes wild and so moves fantasy into act, future-thinking into a hallucinated but enabling present. The artist has to commit herself to the act by strong feeling, as well as preserving reason. Like artist and scientist, Juliet must go wild and stay sane. She must drink the potion in order to finish her story and her author's, and only an abandonment to feeling makes her drink. Her future thinking stretches ahead, forming narrative hypotheses and negating them, selecting and revising versions, arguing likelihood, experimenting with variations, in touch with realism and extravagance. She does not think too precisely on the event, but her thinking is precise, and precise enough, though her imagination, like Hamlet's and everyone's, is contained by history. Because she is a fiction, we can see how.

Like many dramatists and novelists, Shakespeare creates characters who are centres and models of creativity, minds like his own. The activity of such minds, in memory or fantasy, individuates character, contributes to the dramatic narrative and offers models – generative, rational and affective – of narrative acts and forms. The creative register may not always be a major character, like Hamlet and Juliet. One of Shakespeare's congenial fantasists is Gonzalo, in *The Tempest*. It is a critical commonplace that his Utopian fantasy of the ideal society is a piece of colonial and authoritarian dreaming, like much democratic planning by the autocratic imagination. He projects the golden age, realistically as well as idealistically, into the future. He is excited, like Prospero, by an apparently desert island to control and shape. But Gonzalo's excitement is more superficial, his fantasy more frivolous and artificial, than Prospero's. His narrative is not projected quite seriously, though frivolity is undermined by Shakespeare's familiarly uncomfortable ambivalence, and it is not totally discredited either:

> I' th' commonwealth I would by contraries
> Execute all things; for no kind of traffic
> Would I admit; no name of magistrate;
> Letters should not be known; riches, poverty,
> And use of service, none . . .
>
> (II.1)

And on to the contradictory conclusion 'No sovereignty'. But this is a broken ending, not a full stop. The sentence is interrupted by Sebastian's 'Yet he would be King on't', and it must be noticed that Sebastian, and some critics, have leapt to a conclusion that may not have been Gonzalo's. His Utopian fantasy was cut off and might have ended in other ways. He might have imagined an end to sovereignty, the succession of a more democratic law. He might have distinguished between king as planner and king as ruler. But as important as the absent ending is the improvised and freewheeling nature of his project and the conditions of his speculative story. He is inspired by the apparently desert island, but the narrative is made up on the spur of the moment, as a distraction for the sorrows of Alonso, who is mourning the apparent death of his son. Sebastian is rude and callous; Gonzalo rebukes him and changes the subject, since it is foul weather when the King is 'cloudy'. When the King tells him he has failed and said 'nothing', he responds with modest nonchalance, 'I do well believe your highness'. He further deprecates his island dream as merely ministering 'occasion to these gentlemen, who are of such sensible and nimble lungs that they always use to laugh at nothing'. Fantasy is shrugged off, placed at arm's length, serious purpose and effect dismissed. Gonzalo neither answers objections nor objects to interruption. And his audience is hostile from the beginning, composed of the King, scarcely listening, wrapped in grief, and the traitors and cynics whose objections, though shrewd, are discredited as villains' criticisms. Shakespeare is neither putting forward a serious ideal nor creating the conditions for solemn and premeditated construction. The fantasy is benevolent, and perhaps a bit bumbling, but it is not a speech or a pamphlet, and deconstructs itself in every way. It is clearly offered as a text hastily improvised by poetic faith, a Utopian narrative dreamed up in unsettling conditions.

It also corresponds, in a parodic way, to Prospero's fantasy and to Shakespeare's. Prospero too explains that he has responded opportunistically, taking a propitious wind offering its now-or-never chance. And chanciness, rather than providential gravity and unity, is emphasized in the imagery of theatrical and global dissolution. Prospero forgets the conspiracy, his island colony has not educated Caliban, Antonio is unresolved and the books are to be buried. Gonzalo, Prospero and Shakespeare are making trials and experiments, and the fantasy within *The Tempest*, like the play itself, flaunts and admits artifice, provisionality, improbability and playful fragility. Gonzalo's creative fiat is created in and for the context of doubt and impermanence, of fantastic genre as it responds to its author's and to his author's creativity. (Another inset narrative, the masque, is also interrupted before it ends.)

Juliet's narrative is the necessary and desperate projection of a future. In her circumstances she must imagine, and self-analysis and revisionary scruple successfully represent mind's effort, under stress but not overwhelmed. Between the serious and consistent narration of Juliet and the provisionality of Gonzalo are other models, representing creativity, expressing individual character and playing a part in the total narrative trajectory. The storytelling within the stories varies in moral impulse, form and content. In *Twelfth Night* Malvolio ill-wishes others and himself, though his central fantasy, comic and serious, is a rich wish-fulfilling story of promotion and role reversal. In Act II, scene 5, he dreams a future in which he is head of household, Olivia's husband, Sir Toby's boss. Fantasy is made by outside conditions and internal needs: Maria and the conspirators nourish his desires, but his own imagination 'blows' him up before he reads the forged letter. The fantasy is thoroughly particularized, with the nice touch of Olivia's sleep on the daybed, which leaves her complacent husband to rule the roost and pride himself on uxorious success. Equally telling, for idiolect and psychology, is the famous slip in construction, when he forgets he will not be wearing the steward's chain in his future and corrects it with opportunistic creativity to 'some rich jewel', though the lame 'some' signals desperate recovery from a fluff in performance. These fantastic narratives are performances, not only speech-acts but grateful theatrical responses to the author's provision for movement, gesture, costume and props.

Like Juliet, Malvolio is impassioned but rational. He needs observation as well as hearsay, 'Maria once told me she did affect me, and I have heard herself come thus near, that should she fancy, it should be one of my complexion.' He quotes precedent, 'the Lady of the Strachy', and when he picks up the enigmatic text, his reading is careful as well as ingenious, as he fulfils Fabian's prediction, 'Did I not say he would work it out?' He is aware of the passive response to imaginative temptations and of reason, 'I do not now fool myself, to let imagination jade me; for every reason excites to this.'

Malvolio's is a painful case of the most intimate fantasy exposed to public view, but here, as later in the mad scene with 'Sir Topas', he preserves intellectual dignity. In private and public, misled and mistaken, he exemplifies the mind's effort, awareness and weakness as it swims and drowns in the self-generative stream. Like Viola's fiction of a sister's fatal love-melancholy, Malvolio's story of a future is false but not fantastically improbable.

A more malevolent fantasist is the future Richard III, the Gloucester of *Henry VI*, *Pt 3*, who imagines the future with the aid of his author's historical hindsight. Shakespeare's history plays are of course constantly making the historical past, the familiar story of the chroniclers, into fantastic futures, complicating or disguising obvious ironies by a mix of psychological interest in the individual case and habits of mind. In Act III, scene 2, Richard's fantasy is thoroughly motivated, as Edward IV's intention to marry provokes thought about the succession. His generative fantasy is one of Shakespeare's longest and most elaborate self-analysing narratives. Fired by jealous scorn for Edward, Lady Grey and their future progeny, he hopes: 'Would he were wasted . . ./That from his loins no hopeful branch may spring,/To cross me from the golden time I look for!' Placing his golden age in the future, he rationally checks his wishes, since even if Edward were dead or infertile there remain Clarence, Henry, his son Edward, and their 'unlook'd for issue', between him and the crown. 'A cold premeditation for my purpose', he reflects as his premeditation cools. There follows a bridge passage in which he figures himself as idle fantasist, standing on a promontory, seeing a distant prospect and wishing his 'foot were equal with his eye'. Images stimulate more images, and the promontary promotes a Canute-like chiding of the sea and a fantasy about ladling it dry. As he fantasizes he sees the action of fantasy, criticizing its flattery, its speed of action and its unreality. But it grows and goes on growing. He breaks away from dreams of power to entertain alternatives, pleasure instead of political power, but reasons passionately that for him love is less likely than twenty thousand golden crowns. His repulsive images for his own monstrosity shock him into an image of a misshapen body finding a compensatory crown on top, but this is dismissed too, and he reimagines those living obstacles, seeing himself in a thorny wood rending the thorns and rent by them. Like someone playing the game 'stone, paper, scissors' he invents a counter-image of an axe to cut through the thorns, converts this to an image of murder and realizes this in images of creative precedent:

> Why, I can smile, and murder whiles I smile,
> And cry 'Content!' to that that grieves my heart,
> And wet my cheeks with artificial tears,
> And frame my face to all occasions.
> I'll drown more sailors than the Mermaid shall;
> I'll slay more gazers than the basilisk;
> I'll play the orator as well as Nestor,
> Deceive more slily than Ulysses could,
> And, like a Sinon, take another Troy.
> I can add colours to the chameleon,
> Change shapes with Proteus for advantages,
> And set the murderous Machiavel to school.
> (III.2)

He ends his visibly self-generated list with a final energy of decision, like the conclusion of Juliet's fantasy:

> Can I do this, and cannot get a crown?
> Tut! were it farther off, I'll pluck it down.

Creativity grows, is checked, revised, repeats itself, grows again and activates resolution. Richard's inventive storytelling and image-making work through a series of counter-actions, oppositions and corrections like those of his political actions in *Richard III*, all teeming with improvised or organized energy and wit.

Malvolio and Richard fail to predict with complete accuracy of course, but they predict with justifications and reason as they fantasize about their desires. Coriolanus is a character who forces himself to fantasize about an undesirable future. Creature of Volumnia's voluminous 'fancy', on whose creative success she prides herself, he forces himself to imagine what he cannot possibly bring himself to do. His fantasy is articulated in another speech that characterizes individual psyche and temperament and provides another model of dangerous creative energy. Here is one of the best generative models in Shakespeare's drama of forecasts, not compelling action, like Juliet's, Malvolio's and Richard's, but tragically repelling it:

> Well, I must do't.
> Away my disposition, and possess me
> Some harlot's spirit! My throat of war be turn'd,
> Which choired with my drum, into a pipe
> Small as an eunuch, or the virgin voice
> That babies lull asleep! The smiles of knaves
> Tent in my cheeks, and schoolboys' tears take up
> The glasses of my sight! A beggar's tongue
> Make motion through my lips, and my arm'd knees
> Who bow'd but in my stirrup, bend like his
> That hath receiv'd an alms! I will not do't,
> Lest I surcease to honour mine own truth,
> And by my body's action teach my mind
> A most inherent baseness.
>
> (III.2)

This is a failure of extreme fantasy, a paradigm that shows how telling the story of the future can act as a deterrent. It is framed by the attempts of Cominius and Volumnia to 'prompt' the soldier to 'perform a part' he has 'not done before' and followed by the mother's persuasive rejection, 'Do as thou list' which provokes the dangerous submission 'Pray be content./Mother, I am going to the market-place.'

Here, as in the play's last crisis, when Volumnia persuades him not to fight Rome, his capitulation is spontaneous and uncontrolled, cut off from desire and reasons, as mindless as a knee-jerk. Coriolanus's determining acts are determined outside both his reason and his fantasy, his infantilist regression dramatized and analysed in negative, in a demonstration of psychic discontinuity. The attempt at self-persuasive fantasy overreaches itself, generating disgust, as he tells the story of the future in totally unpersuasive terms, his aggressive masculinity diminished to the role of eunuch, virgin, knave, schoolboy, beggar. His stories of the future imagine unactable opposites, roles his martial typecasting cannot play. He imagines himself into uncongenial action, tries on unwearable masks he has to discard. He begins with 'Well, I must do't' and he tries to imagine doing it, talks himself out of the intentions, leaving a chasm unabridged by prospect, into which he falls. That initial 'Well' is hesitant, however resolutely it may be voiced by the actor; it is the hesitancy of intelligence. Shakespeare makes each imagination distinct, but the activities join to make a psychological class. Fantasies of the future are never pure fantasies: Shakespeare's acts of narrative projection all involve reasoning and passion.

The exposures show the dangers of fantasy, of course. Juliet's is a rare example of a justified fantasy, but though she has no alternative in her tragic trap the outcome is destructive. The fantasies of Malvolio, Gonzalo, Richard and Coriolanus, in individualized structures, fail by distortions of present 'reality'. Sometimes such distortion is the focus of the play, as in *Love's Labour's Lost* where a group of fantasists tell the story of their future, of an ideal community, celibacy and academy, impossibly segregated from psychological and political contexts. Berowne is the detached rational man, the realist who points out objections then nonchalantly throws in his lot with fantasy, to be elected leader when the story of learning is exchanged for the story of happy and concluding love. As in *The Tempest*, the correspondence of internal and total narrative is marked. The realistic women, whose presence has been neglected, reject and refuse the conventional ending, as the author deprives his audience of the end they expect. The course of fantasy runs a complicated trail, leading us to a false telos, then substituting another outside the play's time and scope. Comic fantasy is to be tested in the hospitals of the larger world, in a future narrative projection which is open-ended and open-eyed about likelihood and unlikelihood:

> *Ber.* Our wooing doth not end like an old play;
> Jack hath not Jill: these ladies' courtesy
> Might well have made our sport a comedy.

King. Come, sir, it wants a twelvemonth and a day,
And then 'twill end.

Ber. That's too long for a play.
(V.2)

Shakespeare is no more tolerant of fantasy than he was of nostalgia. Like the sentimental and selective story of the past, it does not live in the present. When he creates Richard III, Malvolio, Gonzalo and Coriolanus, he does not merely plot to punish them. He shows their fantasy generating a movement away from the present, like Gonzalo's contradiction, Malvolio's self-persuasion and Richard's ferociously willed story. Shakespeare shows the work of rational creativity and shows how the mind rejects reason. Theseus puts the lunatic, the lover and the poet in the same creative category, 'of imagination all compact', but he speaks with a lover's bias. Shakespeare's passionate and controlled poetry is certainly different from the constructions of his fantastic lovers and lunatics who abandon themselves to irrational fantasy. But the abandonment is always made by rational minds, is a visible abandonment of the rational powers.

Some characters are constructed to show a conspicuous awareness of the nature of fantasy. Brutus's fantasy of honourable insurrection, for example, is carefully developed, first privately and implicitly, then more openly and explicitly. Before he acts out his fantasy of honourable revolution, we are given access to his self-conscious analysis, as brilliantly perceptive as Hamlet's, but in its own fashion feverish and fearful. Brutus comments on the form of his anticipation, not particularizing its content but generalizing in dreadfulness:

Since Cassius first did whet me against Caesar,
I have not slept.
Between the acting of a dreadful thing
And the first motion, all the interim is
Like a phantasma, or a hideous dream:
The genius and the mortal instruments
Are then in council; and the state of man,
Like to a little kingdom, suffers then
The nature of an insurrection.

(II.1)

Faculty-psychology in a classical lexis, revolutionary psychodrama in a play about revolution and a sly theatrical reflexiveness are joined to imagine Brutus's anxiety about projecting the future. Once more Shakespeare brings together reason and mental disorder. Another self-image there, for Brutus is rational and disturbed as he generalizes about mind's government and phantasma, reflecting the play's combination of political debate and doubt. We see later what the acting-out, or 'motion', of Brutus's fantasy is, as Shakespeare dramatizes a familiar self-contradiction and confusion of revolutionary ideals. Brutus fallaciously plays with the fantasy of defeating aggression by aggression, in dangerous innocence: 'Let's carve him as a dish fit for the gods.' The futile and fantastic ideality is endorsed by familiar out-of-context quotation of this tragic oxymoron, as if context is rejected as unbelievable. Shakespeare makes revolutionary innocence just credible. Brutus's hovering on the threshold of credible and astounding fantasy is at the heart of the play. It discovers a revolutionary flaw, particular but not merely particular, and introduces a psychologically interesting analysis of fantasy in a play where so much turns on classical omen. The characters in *Julius Caesar* dream with a Roman superstitiousness, and the play has a future familiarized as history, but within the historical portrayals Shakespeare places the mind's coil and recoil as it fantasizes and observes its own motions. One of the best touches is the rendering of Brutus's sense of unreality, as he makes his fictions: 'all the interim is/Like a phantasma, or a hideous dream'. This language constructs a comparison of wakeful fantasy with dream but also, less obviously, describes the pathology of losing the present.

In *Henry VI*, *Pt 2*, when Richard, Duke of York is supplied with an army he eagerly takes his opportunity. As he plans treason he takes time to comment on the business of his own activity, in a busy self-consciousness that observes mental action and illustrates it. The busy construction of fantasy is given an extra bit of business. As usual, Shakespeare is designating species and genus: this is what fantasy is like, and this is what the successful politician is like – good at limited prediction, reasoning with a sense of probabilities and consequences, seizing the moment with zeal but keeping cool enough to plan effectively, not wildly. It is also in character, proud, pompous, and gleeful. This kind of political–personal inferiority enlivens the chronicle:

> Let pale-fac'd fear keep with the mean-born man,
> And find no harbour in a royal heart.
> Faster than spring-time showers comes thought on thought,
> And not a thought but thinks on dignity.
> My brain, more busy than the labouring spider,
> Weaves tedious snares to trap mine enemies.
> Well, nobles, well; 'tis politicly done,
> To send me packing with an host of men:
> I fear me you but warm the starved snake,
> Who, cherish'd in your breasts, will sting your hearts.
> 'Twas men I lack'd . . .
>
> (III.1)

Hamlet shares the self-consciousness of Brutus and York but inhabits another category. In his character, Shakespeare demonstrates a mind too rational to look far into the future, even though that is what the play's action keeps prompting him to do. Hamlet refrains from planning, and only looks back, in detail, when he can recall with confidence to tell Horatio the story of his voyage and counter-plot. His most famous speech insists on the present. Indeed, one way of describing his predicament would be to say that he is committed to the present but forced to find it unendurable. When he looks back, the past is mostly unendurable too, and he is, like his author, too rational to fantasize about futures. Of course he is made, like Mercutio, to know about wish-fulfilment:

> To die – to sleep,
> No more; and by a sleep to say we end
> The heart-ache and the thousand natural shocks
> That flesh is heir to: 'tis a consummation
> Devoutly to be wish'd. To die, to sleep;
> To sleep, perchance to dream – ay, there's the rub:
> For in that sleep of death what dreams may come,
> When we have shuffled off this mortal coil,
> Must give us pause . . .
>
> (III.1)

It is the most famous pause in Shakespeare, occurring in another meditation both analytic and passionate. This mind is apprehensive but rational as, and in what, it fears. The speech makes one of the most imaginative portrayals of fantasy and the refusal to retreat from fantasy: that liminal tension, after 'what dreams may come' and 'Must give us pause', forces us to imagine a nightmare dreaming, instead of being lulled by the time-worn metaphor of sleep. Hamlet will have nothing to do with the old euphemism, which he instantly converts to a terrifying *occupatio* to give a reluctantly glimpsed hideous prospect. The fantasy of dreams after death has a special context: Hamlet has mentioned his bad dreams to Rosencrantz and Guildenstern, and we have seen something of his waking ones.

In Act II, scene 1 of *Othello*, Othello and Desdemona briefly contemplate their future. Here too we have a sense, as in Hamlet's soliloquy, of mind occupying a present with a full grasp of reality, shadowed for the audience by unreality. Hamlet refuses to imagine, refuses to plan suicide and murder. Desdemona and Othello offer a doubled response to the future, but Othello hesitates, as he imagines. In the reunion after the storm at sea, there is the only moment in the play which for a split second inhabits the present. The greetings 'O my fair warrior!' and 'My dear Othello!' are the verbal accompaniment to an embrace. The action of words and bodies engrosses and presents the present, but as the characters contemplate that present the future begins to make its presence felt:

> It gives me wonder great as my content
> To see you here before me: O my soul's joy,
> If after every tempest come such calmness,
> May the winds blow, till they have waken'd death,
> If it were now to die,
> . . .
> 'Twere now to be most happy, for I fear
> My soul hath her content so absolute,
> That not another comfort, like to this
> Succeeds in unknown fate.
>
> (II.1)

Romeo cheered up Juliet's prophetic soul and Desdemona says, 'The heavens forbid/But that our loves and comforts should increase,/Even as our days do grow.'

A temperate but devout optimism is at once countered by the willed alternative presented by Iago's fantasy of his and their future, 'I'll set down the pegs that make this music.' Again the anticipations of the audience are stimulated by conflicting projects, as the sense of present comfort and joy is permitted and troubled. And the sense of controlled future, in 'unknown fate' and 'heavens', is introduced with a hesitation and doubt appropriate to the tragic consciousness in and of the play. The audience too looks forward reluctantly, impelled to arrest that present tense.

Othello looks ahead with doubt, because the present is too good to last, and he is later compelled to look and face someone else's story of the future, in an action that represents all our passivities. Similarly ironic, though more optimistic, is King Lear's most realistic fantasy. He and Cordelia have been defeated, and his partially instructed imagination settles for much less than his early hopes, 'We two alone will sing like birds i'th' cage' (V.3). His project transforms, while it sees imprisonment. Lear shapes a fantasy unique in Shakespeare, though it has features common enough in the European novel, which habitually constructs minds liable to fashion dangerously ideal narratives of future time and ends. Lear's fantasy almost resists the teleological pattern. It imagines a stasis, a present neither developing nor deteriorating, in which father and child live the impossible dream of enclosed and secluded loving, a dream the more touching for its touches of reality. Lear has learnt, but only a little. His fantasy of compromised love and action has been found not only totally unrealistic but nearly fatal – actually fatal, but he does not know that yet – but his final fantasy touchingly images the artist's grounding of fantasy in reality. The political world is admitted but kept outside the walls, metamorphosing constriction to protection, imprisonment to freedom. Lear is not given the narrative self-consciousness of Juliet or Hamlet, but the audience is kept in touch with the fact of fictions by the image's song, 'old tales' and the ironically distanced news of the world, 'who's in, who's out', a wish for safe distance by creatures tragically 'in' and 'out'.

King Lear, like *Love's Labour's Lost*, is a play the action of which hinges on that exposure of fantasy which was to become a central constructive and thematic presence in the novel, when it developed into the major literary medium for examining individuals in society. Juliet and Berowne are characters designed to endure, or to seem capable of enduring, the rough passage from life as they dream it to life as it is made for them. King Lear can almost endure it: he reconstructs his dream almost realistically. But these small individual dreams are reconstructed by a larger political power. Shakespeare includes, as images of such power, the fantasies made by certain 'individual wills'. Some of his fantasists – punished but creatively successful, stand for political institutions, and as puzzling powerful individuals, like Hitler and Saddam Hussein, who may be seen both as representatives of political institutions and as instrumental in shaping those institutions. Richard III, Iago and Edmund are such fantasists.

Shakespeare spends much less time on the strength of fantasies of the future than European novelists were later to do. He lacks their interest in literature as a formative influence, delightful and dangerous. He read and used narrative romances, but his fantasists do not inherit a literary culture. Hamlet reads, and Macbeth has been scared by 'dismal treatises' (oral narratives), but the forces that make or discourage their fantasies lie elsewhere in the culture. Just as Shakespeare finds nostalgia uncongenial, so too his imagination is hardly ever solicited by indulgence in fantasy, as the imaginations of Cervantes, Stendhal, Jane Austen, George Eliot, Tolstoy and Joyce obviously were, even though they correct and expose the impossibilities of constructing desirable futures. Shakespeare is too rational to look before or after, without placing the narratives of past and future in present consciousness of present time. His intellectual physiognomies are structural, taxonomic and also suggest a psychological, moral and political preference.

CHAPTER SEVEN

Gender and Narrative

'A woman's story by a winter's fire'

Gendered narrative in Shakespeare means in practice woman's narrative, because man's narrative is the norm, not categorically distinguished or typed. There are professional subdivisions of men's narrative, like the stories of the bombastic soldier, the young blade or the tyrant; but woman's narrative, the main form of woman's speech – stereotyped for centuries as garrulous and disordered in form, the old wives' tale, unrestrained, reckless and fantastic in content – is dramatized and discussed by Shakespeare across the genres.* It's a language designed to be spoken by male impersonators, to be variously performed as evaluative, imitative, ambiguous, ridiculous, exaggerated or creative, by the stereotyping sex, and presented to a gender-conscious audience, like that of present-day Japanese

* I have discussed some examples of attack and defence in 'The Talkative Woman in Shakespeare, Dickens and George Eliot', in *Problems for Feminist Criticism*, ed. Sally Minogue, London and New York, Routledge, 1990. One of several classical examples of misogynist typing is in Euripedes' *Hippolytus*: 'Handmaids should ne'er have had access to wives,/ But brutes, with teeth, no tongue, should dwell with them,/That so they might not speak to any one'. Among the defenders of the talkative woman well known to Shakespeare is Chaucer, whose Wife of Bath is given the advantage of a rambling, fast, miscellaneous *écriture féminine*, with insight into the male authorial prerogative: 'Who peyntede the leon?', and Erasmus, whose loquacious and unconventional female narrator, Moria or Folly, in *Praise of Folly*, defends her language: 'If anything I've said seems impudent or garrulous, you must remember it's Folly and a woman who's been speaking.'

No or Kabuki theatre. The acting medium makes the matter of gendered language highly conspicuous. But Shakespeare's men and women, misogynist and misandrist, in commentary or character, are a man's invention, as Mrs Gamp, a male-authored and gender-conscious character, said contemptuously of the steam-engine.

Shakespeare's attitudes to gendered narrative – by no means always clear, of course, as the changing interpretations of *The Taming of the Shrew* over the centuries make plain – show themselves through stereotype, but through a placing and an awareness of stereotype. Stereotyping is dramatized, seen in source and origin. Some of the women characters, for instance, speak against certain categories of male narrative, though the critique does not usually go very far. Portia, in *The Merchant of Venice*, contemplates cross-dressing and thinks of putting on male language with her barrister's gown, telling Nerissa she will 'speak between the change of man and boy,/ With a reed voice, and turn two mincing steps/Into a manly stride; and speak of frays/Like a fine bragging youth: and tell quaint lies/ How honourable ladies sought my love,/Which I denying, they fell sick and died' (III.4). 'Puny lies' and 'bragging Jacks' complete the indictment of the boastful, lying, fighting young man. When Imogen, Cymbeline's daughter, contemplates men's dress, Pisanio advises her to be 'Ready in gibes, quick-answer'd, saucy' (III.4). In fact neither Portia nor Imogen assume the young man's show-off talk.

Rosalind/Ganymede puts on the young man's pertness and wit, especially when talking to Phebe, with whom she is ill at ease and sexually embarrassed, and to Orlando, with whom she affects the 'saucy lackey' in order to 'play the knave'. Her misogyny is fine-grained; it is immediately exaggerated when she is put on guard by Orlando's perception that her accent is a touch refined for a forest-bred youth 'in so removed a dwelling'. She over-corrects her act and betrays anxiety, 'I thank God I am not a woman, to be touch'd with so many giddy offences' (III.2). With Orlando she also wrings out the odd bawdy joke and plays the cynic about love, 'Love is merely a madness' (III.2) and 'men are April when they woo, December when they wed', (IV.1) but there is pain beneath the banter, and her most famous story about stories, a short anthology of famous lovers dying, 'but not for love', (IV.1) is amusing but melancholy too.

The most satisfying of Shakespeare's women critics of men's stories is not a cross-dressing comic heroine, but Desdemona in a brief exchange which goes deep, right to the heart of *Othello*'s theme. Waiting in Cyprus for her husband's ship, she has to pass the time talking to Shakespeare's most consistent foulmouth, her escort Iago. His idea of amusing conversation is good old misogynistic fun, and when Cassio greets Emilia with a social kiss Iago makes the routine joke about talkative women:

> Sir, would she give you so much of her lips
> As of her tongue she has bestow'd on me,
> You'ld have enough.
>
> (II.1)

When Desdemona at once denies it, 'Alas! she has no speech', he cynically proposes that Emilia is insincerely on her best behaviour with her 'ladyship' and 'puts her tongue a little in her heart'. When Emilia briefly protests, Iago launches into a full-scale traditional male attack, hearty, teasing, aggressive, unpleasant:

> Come on, come on, you are pictures out o' doors;
> Bells in your parlours; wild-cats in your kitchens;
> Saints in your injuries; devils being offended;
> Players in your housewifery; and housewives in your beds.

Desdemona chooses exactly the right word in reply, 'O, fie upon thee, slanderer!', and after participating in the exchange – 'I am not merry, but I do beguile/The thing I am, by seeming otherwise' – says just the right thing about such locker-room talk and significantly says it in prose, as if choosing not to join Iago's verse, 'These are old paradoxes, to make fools laugh i' the alehouse.' The play's development and outcome are shadowed here in a kind of joking which is deadly serious.

It is satisfying that Shakespeare makes Iago both racist and sexist, perceiving that the prejudices are intimately connected. It is also satisfying that he sees the connection between racism, sexism, lies and slander: he knows that to stereotype is to tell lies and to slander. He is ironic and shrewd as he makes Desdemona see through the slanderer but only locally or superficially, not making the conceptual generalization but going on, fatally, to trust Iago's honesty, unable to read the man's lack of scruple in his apparently casual incorrectness. Her defence of Emilia begins their sisterly bonding, one of the strongest in Shakespeare – and Shakespeare is strong on women's bonding – and it is for her that Emilia's tongue is loosed, on two important occasions, one private and one public.

When Iago sneers at her 'tongue', Desdemona seems to speak reliably about her having 'no speech', while the whole scene makes it clear that Iago does not. When we see and hear Emilia in her husband's presence her genius is rebuked. She says little, is in his power and compromises her virtue to get the handkerchief for him, in a most crucial physical act in the tragedy. But Iago's comment on her talkativeness turns out to be truer than he knows, and when she talks to Desdemona before the murder she is most informative. After she puts the marriage sheets on the death-bed, Emilia is asked by Desdemona if she thinks there are women who commit adultery and makes a brilliant political speech attacking the double standard, as well as telling us a great deal about her marriage.

Desdemona does not think 'there is any such woman', and Emilia's riposte is powerfully conceptual, hypothetically narrative. It recalls Shylock's speech at his trial, and for good reason. It rises from prose to the formality of verse:

> Yes, a dozen, and as many to the vantage, as would store the
> world they played for.
> But I do think it is their husbands' faults
> If wives do fall: say, that they slack their duties,
> And pour our treasures into foreign laps;
> Or else break out in peevish jealousies,
> Throwing restraint upon us: or say they strike us,
> Or scant out former having in despite,
> Why, we have galls: and though we have some grace,
> Yet have we some revenge. Let husbands know,
> Their wives have sense like them: they see, and smell,

> And have their palates both for sweet, and sour,
> As husbands have. What is it that they do,
> When they change us for others? Is it sport?
> (IV.3)

This is not a narrative speech, but an argument, working through logic and question, though with some generalizing narrative. It is not Desdemona's language, and it does not convince her. Her speech is narrative, and the only way she can articulate her fears and pain is by singing the Willow Song. Her question about adultery was a way of telling and not telling. As in Cyprus, she bravely tries to control herself, in woman's gossip, about the visitor who has seen her husband hit her, 'This Lodovico is a proper man', but can't keep it up. She tells her suppressed story in the song, in an act of bonding, speaking to a woman about another woman, her mother's maid, Barbary.

After Emilia incredulously asks Iago, in the next act, if he told Othello his wife was false and he says 'I did' she releases the word that has been in our mind for a long time: 'You told a lie, an odious damned lie;/Upon my soul, a lie, a wicked lie!' She is told to go home (Brabantio asked who 'let' Desdemona 'out') but answers, gloriously, 'Perchance, Iago, I will ne'er go home', refuses to hold her tongue, and dies for telling her tale. As she dies she sings Desdemona's song, already transformed from a melancholy love-song to a woman's song, a lament for victims of patriarchy, made more than lament by the bonding.

The Winter's Tale is *Othello* rewritten as tragi-comedy, a romance with a happy ending. Like *Othello* it is a play about the morality of narrative, full of lies, slanders and crises of telling and listening. Paulina plays Emilia's role, a heroine of full free speech. She really is a talkative woman, also accused by a foul-mouthed misogynist. She has the same kind of attachment to Hermione as Emilia to Desdemona, and the destructive sexist in the story is Leontes, an Othello who is his own Iago. Shakespeare varies his perceptive collocation of slander, lies and murder, husbands, powerful men and killers. Leontes, like Iago, is afraid of the talkative woman and with good reason.

At the beginning Leontes speaks his version of Iago's sexism: he muses on his son's likeness to him, venting his jealousy and showing its political roots as he repeats the men's common slander, 'Woman say so,/(That will say anything)' (I.2). Later, he focuses his misogyny on Paulina, the only person at court brave enough to defend Hermione, standing her ground to insist with the vehement repetitiveness of Emilia, that the Queen is good. She says 'good' seven times, as offensively as possible, 'I say good queen,/ And would by combat make her good, so were I/A man, the worst about you', and threatens to tear out the eyes of any man obeying Leontes's order to 'Push her out'. Leontes's misogynist abuse uses old stereotypes: 'A mankind witch!', 'A most intelligencing bawd!', 'crone', 'A gross hag', 'midwife', 'Lady Margery' and 'A callat/Of boundless tongue'. In the Chaucerian style and tradition, Antigonus is henpecked:

> Thou dotard! thou art woman-tir'd, unroosted
> By thy dame Partlet here.
>
> (II.3)

This is a pointed and layered allusion, a potted history of misogynist stereotype: in the *Nun's Priest's Tale* Partlet is typed as Eve, tempting Chaunticleer and distracting him from his warning dream by her seductive tongue, and Leontes's destructive jealousy is generalized, and politically placed, by attacking Paulina as well as his wife in this traditionally prejudiced way. The implications of compounded patriarchal power are very clear. Hermione knows that language is useless – 'My life lies in the level of your dreams' – but her responses are personal, whereas Paulina, like Emilia, is being articulately political. She uses *occupatio* as a contemptuous and subversive way to call him tyrant, 'I'll not call you tyrant', and his conventional masculine sneers at Antigonus bring out the perceived relationship between husband and ruler: 'can'st thou not rule her?', 'He dreads his wife', and,

> And, lozel, thou art worthy to be hang'd,
> That wilt not stay her tongue.
>
> (II.3)

Unlike Iago, Leontes is a misogynist in a tragi-comedy, and he is made a misogynist who comes to honour woman's talk and old wives' tales. After the revelation of the oracle is first blasphemously rejected and then accepted, Leontes recants, and listens humbled to Paulina's eloquent vision of attainable penance. She can now repeatedly quote the oracle with the word, 'Tyrant', and develops a brilliant sustained image, synecdochic and hyperbolic, the grotesque poetry of a triumphant old wife, ending with a catachresis to be voiced vituperatively and triumphantly:

> But, O thou tyrant!
> Do not repent these things, for they are heavier
> Than all thy woes can stir: therefore betake thee
> To nothing but despair. A thousand knees
> Ten thousand years together, naked, fasting,
> Upon a barren mountain, and still winter
> In storm perpetual, could not move the gods
> To look that way thou wert.
>
> (III.2)

It is a fine insight on Shakespeare's part to make the contrite and heirless Leontes lap up her abuse and at the same time make a recantation of the misogynist critique. After he begs her to 'Go on, go on', declaring that she cannot 'speak too much' and admitting that he deserves 'all tongues to talk their bitt'rest', he provokes 'a Lord' to rebuke her for the 'boldness' of her speech, emphasizing the sexual politics of speaking. And Leontes comes to approve, explicitly, her earlier talking, 'Thou did'st speak but well/When most the truth.' She had spoken when the rest of the court – those lords and others – were silent.

The triumph is Paulina's, and women's. Mamilius's winter's tale has been cut off, but the story of the play is begun by the wintry King Leontes and completed by the old wife, Paulina, the Queen's friend and midwife of spring. It is Leontes who tells the irrational, fantastic, false, rambling, disjointed and incoherent story of his wife's infidelity, a story wild in style, form and content. Paulina's story of a dead queen and a statue that can move and speak is a good fantasy, a fable that makes sense, a lie that contains a truth, about a fiction that comes to life, a story which is rational and profound in form and content, truthfully and truly mythopoeic.

But Shakespeare did not begin by attacking the misogynist tradition and honouring the articulate woman. In the three *Henry VI* plays, his attitudes to women's narrative are themselves traditional and sexist. The crude misogyny, which is also found in the chronicle sources he is drawing on, is confined to the first play, and the rest of the first English tetralogy, which ends with *Richard III*, shows a change in attitudes to women's language. Almost certainly, Shakespeare's first woman narrator is Joan of Arc, or La Pucelle, in *Henry VI*, *Pt I*. In creating her character Shakespeare's stereotyping of woman is facilitated, and compounded, by his nationalism, as he takes over the hostility of the English historians Hall and Holinshed, to outdo their xenophobia and misogyny. As he revises his sources he makes Joan stronger and more licentious, and she provides a complete model for misogynist stereotype of woman's speech and, in particular, women's narrative. Her language is declared, over and over again, to be irrational, fantastic, false, excessive, garrulous, dangerous and seductive. She is made to use language aggressively and dominatingly, as other warriors in drama do, oratory often taking the place of action, as in the long hyperbolic self-aggrandizing orations of Marlowe's Tamburlaine or the raptures and tantrums of Hotspur; but though she has a couple of good persuasive speeches, one addressed to the Dauphin and one to Burgundy, her narrative idiolect is not especially distinguished. The interest is really in content rather than style, the indictment through what is said about her rather than by her.

As a cross-dressing woman she is not sympathetic, like the later heroines of Shakespeare's romantic comedies – because she is a highly simplified character in an early play (long thought not to be by Shakespeare), because she is fighting the English, and perhaps because she actually fights, unlike Viola, who is afraid to fight a duel, and Rosalind, who faints at the sight of blood. Eventually her vehemence and power are attacked by the French as well as the English, and her unreliability demonstrated, as in the chronicles, in a repulsive image of a liar and betrayer which had to wait to be revised – as politic and pragmatic – by Bernard Shaw. Most of the attack is an attack on her language and is close to the chronicle sources: her narrative is described as 'temptation' (relating her to Eve, first woman storyteller to be blamed) and she is a 'witch': Alençon says 'These women are shrewd tempters with their tongues' (IV.2), in an early extension of the word 'shrewd'. York calls her 'fell banning hag' (V.3). She is said to charm and bewitch Charles with her words and called a 'giglot wench', Talbot calls her 'railing Hecate' (III.2), and in the end her 'incantations' are said to fail. Joan's is a compounded narrative corruption of lies, irrationality, aggression and magic. She is firmly placed in the male traditional stereotype, grouped with the mothers of perverted narrative, the Sibyl whose telling is prophetic, Eve whose story is tempting, a witch whose telling is diabolical and damning. But in her case, Shakespeare makes misogynist stereotypes stick. At the end she lies, desperately, crudely and implausibly pleading her virginity, then denying the pregnancy, finally denying her class and her father. She is, as far as I know, the only consistent and aggressive liar who is not enlivened by Shakespeare's authority. It is as if she cannot even be created as a good liar, like the unreliable men, Iago and Edmund, whose fictions are strong reflections of their author's sense of dramatic timing, impersonated passion and wonderfully inventive circumstantial detail.

Once Joan is dead, her function is transferred to Margaret, who marries Henry VI. Margaret resembles Joan in the assumption of political power, domination of a weak man, and military action, all reflected or represented in narrative power. In Hall she is accused of usurping man's role, 'a manly woman, longing to rule and not be ruled', and Shakespeare follows Hall, criticizing her for talking too much and too wildly, and placing her in the narrative tradition of Sibyl, Eve and witch. But Margaret is a transition point, taking us from a demonizing stereotype to a new image, denigrated, but by unreliable sources, and justified, as Joan never is. The act of demonizing the powerful woman is not endorsed but explicated and judged. Like Joan she is shown as licentious, but subtly, her attachment to Suffolk being partly excused, by the chroniclers and

Shakespeare, by the temptations of a proxy courtship and marriage to a weak youth. Margaret is called 'madding Dido'; Dido is traditionally a listener not a teller but here contributes to the misogynist demonizing. Margaret is placed in the tradition of dishonest fiction-makers, women drawing on fable and fairy-tale, irrational, fantastic, spell-binding and tempting. But her powerful language has none of Joan's crudeness and lapse.

Most important, attacks on her speech are qualified by similar attacks on powerful male eloquence: York as well as Margaret is said to be a great speaker, dangerously persuasive, and she is placed in dialogue and comparison with another dangerous and talkative speaker, Richard III, a liar, slanderer and tempter who puts her in the shade, to illuminate her cause. At the end of *Henry VI, Pt 3* she is rebuked by Richard, then Gloucester, for wearing breeches instead of petticoat (a proverbial insult which has lasted into our time) but defended by her son, who flings the words back in Richard's face 'Let Aesop fable in a winter's night;/His currish riddles sorts not with this place' (V.5), – an important anticipation of Lady Macbeth's attack on Macbeth's susceptibility to horrors, which is clearly gender-significant. Gloucester says, 'For God's sake, take away this captive scold', and her son turns the noun, used of women, into an adjective for Richard, 'Nay, take away this scolding crookback rather' (V.5). (She is described by Hall as 'a scolding woman, whose weapon is only her tongue and her nayles'.) Gloucester wants her dead – 'Why should she live to fill the world with words?' – and he is fully answered by her words in *Richard III*, where she has been transformed from a powerful and cruel ruler to an aged prophetess, valorized not only by her antagonism to Richard but also by her association with two of his victims, Elizabeth, the mother of the murdered princes, and his own mother.

At first they are opposed to Margaret, but the she-wolf of France eventually becomes their sister, ally and mentor. The great antiphonal chorus in Act IV, scene 4 joins the women's voices by onomastic repetitions, 'I had an Edward', 'I had a Richard', 'Thou hadst a Clarence'. Elizabeth recalls Margaret's old prophecy 'That I should wish for thee to help me curse'; Margaret has one of her most splendid lyrical narrations, contrasting past with present, and Elizabeth asks for instruction:

> O thou, well skill'd in curses, stay awhile
> And teach me how to curse mine enemies.

Margaret begins the lesson, Elizabeth asks again, 'My words are dull: O quicken them with thine', and Margaret tells her that words will be sharpened to piercing-point by woes. After her exit the Duchess of York wonders why calamity is 'full of words' and Elizabeth tells her they may be useless, 'Poor breathing orators', but can at least 'ease the heart'. The Duchess concludes with the decision not to be 'tongue-tied' and they join to 'smother' her son in 'bitter words'. No wonder he arrives to say, 'Let not the heavens hear these tell-tale women', but that is what the heavens do, in the rest of the play. A woman's talkativeness is politicized and justified. The justification is ritualized in this strong scene of sisterly bonding and explicit consciousness-raising.*

Lady Macbeth is a strong woman who takes a different course, adopting the man's part. In all her criticisms of her husband she attacks what both sexists and feminists have often identified as the feminine principle of gentleness. It is clearly imaged by her as the nurturing breast, source of that milk she wants to exchange for gall, to be the better destroyer, and which she uses to denigrate the tenderness of Macbeth, 'th' milk of human kindness' (I.5), a phrase whose ambiguity is profound. The image is echoed, in a morally responsive context, when Malcolm, pretending to outdo Macbeth, speaks of pouring 'the sweet milk of concord into hell' (IV.3). Lady Macbeth upbraids Macbeth for not being sufficiently 'manly'. She accuses him of unmanliness just before she sneers at the woman's story by the winter's fire. (To be criticized by Lady Macbeth is to be honoured.) As he starts in horror at Banquo's ghost in the banqueting scene, she asks Macbeth 'Are you a man?'

* Harold F. Brooks, in '*Richard III*: Unhistorical Amplifications: The Women's Scenes and Seneca', *Modern Language Review* 75 (October 1980), shows 'sources' for these women and in all the bonding is absent.

and later exclaims, 'What! quite unmann'd in folly?' These insults frame her misogynist attack on fantasy:

> O! these flaws and starts
> (Impostors to true fear), would well become
> A woman's story at a winter's fire,
> Authoris'd by her grandam.
>
> (III.4)

It is in character with her own desexing and self-demonizing that she equates murderousness with manliness and denies the woman's narrative imagination. Her 'authoris'd' is a brilliant anticipation of modern conflations of authorship and authority and underlines the truthfulness of old wives' fictions. She would have done better to trust the old wives, the Sibylline witches who may or may not be instruments of darkness, looking more like men than women but who speak truths, tripping and teasing Macbeth by faking truth as fantasy, as he comes belatedly to recognize, or the traditional tellers of fantasy, warning against hobnobbing with spirits. In one of his last nihilistic speeches Macbeth speaks of having once been terrified by 'dismal treatises', or old wives' tales, and his indifference to what once made his hair stand on end is a sign of calloused conscience. Shakespeare moved towards sympathy with the old wives, in *Henry VI* and *Richard III*, and Lady Macbeth's antipathy is the other side of the coin.

Two celebrated old wives are the Nurse in *Romeo and Juliet* and Mistress Quickly in *Henry IV, Pts 1 and 2* and *The Merry Wives of Windsor*. They are irrational and rambling but neither is a fantasist like Joan. Like Chaucer and Erasmus, Shakespeare is using irrational woman as a structural base for comic character, and as Coleridge points out, such ungoverned talkativeness is not only a matter of gender but a matter of class. Mistress Quickly's loose language registers her 'easy yielding' nature, but more dominant is the imprint of an unpractised mind, laughable and subversively suggestive of new ways with telling. The features of the relaxed, unperiodic style denote a lack of training, superficially ludicrous, profoundly original. Erasmus scarcely wrote a demotic language, but his avoidance of traditional rhetorical features for Folly, a delightfully unreliable narrator, and his reflexive comments on informality show his interest in the virtues of uneducated talkativeness. More women than men were, and are, outside education, and the talkative woman's lack of surview and method is a social deviation transformed into a literary profit and power.

Coleridge sees that Mistress Quickly is the immethodical mind methodized. While dramatizing a tendency to call memory, not selective power, into play and to relate events 'in the same order and with the same accompaniments, however accidental or impertinent, as they had first occurred to the narrator', Shakespeare creates an affective sequence and connectiveness, 'the fusion of passion' that substitutes for method. What Coleridge says applies to many talkative women characters: the habit of over-circumstantial detail makes for vivid particulars, unselective miscellany and disjointed fragmentariness. All these features isolate and heighten narrative detail like Mistress Quickly's description of the parcel-gilt goblet, round table and sea-coal fire, and the Wife of Bath's slow-motion recollections of love and the 'wo that is in mariage'. In each narrator there is more than excess of particulars: Mistress Quickly's quick-moving, scatty memory is fired by indignation, and the Wife of Bath's motive for sentimental history revealed as passionate nostalgia and melancholy come to the surface, 'The flour is goon, ther is namoore to telle;/The bren, as I best kan, now moste I selle.' The Wife of Bath's talkative lament for mortality makes her eloquence more than a woman's untutored reminiscence, and gender is transcended. Rather differently, driven by mind rather than heart, Erasmus's Folly also goes beyond gendered impersonation, as wit and intellectual argument are used to celebrate intuitive and imaginative powers and defy reason and system. A misogynistic tendency may be at work, superficially or partially, woman satirized rather than seen as victim, but the question of gender is not primary. The talkative woman is Erasmus's means, not his end. (One can feel indignant about such instrumentality, but that question goes far beyond the talkative woman.)

Another remarkably free-flowing idiolect is created for Juliet's Nurse. Like Mistress Quickly she is not a man-hater, scold nor shrew but an easy-yielding woman, serving the culture and deserting Juliet the moment conflict arises between society and individual will. She is a sentimentalist and should not be sentimentalized, as I said in Chapter 5. The Nurse begins her long reminiscence of Juliet's infancy with a mere repetition of Lady Capulet's prompting. 'She's not fourteen', which is elaborated, particularized and repeated with characteristic and stereotypical but creative persistence and self-centredness. The brilliantly internalized upstaging of the Capulets makes it a great part. Not only does the Nurse recall events in the order in which they occurred, she repeats them until her listeners shut her up, amusing the audience off the stage by subversions of narrative and interruption of serious affairs. Lady Capulet is crisper in her dating, and it takes the Nurse a long time (she inhabits time and does not construct it) to identify the birthday, not by calendar date, but by the pragmatic recollection of a startling natural event – an earthquake – and her own child's birth:

Lady Capulet Thou knowest my daughter's of a pretty age.
Nurse Faith, I can tell her age unto an hour.
Lady Capulet She's not fourteen.
Nurse I'll lay fourteen of my teeth –
And yet, to my teen be it spoken, I have but four –
She's not fourteen. How long is it now
To Lammas-tide?
Lady Capulet A fortnight and odd days.
Nurse Even or odd, of all days in the year,
Come Lammas Eve at night shall she be fourteen.
Susan and she – God rest all Christian souls –
Were of an age. Well, Susan is with God;
She was too good for me. But as I said,
On Lammas Eve at night shall she be fourteen.
That shall she; marry, I remember it well.
'Tis since the earthquake now eleven years,
And she was wean'd – I never shall forget it –
Of all the days of the year upon that day.
For I had then laid wormwood to my dug,
Sitting in the sun under the dovehouse wall.
My lord and you were then at Mantua –
Nay I do bear a brain.

(I.3)

Coppélia Kahn's interesting account of the Nurse's role makes a connection between language and function: the subservience that strikes Kahn (and Coleridge) is given a carefully constructed narrative correlative.* Moreover, the Nurse's talkativeness suggests the humanizing subtext of her personal life (dead child and merry husband), to make the traditional identification with 'nature' in the repeated and proleptic anecdote of Juliet's 'fall'. An important aspect of the engrossing narrative is its passivity. Some stereotypes of woman's talkativeness, like Erasmus's Folly, subvert the dominant culture – but others offer a yielding to culture, language and time. The Wife of Bath and Folly are rebels, Mistress Quickly and the Nurse more passive. But volubility is expressive in various ways. The idiolects of the Wife of Bath and Folly are relatively systematic. In narrative complication, looseness and anti-rhetorical language, they are anarchic; but Shakespeare, like Dickens after him, invents lower-class, talkative women to demonstrate grammatical, syntactical, lexical and chronological disorders. There is overlap: all four narrators cram in particularities and keep going with verve and stamina, but two are relatively 'educated', two 'uneducated'. It is the less educated speakers who are more superficially conformist. But their language is not conformist but comically and brilliantly subversive, its fragmentation and fluency anticipating the languages of modernism.

Shakespeare's most problematic play about gender is *The Taming of the Shrew*, a play whose theatrical history is obscured by textual problems. The version which may or may not be Shakespearian, *The Taming of a Shrew*, completes the structural framework story of Sly the tinker, clearly presented as a dreaming ignorant man watching a male wish-fulfilment story and going off to try its method on his own wife. But even *The Taming of the Shrew*, which does not complete the frame but ends with the inset play's conclusion, has a last word of niggling doubt in Lucentio's ''Tis wonder . . . she will be tam'd so.' John Fletcher in his sequel, *The Woman's*

* Coppélia Kahn, 'Coming of Age in Verona', *The Woman's Part* (Illinois, University of Illinois Press, 1983).

Prize, or, The Tamer Tam'd (*c*.1611), explicitly dramatizes the irony, to show the taming as short-lived. The taming of a shrew was proverbially impossible, and Shakespeare's play has proved historically mutable.* Whatever the Elizabethans thought of it – and Fletcher provides some evidence against a straight-faced moral reading of husbandly authority – Victorians and early moderns certainly read it as a satisfactory fable. For instance, in his preface to the New Cambridge edition, Arthur Quiller-Couch makes vaguely liberal remarks about changed attitudes to male oppression but still smugly observes that the play's conclusion is 'satisfactory'. It is worth noticing that he speaks as if the last act did not exist, emphasizing Katherina's capitulation, in Act V, scene 1, to Petruchio's demand 'kiss me, Kate'.

In Act IV, scene 5, she accepts Petruchio's perversion of language and life, calling the sun 'moon, or sun, or what you please' and calling an old man a young woman. Commentators have noticed that she accepts Petruchio's will rationally, and ironically, saying 'as he says', when Hortensio advises her to agree in order to get on with the journey, and it is easy to play Katherina as affecting docility from a politic sense of expediency, but the late twentieth century wants to go further, and Shakespeare's text is happy to accommodate them. Michael Bogdanov's version, produced for the Royal Shakespeare Company in the Aldwych Theatre, London, in 1978, had a wonderfully ironic Katherina in Paola Dionisotti who acted submission before a Mafia-like group of men left wondering if the deferential speech was not too good to be true. This production literally overthrew the prettiness of a romantic set and scenery at the beginning, and allowed the end, even without Sly's completed frame, to present the taming as dream, fiction and theatre. The final speech, (which I have discussed in Chapter 4) once heard as stagy and ironic, cannot easily be re-

* There is a good account of key modern productions, including Michael Bogdanov's for the Royal Shakespeare Company in 1978 and Jonathan Miller's later conservative interpretation, also of critical responses and theoretical issues of historical interpretation, in Graham Holderness's *Shakespeare in Performance: The Taming of the Shrew* (Manchester University Press, 1989).

stored to the sexist tradition. Katherina's injunction to her fellow-wives, who have so swiftly put off submissiveness with marriage, uses the lexis of patriarchy, husband being 'lord', 'life', 'keeper', 'head' and 'sovereign', and moves into a generalized story of man's commitment to the care and maintenance of woman:

> To painful labour both by sea and land,
> To watch the night in storms, the day in cold,
> Whilst thou liest warm at home, secure and safe;
> And craves no other tribute at thy hands
> But love, fair looks, and true obedience;
> Too little payment for so great a debt.
> Such duty as the subject owes the prince
> Even such a woman oweth to her husband.
> And when she is froward, peevish, sullen, sour,
> And not obedient to his honest will,
> What is she but a foul contending rebel,
> And graceless traitor to her loving lord?
> I am asham'd that women are so simple
> To offer war where they should kneel for peace,
> Or seek for rule, supremacy, and sway,
> When they are bound to serve, love, and obey.
> Why are our bodies soft, and weak, and smooth,
> Unapt to toil and trouble in the world,
> But that our soft conditions and our hearts
> Should well agree with our external parts?
> Come, come, you froward and unable worms,
> My mind hath been as big as one of yours,
> My heart as great, my reason haply more,
> To bandy word for word and frown for frown.
> But now I see our lances are but straws,
> Our strength as weak, our weakness past compare,
> That seeming to be most which we indeed least are.
> Then vail your stomachs, for it is no boot,
> And place your hands below your husband's foot.
> In token of which duty, if he please,
> My hand is ready, may it do him ease.
>
> (V.2)

Generations of playgoers and readers have accepted this speech with varying responses, of acquiescence, anxiety, satisfaction, fury and cynicism. Though it will no doubt be produced again by conservative men, it now seems strange that it was ever directed or acted or read as unironic. The speech is ironized by context. The audience on stage is composed of men lolling in comfort, and Petruchio has just uttered Shakespeare's most memorably hedonistic line 'Nothing but sit and sit, and eat and eat.' As I have already said, in Chapter 4, the men have scarcely been seen in painful labour, though they have worked hard to get their rich brides. Katherina's speech also significantly refers to unmercenary motive, as I have said: 'craves no other tribute at thy hands/But love, fair looks, and true obedience;/Too little payment for so great a debt.' This is a story running counter to the play's action, in which wife-hunting and, in particular, the taming of the shrew has candidly proclaimed the financial motives of amusingly indolent men. This is not just a speech which may be spoken ironically but a politic story contradicting the story of the play. Shakespeare's superficially sexist play is his most subtle attack on misogyny. Katherina's speech is in every way too good to be true, as is suggested by Lucentio's final line, ''Tis a wonder, by your leave, she will be tam'd so', and by the comic fiction-asserting and frame-completing end of Sly's naïve acceptance in *The Taming of a Shrew*.

PART THREE

Plays

CHAPTER EIGHT

Hamlet

'To tell my story'

The figure of narration is crucial, central and assertive in *Hamlet* but not presented with Shakespeare's most conspicuous and self-conscious virtuosity. Though *Hamlet* teems with self-conscious comment on diction, figures, wit, hyperbole and theatrical performance, its magnificent plot-precipitating narrations are restrained. When they draw attention to themselves, it is with subtle reserve.

From Coleridge* onward, critics have admired the first scene of the play, where narration is cleverly eluded, postponed and naturalized. We are eventually brought to the brink of formal narration, with the conventional relaxation of 'Well, sit we down' with which Horatio emphasizes, arrests and initiates the shift of drama into storytelling. Bernardo is given three full lines and two half-lines of slow-moving and slow-sounding descriptive introduction, 'Last night of all . . .', to be interrupted by the Ghost's entry, which inhibits and supplants narration. This scene stages narrative inhibition within a frame of inhibition, as the Ghost is questioned, 'charged', stalks away, and is given another opportunity to speak which is lost when the cock crows. In the next scene, Horatio tells Hamlet of the apparition and its silence, 'But answer made it none', and we are kept waiting while Laertes makes his long farewells, in scene 3, before the first nervous expectation is repeated in scene 4.

* *Shakespearean Criticism*, ed. T.M. Raysor (London, Everyman, 1960).

The Ghost makes his appearance, after the distracting general conversation of Hamlet and Horatio, and is followed by Hamlet, to perform the first great narration of the play in scene 5. His story begins with grave emphasis on telling and listening: 'Mark me', 'lend thy serious hearing', 'I will', 'Speak, I am bound to hear' and 'So art thou to revenge when thou shalt hear', before it settles down to formal narration. Even then, the Ghost's exposition is long and tantalizing, turning on a kind of *occupatio*, as he tells how he is 'forbid/To tell the secrets of my prison-house', dwelling on the tale he could but may not unfold, which would make Hamlet's eyes 'like stars start from their spheres' and his hair to stand 'an end/Like quills upon the fretful porpentine'. After a brief interrupting dialogue, the Ghost gets to the point curtly, 'Revenge his foul and most unnatural murder', then elaborates, telling the story slowly and in circumstantial detail, following the false report with his version, which begins with an echo of his words of location:

> Sleeping within my orchard,
> My custom always of the afternoon,
> Upon my secure hour thy uncle stole
> With juice of cursed hebenon in a vial,
> And in the porches of my ears did pour
> The leperous distilment, whose effect
> Holds such an enmity with blood of man
> That swift as quicksilver it courses through
> The natural gates and alleys of the body,
> And with a sudden vigour it doth posset
> And curd, like eager droppings into milk,
> The thin and wholesome blood.

He began by imagining terror and his disappearance is followed by Hamlet's terror, 'shall I couple hell?' and pity, 'Ay, thou poor ghost'. The scene ends as Hamlet pretends to tell, 'How say you then, would heart of man once think it', then refuses to tell.

The Ghost's narration is formal, harrowing and teasing. Hamlet is impatient, 'Haste me to know't', and the Ghost is short of time, 'But soft, methinks I scent the morning air:/Brief let me be', but is allowed to take his time, as he remembers with anguish. Shakespeare varies, interrupts and animates the long narration, marking time, as he often does, in order to personalize the narration, to inject irony into gravity, and perhaps to reassure any members of the audience who are, like Polonius, impatient of narrative oration, by however passionate and weighty a *nuntius*. It is a passionate act of telling and listening: audience, narrator and interlocutor have their nerves stretched: 'O horrible! O horrible! most horrible!' Impatience and patience are mocked, for characters and audience.

Every act of narration in Shakespeare is what Hamlet calls 'a passionate speech'. Most of the acts of narration in this play are distressed. In Act II, scene 1, the 'affrighted' Ophelia disturbs her father – 'what, i' th' name of God?' – and tells the story of Hamlet's wild and dishevelled appearance in her closet, fully registering the pity and horror that we saw in his response to the Ghost. Ophelia's terror tells a terrifying tale. Her response mirrors Hamlet's response to the Ghost's tale, indeed told by one loosed out of hell (or purgatory) to speak of horrors, as I said in the Introduction. The stories join, to represent intimacy, distance, the terror of knowing and the terror of not knowing. Their reflection and interaction emphasizes the act of narration.

The next elaborate narration is explicitly described as 'a passionate speech'. The narration of Aeneas, jointly performed by Hamlet and the First Player, is the most technically self-conscious piece of narration in the play. It is probably Shakespeare's most celebrated formal narration, though relatively little attention has been paid to it as narration. Hamlet asks the Player King, in Act II, scene 2 for the speech heard once, but 'never acted, or if it was, not above once', from the play which was 'caviare to the general', though 'excellent' and 'well digested in the scenes, set down with as much modesty as cunning'. Fictitiously wrenched from its fictitious context, invented by Shakespeare, and introduced with a scornful professional joke, the speech is 'digested', or ordered, and set down with as much modesty as cunning to fulfil its function in *Hamlet*. Remarkable in all the modes of thematic reflection and preparation which have been variously discussed, it is also remarkable because it is a narration. It is commanded as 'a passionate speech' and of course becomes the occasion for a display of histrionic passion, a 'taste' of 'quality'. The passion is performed, on request, out of context, to become the demonstration piece in which the player performs performance, changing colour and weeping real tears. It then of course becomes the occasion and subject for Hamlet's self-analytic and theatrically analytic speech about his lack of response to a real 'motive and . . . cue for passion', which is shamed by the actor's command, and affective energy, 'And all for nothing!/For Hecuba!'

It is true that the actor's control of affective behaviour are what would have been expected as a taste of quality, but it is worth noticing that this is applauded, not in a dramatic but in a narrative rendering of pity and terror. The brilliant performance shows us precisely what is meant by a passionate speech; it is an impassioned narration, in which telling is as passionate as showing. It is not only a tribute to Elizabethan elocution but to Virgil. Hamlet is made to share Shakespeare's affection for 'Aeneas' tale to Dido', which he 'chiefly loved'. Though Shakespeare has to invent a play, from which this invented extract may be conveniently spoken, it is in line with the other similar tributes, which intimately reveal Shakespeare's feeling for a great predecessor. Though Aeneas's speech in *Hamlet* – hardly ever referred to as Aeneas's speech – lacks the critical self-consciousness of the direct Virgilian references in *Titus Andronicus*, it is the culmination of an intimate tribute to a great ancestor, not in the genre of drama but in that genre of narration which the dramatist had to assimilate and master. Coleridge stands out among the commentators in recognizing the speech as one of 'epic narrative', but like Schlegel he uses an insight about generic origin to defend the heightened style as appropriate to epic and differentiated from drama as if drama could do without narrative.

The self-conscious comments are well digested in every sense of that word, ancient and modern. Hamlet and Polonius represent the critical audience. Polonius praises Hamlet's elocution, ''Fore God, my lord, well spoken, with good accent and good discretion', flattering the amateur who begins the speech, with a plausible false start, but he demurs at the Player's longer recital, 'This is too long.' He echoes (again sycophantically) Hamlet's praise of 'The mobbled queen', with 'That's good'. So at one stroke, Shakespeare varies, animates and interrupts narration, while drawing attention to the powers of language and performance. The Player succeeds in controlling and generating passion (forcing 'his soul so to his own conceit'), in speaking what Virgil has taught Shakespeare to register as an act of impassioned memory. When he changes colour and weeps for Hecuba's heaven-rending clamour at her husband's slaughter, he is recounting Aeneas's recollections. Such technical interest is of course subordinated to the thematic relevance but need not be expunged by it. Hamlet loved a speech in an imaginary play, invented as a speech in the real play *Hamlet*. Shakespeare loved Virgil's passionate narration. An appreciation of the anguish of memory has its own thematic point to make in this play: 'Remember thee?' When James Joyce used *Hamlet* in *Ulysses*, which begins with Stephen Dedalus's torment of memory, it is with a similar sense of appropriate tribute. The parallel is not a remote one: what Shakespeare praises in Virgil's affective narration, as I have suggested, is something Virgil learnt from Homer. The recognition of Shakespeare's repeated praise may not illuminate *Hamlet* but gives a backstage view of Shakespeare's sense of his craft.

In Act III, scene 1, Polonius and Claudius 'bestow' themselves to see 'unseen' the encounter of Hamlet and Ophelia. They withdraw as Hamlet comes on to speak his most enigmatic soliloquy, 'To be, or not to be'. In Hamlet's other soliloquies there is always an element of narration, for which there is theatrical and psychological justification. To meditate without narrating is rare. Moreover, the form of meditation makes a peculiarly delicate and subtle vehicle for narration. In the first soliloquy in Act I, scene 2, we are allusively and fragmentarily told about the incestuous and hasty marriage. In the second, in Act II, scene 2, we are given a brief narrative forecast of Hamlet's intention to catch the conscience of the king with the Mouse-Trap. In the soliloquy in Act III, we are told about his intention to speak daggers to his mother. In the brief soliloquy in Act III, scene 3, we are told that he will not kill

Claudius at prayer. In the last soliloquy, in Act IV, scene 4, after a local and general summary of events, taking in the expedition of Fortinbras and his own situation, 'a father kill'd, a mother stain'd', we are told that his thoughts will henceforth be bloody. Each of the soliloquies carries with it some narration, retrospective, prospective or a mixture of both, with the exception of the 'To be, or not to be' speech. There are listeners to this soliloquy.

The convention of soliloquy is a complex one: the actor often performs introspection extrovertedly, addressing the audience with a private stream of consciousness. There is no suggestion that the 'To be, or not to be' soliloquy either is or could be overheard, but Shakespeare's fine dramatic sense may have been alert to the physical proximity of the spying Polonius and Claudius, of whose presence the audience is aware. The listeners are tactfully made to respond only to the dialogue between Hamlet and Ophelia, the soliloquy having a kind of conventionalized inaudibility for them. I think it unlikely, however, that Shakespeare would have ignored the audience within the play as he planned this speech. It may be that a fine sense of theatrical decorum created the soliloquy to give away nothing. We have only to imagine the inclusion of the kind of fragmentary and allusive mention of Ghost, King, murder, Queen, guilt, which occur in all the speeches after Hamlet has heard the Ghost's story, to realize the advantage of this narrative absence. It would be tempting to push conjecture further and suggest that the puzzling and much-discussed allusion to the 'bourn' from which 'No traveller returns' would effectively mislead Claudius, but this is to parody the effect I point to. Shakespeare's scrupulous stage sense, which ensured, as Coleridge noticed, that Ariel and Miranda never met for fear that they neutralize each other, may have been at work to empty the famous soliloquy of all narrative and so of all information. The players do not always tell all. Producers who observe this negation of narrative are free to show their listeners listening without strain. The point is one of purely backstage interest, a possible trace of Shakespeare's craftsman's care, like a detail on the Sistine Ceiling not visible from the floor.

In Act IV, scene 5, there is a brief speech by a Messenger, a fine local dramatization of excited narrative. The Messenger brings urgent news of insurrection. He is preceded by noise, to which Claudius attends, 'Attend!'. Asked by the King, 'What is the matter?' the Messenger replies informally, 'Save yourself, my lord'. His passionate speech has the vigour of alarm. The mob is at the door, and the Messenger's warning is at once fulfulled as Laertes and followers break in. No need for the establishment of a nonce character, as at the beginning of *Macbeth*, or an excursus into the problem of bearing messages, as in *Antony and Cleopatra*. Excitement speaks for itself; it follows imperative with hyperbole:

> The ocean, overpeering of his list,
> Eats not the flats with more impetuous haste
> Than young Laertes . . .

It expresses a social attitude, 'The rabble call him lord', and takes time off for sententious parenthesis, 'as the world were now but to begin,/Antiquity forgot, custom not known'. It ends in revolutionary quotation:

> They cry, 'Choose we! Laertes shall be king'.
> Caps, hands, and tongues applaud it to the clouds,
> 'Laertes shall be king, Laertes king.'

A fast, frightening, breathless, and moral speech – Shakespeare plans for his actors.

An actress who believes that Gertrude's speech is dramatic but not 'in character', will not rise to Shakespeare's text.* Before she speaks the long, formal narration, Gertrude briefly breaks the news: 'Your sister's drown'd, Laertes.' Shakespeare narrates the death twice, freed to expatiate lyrically, decoratively and pathetically, without holding Laertes in suspense. He is given two responses. First, 'Drown'd? O, where?', the perfect cue for the narrator's response which leaves Laertes to listen, showing or veiling emotion, until the end of the narration gives the cue for 'Alas, then she is drown'd.' Like Gertrude he shows a characterized sympathy as he

* For a summary of critical responses to the speech see Harold Jenkins's note in the Arden edition, 1982.

holds back tears with one of Shakespeare's fine morbid jokes, 'Too much of water hast thou, poor Ophelia,/And therefore I forbid my tears.' The narrator and the listener are particularized but share and show grief in a way partly but not wholly echoing Ophelia's transmutation of madness to favour and to prettiness. The pathetic fallacy softens the story of dying by harmonizing creature and elements, though only for a while:

> There is a willow grows askant the brook
> That shows his hoary leaves in the glassy stream.
> Therewith fantastic garlands did she make
> Of crow-flowers, nettles, daisies, and long purples,
> That liberal shepherds give a grosser name,
> But our cold maids do dead men's fingers call them.
> There on the pendent boughs her crownet weeds
> Clamb'ring to hang, an envious sliver broke,
> When down her weedy trophies and herself
> Fell in the weeping brook.
>
> (IV.7)

The lyrical and descriptive narration is unrealistic, related from no single or possible viewpoint: the inferences about Ophelia's death are imaginatively collected as the report of an impossibly omniscient, sensitive, detached and inactive eye-witness. The gains are great, in beauty, tenderness and sympathy. Shakespeare delicately ends the pathetic speech with a touch of reality, as he takes us from the floral and musical imagery of dying to the ugly conclusion:

> But long it could not be
> Till that her garments, heavy with their drink,
> Pull'd the poor wretch from her melodious lay
> To muddy death.

Shakespeare's melodious lay, too, is choked into ending.

Gertrude's narration brings a sense of moral surprise. Like Enobarbus, she is a narrator whose choice is wholly effective, because the viewpoint is startling and enlarging. Gertrude speaks as a woman tender towards a woman, but the gentle elegy is backed by the stern knowledge of her involvement and responsibility. Nevertheless Gertrude is shown as morally off-duty, as well as responsible. The narration deepens and changes our sense of her character. When Shakespeare shows Hamlet talking theatre shop with the players, or philosophizing with Horatio, we see a glint of normality, a freedom from the pressures of tragic necessity. Here is Gertrude's one free (or almost free) speech, showing an available large humanity, which tragedy must constrict. We should not romanticize this. Shakespeare does not; he gives us a glimpse only of the unconditional. The narration is in character. As Gertrude speaks her elegy for Ophelia, we are aware of the bitter maturity of the voice that laments the death of innocence. It is a long time since the speaker was a cold maid. The transmutation of fertility to death – genitals to dead men's fingers – is perfectly appropriate to the narrator, to the dead, to Hamlet and to the play. In a patriarchal tragedy, in which there are only two women, woman mourns woman.

Although Hamlet's soliloquies have narration woven into their meditative form, Hamlet does not speak a formal narrative until he stops soliloquizing. When he returns from the sea-voyage to England, he shifts from soliloquy to colloquy. At last he can tell. He has been able to tell truths to Horatio before, but the telling is either laconic, 'I think it was to see my mother's wedding', or offstage, like the information about the Ghost's story, which Hamlet refuses to tell his companions in Act I, scene 5, but tells Horatio later, 'the circumstance/Which I have told thee of my father's death', (Act III, scene 2). Free and full narration is released after Hamlet returns, invigorated by the voyage. His narration of the adventure is terse, vigorous, almost extrovert. Hamlet who has so often found himself 'alone', comes on in the middle of an earnest and intimate conversation from which narration rises:

Ham. So much for this, sir, Now shall you see the other.
You do remember all the circumstance?
Hor. Remember it, my lord!
Ham. Sir, in my heart there was a kind of fighting
That would not let me sleep. Methought I lay
Worse than the mutines in the bilboes. Rashly –
And prais'd be rashness for it: let us know

Our indiscretion sometime serves us well
When our deep plots do pall; and that should learn us
There's a divinity that shapes our ends,
Rough-hew them how we will –

Hor. That is most certain.

Ham. Up from my cabin,
My sea-gown scarf'd about me, in the dark
Grop'd I to find out them, had my desire,
Finger'd their packet, and in fine withdrew
To mine own room again, making so bold,
My fears forgetting manners, to unseal
Their grand commission; where I found, Horatio –
Ah, royal knavery! – an exact command,
Larded with many several sorts of reasons
Importing Denmark's health, and England's too,
With ho! such bugs and goblins in my life,
That on the supervise, no leisure bated,
No, not to stay the grinding of the axe,
My head should be struck off.

(V.2)

The language is active, and its figures drawn from action. Instead of meditative excess, expatiation and moral see-saw, there is terseness, 'in my heart there was a kind of fighting'. The articulation of conflict seems to dispose of conflict. Self-division is past. The vigour of image is scrupulously qualified – 'a kind of' – as if figurative language must be seen straight for what it is and handled fairly. The narration is full of certainty. Details are specifically physical, expressing feeling through the matter of fact, 'Worse than the mutines in the bilboes', which also particularizes environment. Never before have we been so clearly in the world of physical action. All the details of the waking, the night, the search, the discovery and the action are presented economically. The vivid detail of hasty, informal dressing emphasizes urgency and speed. The syntax works to the same end, as verbs accumulate, from 'grop'd' to 'found'. The brevity and rush of asyndeton and accumulation mounts to the climactic contempt, 'Ah, royal knavery!' New style joins old style, for Hamlet's parenthetical moralizing remains to reflect on providence, clerkly calligraphy, and the amplifications of political syntax. The account of the counterplot has to move more slowly, taking time and inflating style to mime the language of diplomacy, which must be forged. It modulates from the new language of decisive and energetic efficiency; it is conscious of drama, style and writing.

> *Ham.* Being thus benetted round with villainies –
> Or I could make a prologue to my brains,
> They had begun the play – I sat me down,
> Devis'd a new commission, wrote it fair –
> I once did hold it, as our statists do,
> A baseness to write fair, and labour'd much
> How to forget that learning, but, sir, now
> It did me yeoman's service. Wilt thou know
> Th'effect of what I wrote?
> *Hor.* Ay, good my lord.
> *Ham.* An earnest conjuration from the King,
> As England was his faithful tributary,
> As love between them like the palm might flourish,
> As peace should still her wheaten garland wear
> And stand a comma 'tween their amities,
> And many such-like 'as'es of great charge,
> That on the view and knowing of these contents,
> Without debatement further more or less,
> He should those bearers put to sudden death,
> Not shriving-time allow'd.
>
> (V.2)

We are returned to blunt, no-nonsense language from both men:

> *Hor.* So Guildenstern and Rosencrantz go to't.
> *Ham.* Why, man, they did make love to this employment.
> They are not near my conscience . . .

When Hamlet says, 'The readiness is all', we have been prepared. Confiding supplants soliloquy and its novelty, as a form of discourse for Hamlet, is a moral renewal. The narration itself is imbued with a sense of readiness, in what it tells and how it tells it.

In the last scene of Act V, there is the conventional self-consciousness about the fact and act of narrative which marks conclusion. Like Othello, Hamlet is anxious that the record should be put straight and asks Horatio – who better to tell one's story truly? – to accept the narrative burden. Hamlet would like to tell his own story but like the Ghost lacks time; present-tense narration elides with prolepsis:

> Had I but time – as this fell sergeant, Death,
> Is strict in his arrest – O, I could tell you –
> But let it be. Horatio, I am dead,
> Thou livest. Report me and my cause aright
> To the unsatisfied.

Horatio, contemplating a stoic suicide, has to be asked twice. Hamlet seizes the poisoned cup with the vigour with which he had once threatened to make a ghost of anyone who kept him from the Ghost and develops his persuasion:

> O God, Horatio, what a wounded name,
> Things standing thus unknown, shall I leave behind me.
> If thou didst ever hold me in thy heart,
> Absent thee from felicity awhile,
> And in this harsh world draw they breath in pain
> To tell my story.

Horatio, who does not narrate earlier in the play, becomes a narrator. When Fortinbras comes on, with English ambassadors and soldiers, the potential audience for the story is enlarged and particularized. Story is fast turning into history. Horatio conceives the report, for which he has absented himself from felicity, as a public, funereal oration:

> *Hor.* . . . give order that these bodies
> High on a stage be placed to the view,
> And let me speak to th' yet unknowing world
> How these things came about. So shall you hear
> Of carnal, bloody, and unnatural acts,
> Of accidental judgments, casual slaughters,
> Of deaths put on by cunning and forc'd cause,
> And, in this upshot, purposes mistook
> Fall'n on th'inventors' heads. All this can I
> Truly deliver.
> *Fort.* Let us haste to hear it . . .

Horatio adds one more cue and motive for the offstage, post-drama narration: it will be good for law and order to tell the facts, 'Even while men's minds are wild, lest more mischance/On plots and errors happen'.

The function of such concluding assertion of narration here is clear: it neatly and strongly binds retrospect with prospect to strengthen closure. There is also here, as in other plays, a fluid sense of fiction and realistic illusion. We who have spent all this time listening to the total dramatic narration are forced to imagine the viewpoint of characters within the play. They are in partial ignorance, except for Hamlet and Horatio, who emphasise the dangers of such ignorance. While we briefly entertain the idea of fictitious characters 'real' enough to know or not know the story we know, the sense of fiction is asserted. The act of comparison asserts the nature of the art in which we participate. The repeated emphasis of telling underlines all the acts of telling that have been performed. The terminal assertion of artifice – particularly, here, of fictional narration – is flourished. Horatio's summary is a fine blend of prolepsis with *occupatio*, and reminds us of that part of the story he cannot tell, for all his knowledge and truthfulness, because his knowledge and truthfulness are fictions. He makes an intelligent, accurate and fairly comprehensive summary of external events, and his capacity to tell is guaranteed by the preview. We see, in another backstage glimpse, why Shakespeare took care to inform us that Hamlet confided in Horatio: his trust technically qualified Horatio for the creative task. He will not be Shakespeare, but truthfulness, fairness, loyalty, political sense and mastery of passion potentially equip him for painful effort. Like other narrators – Othello, for one – he is particularized and symbolic. He suggests the figure of the artist, who makes order of rough and confused material, who reluctantly survives to assume the tragic story, 'As one, in suff'ring all, that suffers nothing'.

CHAPTER NINE

King Lear

'And hear old tales'

As in other plays, the narrations and narrators in *King Lear* are Janus-headed, looking within, at the rhetoric they exemplify, and beyond, to the world that includes but is bigger than works of art. Narration in *King Lear* is in a way self-centred but always concerned to explore and appraise mind, feeling, speech, ordering and social interaction.

As we have seen, Shakespeare's arts of exposition are brilliantly varied. He rings the changes, sometimes making use of uncompromising and stylized formality, as he does with the duplicated *nuntius* in the second scene of *Macbeth*, sometimes retarding expository narration and using action as physical and polyphonic as possible, as in the active first scenes of *Macbeth* and *The Tempest*. The exposition in *King Lear* is accomplished in compression, complex reference and naturalistic disguise. The collaborative and allusive narrative exchanged between the earls of Kent and Gloucester takes a mere thirty-three lines in which to prepare for conclusion, provide retrospect and prospect, sketch character and motive and begin the dual action of the plot.

Lear's authoritarian government is revealed in his first piece of dialogue. It has the air of ongoing conversation, marked by surprise at apparently recent disclosure, 'now, in the division of the kingdom' (I.1). The surprise itself informs us not only about the counselling habits in Lear's court but makes an affective medium for expository recall. The exchange indicates Lear's capacity for unpredictable decision but also for some moral good taste, as he seems to have preferred Albany to Cornwall. (It is a long time before we know why.) The framing symmetry is begun, bracketing Albany and Kent at beginning as at end.

Narration quickly sketches character through style: Gloucester's easy reminiscence of the byblow conception is coarsely indifferent in content and language, whether the director puts Edmund within earshot or not; and Kent sensitively turns the tactless story into a compliment to Edmund without being offensive to the teller. The scene, incidentally, shows that unmannerly plain-speaking is not Kent's only style but is indeed provoked by Lear's 'madness', as he says. Edmund's repressed speech and presence, as a character insulted by the telling of his story, prepares us by full and fine contrast for his great confidential and exclamatory soliloquy in the next scene. The dramatist's art of preparations creates brief and muted forecasts, which are to be reversed, in Kent's ceremonious and placatory 'I must love you, and sue to know you better' and Gloucester's rough and inflammatory 'He hath been out nine years, and away he shall again.' Then narrative modulates into present-tense activity, 'The King is coming.' Private and political acts are set in motion. The audience is started on the tragic trajectory of expectation and surprise, anticipation and recall.

Here, as elsewhere, narration is a key figure, like lexis or syntax, in creating the illusion of character and providing parts for actors. The *dramatis personae* are defined by their styles of telling and listening. But this means to a theatrical end is self-analytic: narration is examined, socially, psychologically and ethically. As so often, Shakespeare creates a social paradigm, in which communication is corrupt, clandestine, falsified and inhibited. Despotism flourishes on lies, flattery, boasts, betrayals – moral forms of narrative. Lear's government discourages truths. The civil and international wars which succeed his quasi-abdication promote distorted narrative modes. Espionage flourishes, truth-telling is perilous and driven underground. As in later police states, confidences to one's nearest and dearest can be dangerous: Gloucester confides in

Edmund, and loses his eyes. Kent speaks out, assuming that moral truths need not be abashed by despots and is exiled, along with his speech. Cordelia's planned silence – 'What shall Cordelia speak? Love, and be silent' – is impracticable. She too misunderstands the nature of political oppression, in which patriarchy is compounded by paternity, and is forced by her sister' false rhetoric and her father's tyrannical demands to attempt the impossible and speak a pure language. The result is a legalistic declaration which does not even represent what she feels. The Fool knows where Truth must go and where falsehood can get warmed. Edgar's credulousness, compounded by his father's, joins with Edmund's lies and slanders to drive Edgar's rational, well-meaning and educated speaking into deranged and rude dialects. Truthful telling becomes rare. Narration is destabilized. Lear's kingdom is given over to the perversions of narrative, lies, betrayals, secrets.

Correspondence becomes furtive, and its various abuses dominate, to show a society in which spies are 'fee'd' to listen and tattle, where letters are intercepted, where disintegrated communication is the response to despotic government and war. It is a spy-story. Shakespeare likes to show underground communications, virtue working in the dark against the false-seemings of news and reportings which are doubtful, deceptive, unreliable. The play is full of letters, an epistolary drama, an Elizabethan anticipation of *Les Liaisons dangereuses*, in which dangerous relationships are shown through, and as, dangerous communications. Kent reads a letter from Cordelia, who has been informed of his obscured course, in the stocks, after he has attacked the false messenger, Oswald. Lear calls him 'my messenger' and the collision between him and Oswald, Goneril's 'reeking post' and 'the other messenger', whose welcome poisons his, is shown as a war of messages. 'Stocking his messenger' is a political act and visual emblem, correctly read by Gloucester in Act II, scene 2 as an insult to the sovereign, 'the King must take it ill' . . . so slightly valued in his messenger'. In Act III, scene 1 Kent instructs an anonymous Gentleman to speed to Dover and make a 'just report' to 'Some that will thank you'. He tells him that Cornwall and Albany have spies among their servants, 'Which are to France the spies and speculations/Intelligent of our state', though he is not thoroughly acquainted with their information. In Act I, scene 2, Edmund pretends to hide the letter which he has forged, and gives it to Gloucester. Only a little later, in Act II, scene 1, he is asked by Curan if he has heard 'the news abroad . . . the whisper'd ones . . . ear-bussing arguments'. Gloucester tells Edmund of a dangerous letter locked in his closet. Edmund instantly informs on him, Cornwall tells Goneril to 'post' to her husband with a letter telling that France has landed. Gloucester interrogated by Cornwall and Regan protests that the letter is 'guessingly set down/Which came from one that's of a neutral heart', but he has just told Kent that he has heard of a plot to kill Lear. News, reports, information are dubious, urgent, impeded and crucial. Letters and messages show the haste, suspicion, fear and insecurities of the state. Espionage and counter-espionage prosper. Gloucester is a wonderful example of a well-meaning, not too sensitive, bungling but in the end tremendously loyal and brave man, caught and wounded in the web of slanders and informers' reports.

News, letters and messages are diffused throughout the action. But there is one concentrated report scene, in Act IV, scene 3, where that Gentleman commissioned by Kent to take the bad news to Cordelia meets Kent again at the French camp in Dover, gives the only partly explained news about France's enforced return to France and is asked about Cordelia's response to the message, now exalted and elaborated into 'letters', probably because Shakespeare imagines her response to reading a text as more isolatable than listening to a messenger.* The messenger tells the story of her response, in one of the play's most beautiful narrations, graceful both in content and affective medium. The tone is appreciative

* This narration is not in the Folio edition, and Stephen Urkovitz, in his valuable study *Shakespeare's Revision of King Lear* (Princeton University Press, 1980, pp. 53–4), says 'When the scene is cut the play improves', because it contradicts later information about Lear's knowledge of Cordelia's presence in England, and is 'in the plot . . . at best forgettable and at worst seriously misleading'. I find the speech more interesting than Urkovitz suggests, because it keeps Cordelia and her emotions imaginatively present, but his case is a strong one, unlike his judgement of the cuts in Edgar's long narrative (see p. 199). Both discussions show the usual lack of interest in narration as a dramatic form.

and admiring, and Cordelia's response, as she reads the story of her father's sufferings, is compassionate and outraged. Her feelings are dramatically rendered, in direct speech within the Gentleman's report, and her words make a brief and eloquent recapitulation of the storm-scene, which the audience has witnessed, as she reads, then pauses to ruminate on, the letter:

> Cried 'Sisters! sisters! Shame of ladies! sisters!
> Kent! father! sisters! What? i'th'storm! i'th'night?'
> (IV.3)

Reading is turned into writing, repetition confirms and intensifies pity and consternation, in a form whose contraction is not only characteristic of the speaker's rhetorical pith, purity and economy but is also a register for emotion. The event is relived, in imaginative apprehension. The few compassionate and horrified exclamations and questions are substantive, needing no verbal forms, summarizing the bare facts and reducing response to a morally significant familial minimum, eloquent as Cordelia's 'nothing'. Her minimal narration is a complex outline; it is also part of a speech which is convoluted, containing narration within narration, drawing attention by repetition and stress to its form and its categories of communication. It is also a rare example, in this play and in Shakespeare's tragedies, of benign narrative: sympathy is compounded. Though the story within the Gentleman's story is Cordelia's emotional and moral paradigm of reception and narration, it is typical of the dramatist's handling of messages and messengers that the larger loving speech should be given to an anonymous speaker. *King Lear* is a play where there are several nonce characters whose very lack of centrality and identity is telling. The beauty and complexity of the speech is a striking instance of Shakespeare's tact in handling the functional event and functional character, caring for fullness of representation and the opportunities for players of small parts. (Whether such parts are played by inferior or novice actors or doubled by performers of major roles makes no difference to our recognition of the dramatist's producing hand, cunning and caring.)

But Shakespeare gives his narrative norm briefly, almost marginally. There is no suggestion in this play that we can do more than uncertainly glimpse true telling. Cordelia's 'nothings' make the point clearly, and their minimalization of narrative is made more clear and poignant when we see how easily the word 'nothing' can become a lie, as Edmund echoes it to pretend, briefly, that the letter he is reading, purportedly from Edgar, is something he would like to keep from, instead of reveal to, his father. The Lady's Brach stinks by the fire while Truth hides in a kennel.

The Fool hides truths in various distorted and disguised narrations. He uses the cunning generality and allegory of proverb and brief exemplum, gnomic saying, wild jokes, and snatches of verse or song. He speaks covertly to Lear, but the covertness maddens Lear because it is so readable. The Fool has to speak in code. So does the other great truthteller, Edgar, whose disguise of costume also involves disguise of discourse. Like the letters, news, reports and messages, Edgar's babblings reflect the tyrannies of the state. His brother's lies and betrayals are treated as social norms, welcomed as truth and loyalty. His speeches are dislocated in many ways, but in spite of interruption, digression and broken sequence, his very dilapidations depend on a narrative sequence. It is one that draws on personal experience as well as fantasy. So as he answers the customary social curiosity which makes us ask each other, on meeting, to summarize life and occupation, here framed with social self-possession only by Kent's, 'Who's there?' and 'What art thou that dost grumble there i'th' straw?' (III.4), he begins with the sequential narrative of his possession by the foul fiend but soon modulates to tell a more realistic and truthful autobiography. Before he does this, however, he is interrogated less lucidly by manic Lear's mania, imagining that everyone's story is his own, 'Didst thou give all to thy daughters?' Lear eventually asks the ordinary and conventional question, 'What hast thou been?', and Edgar responds by telling the story of a proud and lecherous serving-man. It is not his own history, but one coloured by experience of the corruptions of high places. As soon as Gloucester appears Edgar reverts to his horror-story of the foul fiend Flibbertigibbet, a present-tense and impersonal narration, swerving out of prose into verse. When Gloucester asks the social question – observing the forms of everyday intercourse even in storm and dark – 'What are you there? Your names?' – he is also asking urgent and fearful questions. They are answered only by his son, recovered sufficiently to introduce himself by name, 'Poor Tom'. For the first time he joins his two stories, the story of diabolical possession and the story of past sophistication, of one 'who is whipp'd from tithing to tithing, and stock-punish'd, and imprison'd; who hath had three suits to his back, six shirts to his body, – /*Horse to ride, and weapons to wear*'.

Shakespeare is doing several things in this narration, giving a psychologically realistic response to a changing group of listeners, but also making bedlam inventions recast and anticipate stories that the play will enact. Tom's fantasies are truths elsewhere: those autobiographical details about lechery, cohabitation with his mistress, the surplusage of luxury, aggressive arms, nakedness, exposure, darkness, and – of course – madness itself, all turn out to be more than mere horrible imaginings. It would be tempting to say that nothing is too outlandishly evil to appear in action, except of course that Shakespeare moves us – and Edgar – to realize that life not only shocks by converting nightmare surrealism to everyday reality but can shock more by unanticipated events. What Goneril calls so succinctly 'all the building' of fancy does not match the constructions of the play's larger narration, within which individual fancies play their imperfect and contingent parts. So Edgar comes to see how dangerous it is to say he has reached the bottom, being 'worst./The lowest and most dejected thing of Fortune' (IV.1), because no sooner has he consoled himself, like Genet's imprisoned criminals, with the thought that 'the worst returns to laughter', than the world comes up with a worse mutation, his blinded father. He changes his story, 'Who is't can say "I am at the worst?"/ I am worse than e'er I was' and 'And worse I may be yet'. He has reached the limit of forecast.

After the succeeding lies and shifts of dialect, which include the fantasy of Gloucester's leap and the fiend with a thousand noses and whelk'd horns, he eventually comes to his only full and true narration, which is one of the longest and most complex narratives in the play. In V.3, he refuses to tell his story before he fights his brother, 'my name is lost', though there is the minimal narration, 'Yet am I noble as the adversary', and after his victory, he reveals himself and is given the perfect interrogative cue for his revelations. Albany asks where he has 'hid' and how he has known 'the miseries of [his] father', and he gives first a perfect and laconic answer, 'By nursing them', then formally announces the narrative, as do so many of Shakespeare's tellers, with 'List a brief tale'.

Edgar's character is revealed, released and expanded through his one uninhibited narration. It encompasses what the audience has seen dramatized – his disguise, the blinding and the journey, the despair and the rescue – all marvellously condensed in what is indeed the promised 'brief tale', told in less than nine lines. It also includes, again tersely, what the audience does not know, the death of Gloucester. It is recapitulation and shocking news. The teller wants to tell and 'when 'tis told, O! that my heart would burst!':

> The bloody proclamation to escape
> That follow'd me so near, – O! our lives' sweetness,
> That we the pain of death would hourly die
> Rather than die at once! – taught me to shift
> Into a madman's rags, t'assume a semblance
> That very dogs disdain'd: and in this habit
> Met I my father with his bleeding rings,
> Their precious stones new lost; became his guide,
> Led him, begg'd for him, sav'd him from despair;
> Never – O fault! – reveal'd myself unto him,
> Until some half-hour past, when I was arm'd;
> Not sure, though hoping, of this good success,
> I ask'd his blessing, and from first to last
> Told him my pilgrimage: but his flaw'd heart,
> Alack, too weak the conflict to support!
> 'Twixt two extremes of passion, joy and grief,
> Burst smilingly.*
>
> (V.3)

* In the source for the Gloucester sub-plot, the story of the Paphlagonian king in Sidney's *Arcadia*, Edgar does not delay revealing himself to his father: Shakespeare chose to make Edgar postpone his telling and blame himself – 'O fault!' – with important consequences which include the emotional complication of Edgar's character, Gloucester's fatal heartbreak at hearing the story and a more extended, compounded, dialogic and reflexive narrative speech for character and actor.

The narrative form is characteristic of the speaker. Edgar interrupts his record of events by anguished moralized observation, 'O! our lives' sweetness' and 'O fault!' The story is convoluted and analytic; the effects of narration are discussed and demonstrated as he tells the story of the storytelling which was too much for Gloucester to bear. As he tells, the recapitulation transforms the blinding into metaphor, but the shift is still compassionate, even though physical suffering has been exquisitely re-imaged, for the re-imaging forces us to remember the subject before it could be so metaphorically revalued. Narrative accumulates, as Edgar goes on:

> This would have seem'd a period
> To such as love not sorrow; but another,
> To amplify too much, would make much more,
> And top extremity.
> Whilst I was big in clamour came there in a man,
> Who, having seen me in my worst estate,
> Shunn'd my abhorr'd society; but then, finding
> Who 'twas that so endur'd, with his strong arms
> He fasten'd on my neck, and bellow'd out
> As he'd burst heaven; threw him on my father;
> Told the most piteous tale of Lear and him
> That ever ear receiv'd; which in recounting
> His grief grew puissant, and the strings of life
> Began to crack: twice then the trumpets sounded,
> And there I left him tranc'd.
>
> (V.3)

The details of rhetoric draw attention to themselves, as Edgar says of Kent's narrative what the audiences will feel about his own, 'This would have seem'd a period' and 'To amplify too much, would make much more', insisting on the technical terms of 'period' and 'amplification'. Edgar's narration is presented as self-generated, powered by unpremeditated passions, but Shakespeare's narration is cunningly constructed, built on the armature of the three references to heartbreak, 'O! that my heart would burst!' (Edgar), 'his flaw'd heart . . . Burst smilingly!' (Gloucester) and 'the strings of life/Began to crack' (Kent). This organizing figure draws attention to the unbearable strain of knowledge which does not quite kill Edgar, which kills Gloucester, and which is to kill Lear and Kent. Even Albany says, before the story is amplified, 'I am almost ready to dissolve'. There is the combination of explicit self-reference to modes of narration with an impassioned drama, which allows Edgar to take his place, with authority, pain and truth. Telling and listening are demonstrably heart-breaking.

In the Folio edition, this two-part narration, which is in the Quarto, is confined to the first part and ends when Albany asks Edgar to 'hold it in': Albany's request is immediately followed by the announcement of Goneril's and Regan's deaths. Stephen Urkovitz (see note on p. 193) says 'it is Albany's role which is most affected by the change.' This is true, if we only think of character, and only of the characters of Edgar and Albany. The judgement is a striking example of the neglect of narration – its form, function, self-analysis and content – since this omission not only breaks the structure of narration, depriving us of the balance of heartbroken listener (Gloucester) and heartbroken teller (Kent) but cuts the first stage in Kent's 'journey' to death, begun in the story within Edgar's story and resumed when he says at the end that he must follow his master.

As I said in Chapter 6, *King Lear* contains a kind of narration which is rare – perhaps unique? – in Shakespeare. This is a story projected into the future, an idealizing fantasy of the kind familiar in French and English nineteenth-century novels. Earlier in Act V, scene 3, Cordelia wants action, 'Shall we not see these daughters and these sisters?', but Lear proposes a flight into the free and unconditioned world of prison:

> We two alone will sing like birds i'th'cage:
> When thou dost ask me blessing, I'll kneel down,
> And ask of thee forgiveness: so we'll live,
> And pray, and sing, and tell old tales, and laugh
> At gilded butterflies, and hear poor rogues
> Talk of court news; and we'll talk with them too,
> Who loses and who wins; who's in, who's out;
> And take upon's the mystery of things,
> As if we were God's spies: and we'll wear out,

In a wall'd prison, packs and sects of great ones
That ebb and flow by th' moon.

(V.3)

Here there is conspicuous convolution, a story within the story; Lear proposes that they tell old tales and relate the gossip of the outer world, 'who's in, who's out'. Since *Lear* has a fairy-tale origin and plot, the old tales point inward. The fantasy turns on a combination of possibility and impossibility. Prison will not provide a refuge. Like other prisoners, Cordelia will not tell stories and sing songs but be killed. But Lear strenuously tries to imagine what is possible, a prison which exists in an environment of worldly ambition and competition, 'who's in, who's out'. Shakespeare imagines Lear, whose imagination has been instructed, as imaging ideally but not wildly, as he tells of a space and time for love and innocence which the play cannot provide. Like Shakespeare's own stories, narrated through the plays, Lear's joins artifice with truth. The contamination of narrative is insisted on, with clear political significance, even while the dramatist glimpses, and lets us glimpse, what truth-telling might be like. The narrations in *King Lear*, like the whole play, tell the audience tragic truths.

CHAPTER TEN

Macbeth

'A tale told by an idiot'

The most famous narrator in *Macbeth* – whose incapacity has been promoted and compounded by Rose Macaulay's *Told by an Idiot* and William Faulkner's *The Sound and the Fury* – is that pure example of what critics of fiction have called the unreliable narrator, the idiot of Macbeth's metaphor. The idiot's tale, like Shakespeare's, is full of sound and fury, unlike it in signifying nothing. To project even such a brief abstract of artistic incompetence – and Shakespeare, like Cervantes, Thomas Hardy and James Joyce, can elaborate fuller demonstrations – is to signal artistic control and confidence.

The first acts of narration in Act I, scene 2, are energetic. In Act I, scene 1, a context is created for this energy; the play arrests the attention of its audience by a device also used in *Othello* and *The Tempest*, a conspicuous gap in exposition. Pure action, an absence of narrative, in the first uninformative speeches of the weird sisters, creates a need, posing a question which yearns for an answer. Their laconic storm-set questions, answers and riddles are wild but elegantly organized in couplets, single lines and shared lines for three separate voices, with a final ensemble. It is a lyric overture which tells little, an action actively isolated. After it, Shakespeare meets and matches absence with expansive presence, concentrating exposition in a double narration which is framed, formal, contrastive, dynamic, theatrically ominous and politically suggestive. The expository narration is divided between two specialized narrators, the bleeding Captain and the thane Rosse. Each supplies information in ways dear to Shakespeare's art. The bleeding Captain is one of Shakespeare's most vivacious nonce characters. He dominates the scene. His outside perfectly matches his style and subject, and the part is a joy to the actor, whether or not he combines it with another role. Rosse is a character open to a range of histrionic interpretation. He is not dominant but theatrically sustained and developed, reporting in this first scene and still telling away in the last, within thirty lines of the end. He is given a series of crucial and plot-precipitating narrations. His subordination is vital.

These two tellers are contrasted and linked. The Captain comes on bleeding and in pain. Rosse arrives with haste looking through his eyes, 'So should he look/That seems to speak things strange.' The Captain is a frontline soldier. Rosse is an officer and an ambassador or diplomat. The Captain comes straight from the fighting and can 'report . . . of the revolt/The newest state', but he is given a traditionally epic style, which is continued, less loftily, violently and intensely by Rosse. Each narrator is formally identified, introduced and questioned. Each speaks in an exalted, metaphorical and hyperbolic style.

The Captain's expansive three-paragraphed speech is twice the length of Rosse's two-part address, and elaborated by many retarding elements:

Cap. Doubtful it stood;
As two spent swimmers, that do cling together
And choke their art. The merciless Macdonwald
(Worthy to be a rebel, for to that
The multiplying villainies of nature
Do swarm upon him) from the western isles
Of Kernes and Gallowglasses is supplied;
And Fortune, on his damned quarrel smiling,
Show'd like a rebel's whore: but all's too weak;
For brave Macbeth (well he deserves that name),
Disdaining Fortune, with his brandish'd steel,
Which smok'd with bloody execution,
Like Valour's minion, carv'd out his passage,

Till he fac'd the slave;
Which ne'er shook hands, nor bade farewell to him,
Till he unseam'd him from the nave to th' chops,
And fix'd his head upon our battlements.

Dun. O valiant cousin! worthy gentleman!

Cap. As whence the sun 'gins his reflection,
Shipwracking storms and direful thunders break,
So from that spring, whence comfort seem'd to come,
Discomfort swells. Mark, King of Scotland, mark:
No sooner justice had, with valour arm'd,
Compell'd these skipping Kernes to trust their heels,
But the Norweyan Lord, surveying vantage,
With furbish'd arms, and new supplies of men,
Began a fresh assault.

Dun. Dismay'd not this
Our captains, Macbeth and Banquo?

Cap. Yes;
As sparrows eagles, or the hare the lion.
If I say sooth, I must report they were
As cannons overcharg'd with double cracks;
So they
Doubly redoubled strokes upon the foe:
Except they meant to bathe in reeking wounds,
Or memorize another Golgotha,
I cannot tell –
But I am faint, my gashes cry for help.

(I.2)

It contains several similes, brief but circumstantially expansive enough to remind us of Homer, like a similar one in the First Player's demonstration speech in Act III, scene 2 of *Hamlet*. It is punctuated by parentheses and clear caesural pauses. Its narrative markers and fillers respond to Malcolm's formal imperative, 'Say to the King', with 'Mark, King of Scotland, mark' and 'If I say sooth, I must report'. The penultimate line, 'I cannot tell', breaks to resonate in complex conclusion. The narration's irregular lineation, formality, lexical grandeur and slow stately progress make a perfect register for the actor's passionate voicing of praise, pain, exhaustion and breathlessness – Shakespeare knows the pangs of certain acts of telling; he takes care to provide for his functional characters and the Captain is no exception. Stage records and reviews are rich in illustrations of this acting part, reporting narrators who fall, collapse, reel against the King, nearly strike him with a sword, and are brought on in litters.* Joseph Mydell in the Royal Shakespeare production, 1986, gave a robust rendering, bloody but not breathless, not using caesural pauses, short lines and other cues for gasps, nor joining portentousness with pants in 'Mark, King of Scotland, mark'. His gashes never cried out for help till the last line.

Rosse's report is terser, more self-controlled and political, bringing news of victory and settlement, even specifying the gain in dollars, and continuing though not completing the Captain's story. He tells us more about Norway and adds the new character of the Thane of Cawdor. Duncan has to be told that he comes from Fife:

Rosse Where the Norweyan banners flout the sky,
And fan our people cold. Norway himself,
With terrible numbers,
Assisted by that most disloyal traitor,
The Thane of Cawdor, began a dismal conflict;
Till that Bellona's bridegroom, lapp'd in proof,
Confronted him with self-comparisons,
Point against point, rebellious arm 'gainst arm,
Curbing his lavish spirit: and, to conclude,
The victory fell on us;-
Dun. Great happiness!
Rosse That now
Sweno, the Norways' king, craves composition;
Nor would we deign him burial of his men
Till he disbursed at Saint Colme's Inch
Ten thousand dollars to our general use.
(I.2)

His rhetoric echoes, develop and promotes the Captain's personification, 'Valour's minion', in the equally ominous alliterative prolepsis, 'Bellona's bridegroom'. His mission is extended, so we follow him into the next scene, where he gives the crucial information about Macbeth's elevation to Cawdor's title. In later narra-

* Marvin Rosenberg, *The Masks of Macbeth*, University of California Press, Berkeley, California and London, 1978.

tions he tells of the portents on the night of the murder, fearfully and guardedly discusses Macduff's reasons for flight with Lady Macduff and reports the murder of Lady Macduff and the children to Macduff in one of Shakespeare's subtlest tellings of evil tidings, nervously sensitive both to distressed messenger and stricken listener. In the final scene of the play it is Rosse who tells Siward of his son's heroic frontal wounding. In Act II, after Duncan's Murder, Rosse is given one bizarre speech, unlike his more professional narrations, in which he joins in a duet with the Old Man, contributing an amazing and amazed eyewitness report of the sinister equine cannibalism;

> *Old M.* Threescore and ten I can remember well;
> Within the volume of which time I have seen
> Hours dreadful, and things strange, but this sore night
> Hath trifled former knowings.
> *Rosse* Ha, good Father,
> Thou seest the heavens, as troubled with man's act,
> Threatens his bloody stage: by th'clock 'tis day,
> And yet dark night strangles the travelling lamp.
> Is't night's predominance, or the day's shame,
> That darkness does the face of earth entomb,
> When living light should kiss it?
> *Old M.* 'Tis unnatural,
> Even like the deed that's done. On Tuesday last,
> A falcon, towering in her pride of place,
> Was by a mousing owl hawk'd at, and kill'd.
> *Rosse* And Duncan's horses (a thing most strange and certain)
> Beauteous and swift, the minions of their race,
> Turn'd wild in nature, broke their stalls, flung out,
> Contending 'gainst obedience, as they would make
> War with mankind.
> *Old M.* 'Tis said, they eat each other.
> *Rosse* They did so; to th' amazement of mine eyes,
> That look'd upon't.
>
> (II.4)

A messenger with authority and power, whose role expands with the action, Rosse is ambiguous and suggestive enough to have been interpreted as a liar (in the horse-story) by William Empson and a traitor and spy by the Victorian scholar, M.F. Libby.* The film director Roman Polanski shows him letting in the assassins at Fife after the tender farewell to his cousin's family. It is easy to defend him against the charge of unreliability, but it is an implausible rather than preposterous response to a play where information is so often incomplete, obscure, oblique, unreliable and ambiguous, where truths and lies so commonly change places and faces.

The Captain and Rosse are the first of many messengers. The Captain is a nonce narrator, and so are the Old Man, the breathless messenger who croaks the news of Duncan's arrival to Lady Macbeth, the rough and humble messenger aware that his hasty warning terrifies Lady Macduff, and several servants abused by Macbeth. Messengers and messages fill the interstices of many classical, medieval and Renaissance plays to inform audiences inside and outside the drama, to create motive, precipitate action, move the plot on its way. Like Sophocles, the author of the morality play *Everyman* and Samuel Beckett, Shakespeare likes to animate and individualize the messenger or *nuntius*, or the *nuncio* as he familiarly names Viola/Cesario in *Twelfth Night*. The bleeding Captain, Rosse and the Old Man are fine instances of 'the passionate and weighty *Nuntius*' as John Webster called him in that great iambic pentameter which rises from the weighty prose of his Address to the Reader in *The White Devil*. All the messengers in *Macbeth* 'enlifen death' in ways probably not intended by Webster. They swell that company of memorable messengers which includes the soldier in *Antigone*, the 'mighty messenger' Death in *Everyman*, the ambiguous boy or boys in *Waiting for Godot*, and Shakespeare's brief shadow, the vividly dark Marcade in *Love's Labour's Lost*. Impassioned narrators like these intensify and dignify the role. They are also thematically responsive to their play. In *Macbeth* the messengers' narrative behaviour develops the theme of dangerous, compromised and passive discourse. Messengers are traditionally vulnerable. Shakespeare's are bearers of evil tidings who are not killed but have a bad time. The escape imagined by Robert

* M.F. Libby's book *Some New Works on Macbeth* (1893) is mentioned by Empson in *Essays on Shakespeare* (Cambridge University Press, 1986).

Frost for his 'Bearer of Evil Tidings', who prudently gives up the mission and settles down in the middle of the journey, is not open to the oppressed and serviceable messengers here. Macbeth is often refused and snubbed, as well as tricked and teased, by the oracles and heralds of the play's darkness, and his inferiors are often put down and insulted too. The timid or terrified serving-messengers are patronized and bullied, but they come off better than Kent in *Lear*, who is stocked, and do not suffer as badly as the messenger who is beaten, haled up and down and threatened with pickling by Cleopatra, or the man so shamefully whipped on Antony's orders. (The servants in *Antony and Cleopatra* draw on Shakespeare's experiments in message-bearing and message-receiving in *Macbeth*.) One servant's terrified pallor is finely abused as cream-faced and goose-like as he stutters out news of the ten thousand approaching English soldiers. Though another is understandably frightened at having to report a wood on the move, he is merely threatened with hanging if his news is not true and invited by Macbeth to do as much for his master if it is. But most of the messengers are demonstrably and clearly victims of despotism and tyranny. Shakespeare never lets us forget the politics of power.

The subservience of messengers emerges as messages multiply. Messengers are structurally dependent on each other, their messages fitting, or nearly fitting, together in an imperfect jigsaw. In scenes 1, 2 and 3 of Act I, we only get the complete story of Macdonwald's rising after listening to four narrators – the Captain, Rosse, Angus and Malcolm – and we never come to know exactly how the Thane of Cawdor 'combined' or with whom. Unlike Hamlet's players, Shakespeare does not tell all, and his reserve is purposeful:

Angus Who was the Thane, lives yet;
But under heavy judgment bears that life
Which he deserves to lose. Whether he was combin'd
With those of Norway, or did line the rebel
With hidden help and vantage, or that with both
He labour'd in his country's wrack, I know not;
But treasons capital, confess'd and prov'd,
Have overthrown him.

(I.3)

Details accumulate: the audience is like Desdemona busy about the house while Othello tells his life-story, hearing history 'in parcels, not intentively'. Individual speakers don't know the whole truth: 'I cannot tell' (the Captain) and 'I know not' (Angus). There is the politically significant irony of Macbeth's ignorance about his enemy and predecessor: 'The Thane of Cawdor lives' he protests, first to the witches, then to Rosse and Angus. *Macbeth*'s dissemination of news brings home the bitter reality of a frontline lack of military information, not only about political causes and effects but even about the identity of the enemy. Shakespeare's rendering of war reports has been called careless or textually corrupt, while Stendhal has been praised for his politically astute rendering of the ramshackle, backyard, piecemeal and obfuscated experiences of war in *The Charterhouse of Parma*. Fabrizio wanders in the maze of Waterloo, and on his way back to Italy wonders if he has been in a battle, if the battle was Waterloo and if he can find out what has happened to him from reading a newspaper. At Fife too the news is uncertain, the battle dispersed, the terrain doubtful, and you are rewarded with your enemy's title and estate before you know he is your enemy. The arbitrariness, mess, fragmentations and obscurity of war are thoroughly, harshly and quietly imagined by Shakespeare as he uses messages and messengers to delineate and define political communication and power, as well as get the action rolling. Macbeth becomes a tyrant who controls the lines of communication, but he starts off as a submissive soldier, fighting in the dark.

The characteristic message in *Macbeth* is refracted, indirect and secondhand. Reports accumulate doubt and lose clarity as they pass from one mouth to another. Communication is dilapidated, like all personal and political relationships in this play. Duncan says that the bleeding Captain 'seems' to be a likely reporter of war. Lennox says Rosse looks like one 'that seems to speak things strange'. Macbeth and Banquo repeat to each other the witches' promises, bewildered, incredulous, suspicious. Malcolm tells Duncan what he has heard from others of Cawdor's death. Lady Macbeth reads or rereads Macbeth's letter. A servant says one of his fellows has arrived 'almost dead for breath, with scarcely more than would make up his message', and the breathless messenger is memorialized by Lady Macbeth, after her off-guard, 'Thou'rt mad to say it', as the hoarse raven 'That croaks the fatal entrance of Duncan/ Under my battlements'. After the cauldron-scene, Lennox tells Macbeth that messengers have brought news of Macduff's departure to England; this is one of the few slips in the communication of communications in the play. In the previous scene (III.6) a Lord, another nonce messenger, has already told Lennox that Macbeth has been exasperated by the news of Macduff's departure and related how Macbeth's messenger was rebuked. This Lord's report of reporting particularizes the messenger in the image 'cloudy', imagined imaginary dialogue, and the lively stage direction 'hums':

> *Lord* . . . with an absolute 'Sir, not I',
> The cloudy messenger turns me his back,
> And hums, as who should say, 'You'll rue the time
> That clogs me with this answer.'
>
> (III.6)

Malcolm tells Macduff about the false agents sent by Macbeth to lure him back to Scotland, whose deceptions have shaken his faith in embassy. All these refracted messages are excellent economies, curtly selecting and summarizing as they re-report reports. Convolutions and compoundings draw attention to the narrative forms and figures being used. Most important, news and reporting are compromised.

Vivid first-hand reports also highlight indirections. The urgent messenger in Act III, who tells Lady Macduff to escape with her children, apologizes for frightening her with his savage telling. He comes too late. The scrupulous waiting gentlewoman in Act V, scene 1 refuses to repeat what she has heard Lady Macbeth say in her sleep because there was no one else present to 'confirm her speech'. Perhaps she gives a cue to the doctor who decides to take notes while watching and listening as the queen walks and talks in her sleep: 'I will set down what comes from her, to satisfy my remembrance the more strongly.' In Act V, scene 5, Seyton, never rebuked by Macbeth, is brief and possibly sympathetic: 'It is the cry of women, my good Lord', and 'The Queen, my Lord, is dead.' Like Shaw's after him, Shakespeare's forms of address vary finely, and each message and messenger appropriately registers relationship and occasion. There can be a touch of compassionate or tender respect in Seyton's 'my good Lord' and 'my Lord', though the phases can also be neutrally or coldly formal. Shakespeare never forgets the actor, in major or minor roles.

The messengers are professional narrators, their theatrical function traditional and stylized. They are plainly much more than artistically functional, used by the play to expose and analyse acts of social correspondence and communication in particular power-structures. But professional narration in *Macbeth* has greater psychic, ethical and social complexity than these minor messengers exhibit. Shakespeare is interested in the narrative acts and arts of his more important public men and women. In many of the plays he uses a major narration to swell or extend or centralize a character whose role might be too backgrounded, too simplified or too stereotyped. Gertrude, Enobarbus and Edgar, for instance, are characters who are deepened and complicated by a single long narration. In *Macbeth* the two characters in danger of being outshadowed by the principals are Malcolm, son and heir of Duncan, and Macbeth's successor, and Macduff, the chief opposition thane. I have already discussed their expansive narration-scene which shows that Shakespeare knew people do not switch emotions in an eyeblink, but that a passion once generated will survive after the cause has been withdrawn. He also wants to stress the continuity of that political distrust which motivated Malcolm's experiment and which runs right through the play. Macbeth's false agents have poisoned Malcolm's faith, and he in turn poisons Macduff's mind. Malcolm has compromised integrity in telling lies for the sake of truth, and Macduff responds with distaste to the opportunism of the next king of Scotland. Theatrical records show how actors have responded to this subtlety, refusing to shake hands, for instance, or slowly coming to shake hands, in what H. Granville-Barker in his *Preface to Macbeth* (London, Nick Hern, 1993) called 'tame puzzlement . . .

man torn between hope and despair' and what M. Rosenberg in *The Masks of Macbeth* called 'injured scepticism'. The scene shows Shakespeare's knowledge of the powers and effects of performance, on and off stage.

In the next two parts of the scene, narration is varied. Malcolm is given a beneficent narration to counter his false-speaking, as he tells the healing tale of the healing of the King's Evil by Edward the Confessor, in a ritualized passage of considerable symbolic significance. The initial narration of the Doctor, and its expansion by Malcolm, also give Macduff time to convalesce from his distrust and contempt. Communication is healed and emotion modulated. No sooner has Macduff recovered, under cover or through the agency of the impersonal and benign episode of telling and listening, than he is made to listen to another terrible story, this time a true one. Rosse comes on, to tell slowly, reluctantly, truthfully and selectively, the play's most horrible piece of news, the report of the massacre at Fife:

Rosse Would I could answer
This comfort with the like! But I have words,
That would be howl'd out in the desert air,
Where hearing should not latch them.
Macd. What concern they?
The general cause? or is it a fee-grief,
Due to some single breast?
Rosse No mind that's honest
But in it shares some woe, though the main part
Pertains to you alone.
Macd. If it be mine,
Keep it not from me; quickly let me have it.
Rosse Let not your ears despise my tongue for ever,
Which shall possess them with the heaviest sound,
That ever yet they heard.
Macd. Humh! I guess at it.

Rosse Your castle is surpris'd; your wife, and babes,
Savagely slaughter'd: to relate the manner,
Were, on the quarry of these murther'd deer,
To add the death of you.

(IV.3)

Shakespeare returns to the friction between Malcolm and Macduff as Malcolm instructs his elder in manliness, that much discussed theme in the play: 'Dispute it like a man.' This detached moral advice provokes the fine response 'But I must also feel it as a man.' Malcolm's 'Be comforted' is answered by the ambiguous lines, 'He has no children', which may be performed with equal propriety as a reference to Macbeth or Malcolm. This whole scene, like Act I, scene 2, is a continuous sequence of contrasts: facts and doubts are revealed by concentrating and permuting acts of narrating and response. Like the other messages and messengers, this masterpiece shows the instabilities and corruptions of telling, with the pains and perils of listening.

Telling in *Macbeth* is corrupted in many ways. There are the fragmentary, riddling and imagistic snatches of narrative used by the witches, and their topsy-turvy transformations of truth to lie and lie to truth. There are the inhibited and violently released stories that Lady Macbeth does not tell or hear but has to hint in her sleep. Like *Hamlet* and *King Lear*, this is a play where letters are important: there is Macbeth's letter to his wife in Act II, scene 1, and the letter we and the Doctor hear about from the gentlewoman, which Lady Macbeth writes, seals and locks away in her closet, and whose contents are never disclosed. (It is one of the secrets the play refuses to divulge.) The letter written and read in sleep is a fellow of the letter from Macbeth which Lady Macbeth reads alone but to the audience. In both episodes, one on stage, one off stage, Shakespeare shows his interest in the conflations of reading with writing. In Act II, scene 1, the actress playing Lady Macbeth makes Macbeth's letter her own, either reading it as for the first time, and stressing amazement, gratification, expectation and surprise, or performing a revisionary rereading, as many actresses, including Sarah Siddons and Judi Dench, have played it, miming a pondered purpose. Dench quoted instead of reading the script, to show that the narration had already become assimilated and re-created. Both interpretations counterpoint a reader's explicit responses on a writer's implicit passions.

Lady Macbeth's narrations are mostly private, and many of

Macbeth's are too. He plans, ponders, fantasizes and remembers, in the common narrative activity of inner life. Prominent among the forms and figures of his narrative language is circumlocution. This is a form of deception or equivocation shared by Macbeth and the witches, who deceive with actualities, like a Caesarean birth (Macduff's) or military camouflage (Birnam Wood), disguised and surrealized as fantastic impossibilities. Circumlocution is not Lady Macbeth's style. Her dreamt recall, 'who would have thought the old man to have had so much blood in him', and her dream's imperative, 'Out, damned spot!', name things bluntly and plainly, in a fragmentary but specific telling which is the opposite of circumlocution. Her Johnsonian habit of calling spades spades and kicking stones to refute ideas and ideals is in marked contrast with Macbeth's visions and fantasies: 'When all's done'/You look but on a stool' (III.4) and 'A little water clears us of this deed' (II.2). These interpretations are coarse simplifications, not truths. They offer themselves as closer to 'reality' – which the play shows as a subjective and elusive concept – than Macbeth's images or his hyperbole, 'this my hand will rather/The multitudinous seas incarnadine,/Making the green one red' (II.2). His circumlocutions are more to the point than her plain-saying, they image guilt's horrid sufferings, she reduces them to objective-sounding stool and water. She comes to revise her pragmatism, at least in sleep, where she offers her version of the 'multitudinous seas' in 'all the perfumes of Arabia', forgoing her former rhetoric of deceptive understatements. Macbeth's habit of circumlocutory narrative is not a decent recognition of events, however, but a way of meeting them evasively, partially, ideally, abstractly or impersonally. He compulsively imagines the future, for instance, but in defensive figures which generalize and externalize hideous particularities, so making them easier to handle:

> Nature seems dead, and wicked dreams abuse
> The curtain'd sleep: Witchcraft celebrates
> Pale Hecate's off'rings; and wither'd Murther,
> Alarum'd by his sentinel, the wolf,
> Whose howl's his watch, thus with his stealthy pace,

With Tarquin's ravishing strides, towards his design
Moves like a ghost

(II.1)

These images are not 'unreal', in a play where we see and hear witches, Hecate and ghosts, but for Macbeth they are convenient metamorphoses of specific acts. He transforms his imminent sin of bloody murder into a Morality Play, with Murder generalized, not individualized. His murderer's stealth too is externalized and made literary or historical, in the reference to Tarquin's strides, itself distanced by metonymy and metaphor. Before Banquo's murder he is similarly imagined as imagining in animal images and impersonalizations which evade and disguise:

Light thickens; and the crow
Makes wings to th' rooky wood;
Good things of Day begin to droop and drowse,
Whiles Night's black agents to their preys do rouse.

(III.2)

Earlier, such evasion is used to tell and yet not tell Lady Macbeth, keeping her literally 'innocent of the knowledge' but alive to the moral imperative and – however elaborately and retardingly – condemning the 'deed':

Ere the bat hath flown
His cloister'd fight; ere, to black Hecate's summons
The shard-born beetle, with his drowsy hums,
Hath rung Night's yawning peal, there shall be done
A deed of dreadful note.

(III.2)

More publicly, hysterically registering fear and guilt as well as deceit, Macbeth accumulates dignifying metaphor to break the news of murder to Malcolm: 'The spring, the head, the fountain of your blood/Is stopp'd'. His subliming circumlocutions are translated, corrected and snubbed by Macduff's directness, 'Your royal father's murther'd' (II.3). Much has been said and unsaid about what A.C. Bradley, in *Shakespearean Tragedy* (London, Macmillan, 1904), called Macbeth's poetic imagination, but the rhetoric with which the dramatist endows his hero is a characteristic language which shows how it is possible to exalt, decorate, facilitate and so live with killing. It is the language of a complex tragic consciousness, creating a figure who is an un-Aristotelian tragic hero in his interiorized wickedness. It is also the dangerous language of politicians, impersonalizing, abstracting, beautifying, deceptively detaching agent from deed. We hear it all around us every day. It is not usually as responsible or conceptually candid as Macbeth's style, which at least judges his moral actions for what they are, while holding their corruption at arms' length as he tells their story.

Rhetoric itself draws attention to its modes. Shakespeare's constant use of contrastive and convoluted structures makes his narration, like other figures of his craft, conspicuous and self-conscious. Narrative self-consciousness shows itself in *Macbeth* directly, through explicit namings of narration, tale, story, writing, reading and listening. Although the society in *Macbeth*'s Scotland is less polished and civilized than the society in Shakespeare's Troy, Venice or Elsinore, it is a literate one, closer to the seventeenth than to the eleventh century. A small cluster of literary images, supported by actions, makes a pattern barely visible until it is powerfully concentrated towards the end in Act V, scene 5.

Macbeth is told in quick succession about two crucial and terrible events: his wife's death, reported by Seyton, and the sight of 'a moving grove' coming to Dunsinane, reported by an anonymous messenger. His response to the first news is registered in imagery drawn from history, language, theatre and narration:

> To-morrow, and to-morrow, and to-morrow,
> Creeps in this petty pace from day to day,
> To the last syllable of recorded time;
> And all our yesterdays have lighted fools
> The way to dusty death. Out, out, brief candle!
> Life's but a walking shadow; a poor player,
> That struts and frets his hour upon the stage,
> And then is heard no more: it is a tale
> Told by an idiot, full of sound and fury,
> Signifying nothing.
>
> (V.5)

Such compounding of self-conscious artistic references is found in intense scenes of crisis in other plays. Shakespeare often provides his actors with a combination of impassioned lines and reflexive technical references, mixing introverted and extroverted forms. He does this, for instance, in the prison scene in *Richard II*, where Richard discusses and illustrates analogy, order and music, as he waits to die; and again in Hamlet's soliloquy, 'What a rogue and peasant slave am I', which reflects passionately and analytically on an actor's remarkable performance of passionate narration. Unlike the cultivated Richard and Hamlet, Macbeth does not analyse art, but he refers to it sensitively. The images or references to books and stories in the play are few, but whether we notice them or not they habituate the mind to such subjects and such self-reflection.

In Act I, scene 3, Macbeth thanks Rosse and Angus for bringing him good news, saying that their pains 'Are register'd where every day I turn/The leaf to read them'. Memory is a book, to be opened, turned and read. In Act II, scene 4, the Old Man's 'volume' contains 'things strange', made trifling by 'this sore night'. Truth is stranger than fiction. In Act I, scene 5, Lady Macbeth says, 'Your face, my Thane, is a book, where men/May read strange matters.' Consciousness is a book, dangerously open, to be closed, and not read. In the banqueting scene she tells Macbeth, who is unnerved by Banquo's ghost, that his 'flaws and starts . . . would well become/A woman's story at a winter's fire/Authoris'd by her grandam'. His moral fears are relegated to frivolous fantasies. Winter's tale and old wives' tales are compounded in dismissal, and folklore authority dangerously belittled, in a sexism characteristic of Lady Macbeth's attempt to masculinize herself and join the man's world. Her judgement must be reversed: trust the woman's tale authorized by the grandams; read the winter's tale of *Macbeth*. In Act V, scene 3, Macbeth asks the doctor if he can 'Raze out the written troubles of the brain'. Memory is a text inscribed, read and reread, like Macbeth's letter and Lady Macbeth's letter which she writes in sleep; neither is to be erased.

These are the explicit preparations and the matrix for the image-cluster in Act V, scene 5. (We may add to them one more image of the tale, which may provide a pre-echo of sound rather than sense. This is a crux in Act I, scene 3. In one of the frequent refracted narrations, Rosse tells Macbeth that his prowess in battle has been reported to Duncan by many messengers (of which the audience has heard two, the bleeding Captain and Rosse himself) who have come 'post with post', 'as thick as tale'. Theobold's emendation of 'tale' to 'hail' is still followed by Kenneth Muir in the Arden edition; in the last impression (1995) he mentions but does not answer Hilda Hulme's defence of the Folio 'tale' in *Readings in Shakespeare's Language* (London, Longman, 1962) where she argues, with alertness to nuance, knowledge of language use, and textual conservatism – the only kind of conservatism she endorsed – that 'tale' may mean 'talk'. Even if 'tale' refers to enumeration – and the etymology of enumeration is interestingly bound up with that of narration – the emendation is redundant, and I take this 'tale' as a phonic contribution to the pattern.)

The image of the tale told by an idiot originates in two less forceful narration-images in *King John*, a play with several pre-echoes of *Macbeth*, which Shakespeare may have recalled when writing his new play about a tyrant and murderer. In *King John*, Lewis of France, the Dauphin, images his *ennui* and disappointment at failure by calling life 'as tedious as a twice-told tale/Vexing the dull ear of a drowsy man' (III.4). This is dullness compounded in teller and listener, object and subject. Shortly after, King John's second coronation is not only said to gild refined gold and paint the lily but compared to 'an ancient tale new told,/ And, in the last repeating, troublesome,/Being urged at a time unseasonable' (IV.2). This again compounds denigration, but this time it is the timing and urging of narration which is blamed, no doubt because Shakespeare wished to qualify and vary the self-conscious joke about new telling of ancient tales, which is what he is doing in writing the histories.

Macbeth continues the subject of *ennui*, and the habit of rhetorical compounding. 'Idiot' is suggested by or echoes the abusive 'loon' in the previous scene. 'Recorded time' may owe something to the doctor's records, though it also refers, like the *King John* image, to

Shakespeare's work on historical chronicles. The 'dismal treatise' is a startling image, standing as it does between two references back to non-literary sources – night-shrieks and supping with horrors:

> *Macbeth* The time has been, my senses would have cool'd
> To hear a night-shriek; and my fell of hair
> Would at a dismal treatise rouse, and stir,
> As life were in't. I have supp'd full with horrors . . .
> (V.5)

Two unforgettable experiences in the play are oddly joined by the reference to Macbeth's susceptibility to a horror-story. It echoes the reference to his hair 'unfixed' by his 'horrid image' of Duncan's murder (I.3) but has no experiential source in the play and refers to the implied pre-existence of characters. (It is also an echo of that oral culture dismissed by Lady Macbeth.) It is an important reminder, very rare in this play, though frequent in the other major tragedies, of past or potential ordinary life, free from tragic necessity.

The tale told by an idiot is bracketed with the meaningless performance of the poor player, whose poverty of performance is only one possible nuance. Theseus reminds us that 'the best in this kind are but shadows' (*A Midsummer Night's Dream*). Strutting or fretting is show-off or uncontrolled acting, but not only this. We are all poor in our mortality. Shakespeare made money from the theatre but many actors were poor. The images are literal, metaphorical, metonymic. The walking shadow contains the shadow of Theseus's image.

One of Macbeth's rhetorical habits is negation. His Faust-like capacity to see the best while following the worst is shown in the frequently and feelingly summoned presences of virtue and value: 'Stars, hide your fires. 'Pity, like a naked new-born babe', 'Scarf up the tender eye of pitiful Day' and 'Cancel, and tear to pieces that great bond/Which keeps me pale!' Divine light, pure pity, unbearable compassion and moral dread are asserted through negations, and rejected or shunned. These images dramatize the apprehension of a moral system. A specific sensitivity to pity and fear is established in Macbeth, through indirections which direct us. His yearning after human kindness is a more vivid conjuration of moral force than any of the positives affirmed by the virtuous characters, like Macduff or Malcolm. We have already seen how Malcolm's virtue is presented unstably; his negation of evil is the obverse of Macbeth's negation of good. Malcolm's intense, hyberbolic, multiplied image of tyranny is the play's strongest imaging of evil. Macbeth's rejections are its strongest imagings of good. Both characters tell their story in negative. The audience has to develop a positive. Macbeth's 'tale told by an idiot' is in keeping with his other assertions; by the time he imagines it, the audience has learnt how to read his language by reversal. The habit of negation is exquisitely appropriate to hell. The porter pretends to be porter of hell's gate, but Inverness is really hell's gate. Malcolm pretends to be a worse villain than Macbeth, projecting an image of deepening and widening violence not 'literally' acted out but acted in the performance within the performance. (Macbeth's own villainy is 'only' acted.) It is apt that Macbeth's list of negations should end with a tale's absent significance. Meanings in Shakespeare are commonly grasped and summed up as actors, play and audience come to an awareness of ending.

In *Macbeth* hell is an absence like the hell of Marlowe's Mephistopheles. It is like the use of photographic negative by Cocteau in his film *Orphée*, for the crossing to Hades, recalled by Godard in *Alphaville*'s systematic defamiliarization of colours and values. The tale told by an idiot is a dark and covert assertion of Shakespeare's positive. It makes a muted claim to remind us of this tale of *Macbeth* and to enlarge metaphysical expectation. *Macbeth* is also full of sound and fury but told by impassioned reason, signifying something. At one stroke Shakespeare is defining Macbeth's nihilistic *ennui*, and using a negative, most reticently, to claim a positive for his play, for art and perhaps for human existence. The language of the claim is not irony or understatement but proposes a compromised and tentative positive. It is not unlike Malcolm's reversal of role and tale.

I am the more confident in asserting the importance of this tale which signifies nothing, because it offers a negative version of that typical reference to narrative or story or tale which occurs at the end of many of these plays and which I discussed earlier (see Chapter 3). The characteristically Shakespearian closing invocation of narrative order, which *Macbeth* and Macbeth both lack, reminds the audience of fictionality by providing the characters with a little touch of 'reality'. The actors are acting real people who are turning into stories. They are also inviting the audience to compare its knowledge of the story with the ignorance of the story's participants. Macbeth's words about language, acting, history and story perform a survey of artistic constituents which is most specific in self-reference. The words 'last syllable' occur in an extra-syllabic line, drawing attention to its last syllable. The suggestion of professional inefficiency in 'poor player' (like Cleopatra's reminder of the squeaking boy) gives the good actor an extra nuance in performance. The rejection of narrative signification is demonstrated and contradicted, as the word 'nothing' is immediately followed by the entry of a messenger too overwrought to say anything, provoking Macbeth's 'thou comest to use thy tongue; thy story quickly.' His command also shows the pragmatic persistence of Macbeth's old thirst for meanings even as he is rejecting them. It is obeyed by a grim demonstration of the narrative significations in those tales full of sound and fury told by the witches. Macbeth comes to recognize meanings he has misread; he has read the witches' negatives as positives and their positives as negatives. After imagining meaninglessness, through his customary evasive depersonalizing imagery, in the tale told by an idiot, he comes to feel the particular horror of the absence of expected meaning, and the presence of unexpected meaning, in substantial events that demonstrate 'the equivocation of the fiend,/That lies like truth'. He quotes the lie which sounds like a truth, 'Fear not, till Birnam Wood/Do come to Dunsinane', in one more refracted narrative.

Malcolm's final speech contains no large recapitulations of history or story, only more doubts, continuing the play's habits of undermining information:

> . . . What's more to do,
> Which would be planted newly with the time, –
> As calling home our exil'd friends abroad,
> That fled the snares of watchful tyranny;
> Producing forth the cruel ministers
> Of this dead butcher, and his fiend-like Queen,
> Who, as 'tis thought, by self and violent hands
> Took off her life . . .
>
> (V.9)

Lady Macbeth's suicide is reported, doubtingly, 'Who, as 'tis thought, by self and violent hands . . .' and the gross description of the tragic pair as 'this dead butcher, and his fiend-like Queen' does not elicit assent but is there to remind the audience of its access to a larger, more intricate and more subtle story than the one Malcolm knows and crudely summarizes. As Macbeth's metaphor of the idiot's tale reverses the usual Shakespearian call for meanings and orderings of narrative, it follows the bent of the whole play, from the beginning to end.

Index